GUTS

The Seven Laws
of Business
That Made Chrysler the
World's Hottest Car Company

ROBERT A. LUTZ

John Wiley & Sons, Inc.
New York • Chichester • Weinheim • Brisbane • Singapore • Toronto

Published by John Wiley & Sons, Inc.
Published simultaneously in Canada.

This publication is designed to provide accurate and authoritative information in regard to the subject matter covered. It is sold with the understanding that the publisher is not engaged in rendering professional services. If professional advice or other expert assistance is required, the services of a competent professional person should be sought.

Library of Congress Cataloging-in-Publication Data:

Lutz, Robert A.
    Guts : the seven laws of business that made Chrysler the world's hottest car company / Robert A. Lutz.
      p.   cm.
    ISBN 0-471-29561-2 (cloth : alk. paper)
    1. Chrysler Corporation—Management.   2. Automobile industry and trade—United States—Management.   3. Corporate turnarounds—United States.   I. Title.   II. Title: Unconventional business wisdom that made Chrysler the world's hottest car company.
HD9710.U54C4695   1998
338.7'6292'0973—dc21   98-29124
                                             CIP

Printed in the United States of America.

10 9 8 7 6 5 4 3 2

This book is dedicated to the two men who have had the profoundest impact on my life.

Robert H. Lutz, my father, mentor, critic, and coach who, at age 90, still teaches me a lot.

Colonel John C. ("Jack") Vernon, Jr., USMC (retired), my best friend, recently deceased. A fine officer, superb pilot, honest and caring attorney, a role model of courage and integrity.

AUTHOR'S NOTE

Several of the best legal minds of our time, knowing my unsurpassed gift for inciting controversy (or in layman's terms, for putting my foot in it), have suggested I might want to preface my remarks at the earliest opportunity with a small disclaimer of some sort. This is it: The opinions here expressed aren't anyone's but mine. They are not Chrysler's. They are not DaimlerChrysler's. They are not the Man in the Moon's. There. Does everyone feel better? Keep in mind, please, before you get too comfortable, that diplomacy has never been my strong suit. When confronted by a spade, I don't say, "nice shovel." So buckle up tight, then, and we'll motor on.

CONTENTS

Contents

PART III

LUTZ'S COROLLARIES, OR "THE *REST* OF THE STORY!"

FOREWORD

Bob Eaton
Chairman and CEO, Chrysler Corporation

This book is full of contradictions because Bob Lutz has never been hobbled by a slavish concern with consistency. With a martini in one hand and a cigar in the other, he will wax passionate on the blessings of vegetarianism. He's deeply upset that our schools today will tolerate students who behave like he once did. Largely responsible for a monumental transformation in the way Chrysler develops, builds, and markets its products, Bob has a healthy skepticism about what he calls "unexamined change." He's a curmudgeon about casual dress at the office, but trusts the gut instincts of the bedenimed creative types before the numbers and charts of buttoned-down analysts.

Mavericks like Bob Lutz stand out in industries like the car business that revere predictability. Profitably mass-producing automobiles requires highly disciplined engineering and manufacturing processes, financial controls, marketing strategies, and other business practices. And in spite of some of the impressions he might leave in this book, Bob is a disciplined Marine who knows how the system has to work, and respects it. First and foremost, that's why he was so effective at Chrysler in helping to change that system, even getting it to accept something as outrageous as a Viper.

In the auto industry, as with most others, you don't have the luxury of breaking a system in order to fix it. That's the easy way. Instead, changes have to take place on the fly. The unique management theories embodied in "Lutz's Laws" can help guide executives through the difficult change process that someone in our company once compared to rewiring a 747 in flight.

It always made me nervous to hear him say in speeches that "the customer isn't always right," "too much quality will ruin you," and "teamwork isn't always good." Fortunately, the press *usually* allowed him to explain himself, and the explanations, as you'll see, are simply judicious doses of common sense applied to some of the business world's more perfunctory platitudes. When he writes that "disruptive people are an asset," he's talking about people like himself who challenge conventional thinking—not to be difficult, but to be sure it's still relevant.

Bob's last six years at Chrysler were undoubtedly the most creative period in the company's history. The platform team concept took root and blossomed. We introduced more all-new cars and trucks in the nineties than in the previous two decades. We won one award after another for the design and execution of our cars and trucks. We became the acknowledged world leader in developing exciting vehicles, and doing it faster than anyone else. And, to prove the point that Bob makes in his chapter "The Primary Purpose of Business Is Not to Make Money," we made more money than in all the previous six decades of Chrysler's existence put together.

Chrysler has a rule that requires executives to retire at 65. We broke it for Bob and gave him the title of Vice Chairman, which he immediately changed to "coach." During his final 18 months, he would attend our major meetings, lean way back in his chair, mouth the ever-present cigar (unlit, in compliance with company policy), and blow imaginary smoke rings. He spoke as often as before, but always as a coach.

This is his playbook.

July 1, 1998

ACKNOWLEDGMENTS

First-time authors are, I suspect, overwhelmed (as I was) at the complexity of the job of getting a book written and published. It would have been impossible for me without the dedicated help of many people, too numerous to list. Some, though, stand out for the magnitude of their contribution. In no particular order, they are:

T. Quinn Spitzer, Jr., Chairman of the Board of Kepner-Tregoe, Inc., who originally said, "You should write a book," hounded me until I said "yes," and then helped me find a collaborator and publisher.

Robert J. Eaton, Chief Executive Officer of Chrysler Corporation, my boss, who could easily have said "No way!" when I told him I was planning to write a book, but didn't.

Alan Farnham, author and *Fortune* magazine contributing editor, who, as my creative partner, not only helped turn my often-wooden prose into language people might actually want to read, but shepherded this book from proposal to finished manuscript.

Timothy L. Yost, Manager of Editorial Services and Core Processes Communications at Chrysler, a fine writer in his own right, who, through generous contributions of his personal time and intellect, played an indispensable role in this project. As the person who, among other things, helped me write many, many speeches over the years, it long ago became difficult to distinguish his intellectual contributions from my own.

Henning Gutmann, my editor, whose vision for the book exceeded even my own, and who brought to bear on its behalf the full logistical and marketing support of John Wiley & Sons, publishers.

Peter M. Tobia, my agent and business manager, who deftly handled all negotiations and managed all business aspects of this venture.

Judith M. Butkiewicz, my executive assistant at Chrysler, who competently and cheerfully managed her huge normal workload plus the book.

Floyd R. Jamieson, driver, security professional, and friend, without whose motoring and organizational skills, my hours of road-time would have been wasted instead of productive.

Other of my Chrysler colleagues, including (in alphabetical order): Dan Bodene, Julianne Butkus, Joe Guy Collier, Josh Davidson, Derek Fiebig, Barbara Fronczak, Thom Gillis, Ken Gluckman, Steve Hantler, Steve Harris, Peter Hollinshead, Rick Houtman, Van Jolissaint, James Kenyon, Carol Lieber, Cindy Marasco, Mike Morrison, Bill Stewart, and Patrick White.

And last, but not least, my wife, Denise S. Lutz, who always provided support, advice, encouragement, love, and understanding when I was robbing her and all the kids and animals of quality time.

GUTS

THE *FLASH-FLASH-FLASH* OF THE CAMERA STROBES WAS NEARLY BLINDING as I rose to my feet, buttoned my jacket (my "incongruous-from-the-beginning" mix of a Swiss-German upbringing coupled with my decade of service in the United States Marine Corps taught me that a gentleman *always* buttons his suit coat upon standing), and posed for a picture I most certainly did not want to pose for.

Standing beside me was Bob Eaton, the incoming (from General Motors) CEO-designate of Chrysler Corporation, and standing beside *him* was Lee Iacocca—the still-reigning CEO of Chrysler, the architect of Chrysler's famous turnaround of the early 1980s, a bona fide American business icon, and the man who had prevented me—the president of Chrysler—from getting the job Bob Eaton just got. The date was March 16, 1992, and the location was the dais at the front of a small, shabby, ground-floor room that served as Chrysler's press room at its old headquarters in Highland Park, Michigan.

Just minutes earlier, after Lee had announced the news, I'd read a short statement I'd written in longhand at home the night before. I'd said in that statement that I considered myself a team player, and, as

3

such, I saw no reason whatsoever to pack up my ball and go home just because somebody else had been named captain of the team. And I meant every word I said.

But those damned cameras just kept flashing. And then came *the question:* "Mr. Lutz, are you *really* going to stick around Chrysler? You've *got* to be incredibly disappointed."

You know those moments that seem to last a lifetime, when your whole life appears before you? *This* was one of those moments.

What, exactly, was going through my mind at that instant? I quite honestly can't remember. The sands of time, as they say, have washed it away. My friends, though, tell me that—much to their amazement—at this moment of supreme tension and high human drama . . . I somehow had a sly, impish *grin* on my face! They say, too, that on second thought they really *weren't* all that amazed—that it was, in many ways, "typical Lutz."

Given that insight from my friends, I'll tell you a couple of things that *could* have been going through my mind: For a guy who didn't graduate from high school until age 22 and didn't leave the college campus till age 30, I'd already done pretty well in life. For a guy who was once called (by the *Wall Street Journal*) "a common man's aristocrat," I certainly knew a thing or two about "paradox," including about how things can be both good and bad at the same time. For a guy who liked to pilot his own helicopter to work and who was about to buy a Soviet-bloc military jet for weekend recreational sorties, I'd learned the hard way that some days are "blue skies and an unlimited ceiling" and some days it's "thunderstorms everywhere you look."

And, finally, there's a distinct possibility that going through my mind that day in 1992 was the thought that, for a guy who got into the car business in the first place because *I liked cars* (what a concept!), there actually wasn't, in my view, a more promising place in the world to be at that time than Chrysler—top job or not.

I'll also tell you a few other things that most certainly *weren't* going through my head during that frozen moment in time: That just a couple of years later, Lee would join Las Vegas billionaire Kirk Kerkorian in an unsolicited (and, ultimately, unsuccessful) takeover attempt of Chrysler. That, as a result of the official legal resolution of that takeover attempt, I would learn what the term "mutual nondefamation agreement" is all about! And, last but by no means least, not in my wildest dreams on that day in 1992 could I have imagined that, five years later, there'd be *another* camera flash shriveling my pupils—this one from a photographer from *Forbes* magazine shooting Bob Eaton and me for their January 13, 1997 "Company of the Year" cover, meaning that Chrysler had bested such great and innovative companies as Microsoft, Intel, Merck, and General Electric for that coveted honor.

. . .

After my life finished flashing before my eyes on that day in March of 1992, my rather clumsy and totally unrehearsed response to that question about my future was, "Well, you see me here, *apparently* happy."

My friends also tell me that the word "apparently" spoke volumes. I guess, in a Freudian sort of way, it did. But, you know, I've learned something about myself over my 30-plus-year business career, just as (I hope) I've learned a few things about business—things I'll try to impart to you in this book. You may be wondering, in fact, why I'm already being so personal in what is really a business-management book, *not* a traditional memoir. The reason is this: I believe perhaps the single most important thing I've learned in my business career is that you *can't* totally separate the objective from the personal, the rational from the emotional, the (a couple of terms you'll hear a lot about in this book) *left-brained* from the *right-brained*. That stuff gets all tangled up together (whether most business people realize it or not), and the reason for that is, at the end of the day, what business is all about is serving the needs of *people*—complex, multifaceted, mercurial, and, yes, *paradoxical* people. And learning that about business has, in turn, helped me learn something about life: Sometimes the way you get rid of the "apparently" in front of the "happy" is by accepting your fate and making the most of it.

Later in this book you're going to read about what I call, *somewhat* tongue in cheek, "Lutz's Laws" of business. Let me send you off on that journey by putting forth "Lutz's Law of Life" (one that—typical, I guess, of my "eclectic" nature—I borrowed from an old Rolling

Stones song): "You Can't Always Get What You Want—But if You Try Sometime, You Just Might Find, You Get What You *Need.*"

I've found that a pretty good law to live by—and perhaps you might, as well.

. . .

A Postscript: As this book was going to press, two major events occurred. Chrysler and Germany's Daimler-Benz, two of the most profitable car companies on the planet, agreed to pool their resources in the largest industrial merger in history; and I, at age 66½, finally retired from Chrysler (having stayed on a year and a half beyond the company's usual retirement age). Today, my eyes are no longer blinded by flashbulbs; though, to paraphrase an old Swiss proverb, I must admit that I look upon the merger of Chrysler and Daimler-Benz with "one crying eye" (that is, with a certain amount of wistfulness at the passing into history of the stand-alone, 73-year-old Chrysler Corporation) . . . but, mostly, with "one laughing eye." That's because, unlike some of the proposed shotgun weddings in Chrysler's not-too-distant past, this merger has been aptly described as a "marriage of equals." (See my Epilogue for more on the merger.) The creation of "DaimlerChrysler" is, I believe, not just a terrific business deal but something that may well go down in history as the beginning of a true New World Order in the business community . . . and, who knows, maybe even in the community of humankind, as the world continues to shrink. And to the extent that I played a role in helping make all that possible, I feel not just proud, but humbled!

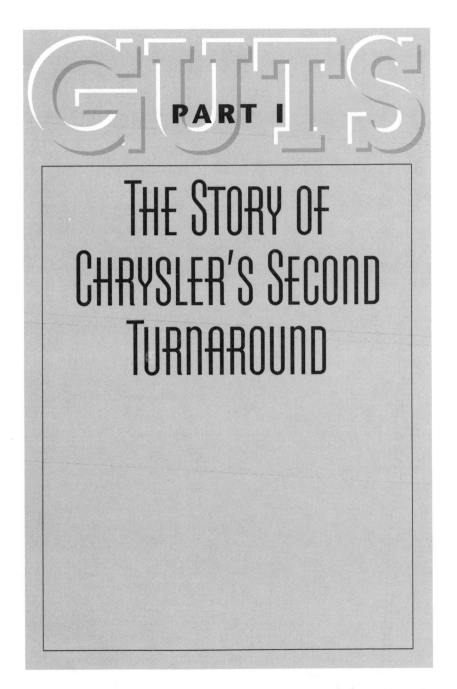

GUTS

PART I

The Story of Chrysler's Second Turnaround

Déjà Vu All Over Again

CHAPTER 1

A FUNNY THING HAPPENED TO CHRYSLER IN THE EARLY 1990s. THE COMPANY
that, just a decade before, had been saved with the aid of historic—
and very controversial—federal loan guarantees, was in deep trouble
again.

How did this happen?

It would be easy, I suppose, to paint the reasons in stark black and
white, complete with stock villains from Central Casting—as writers
of books and articles are so often wont to do. But I hate it when writers do that, when they oversimplify the reality of what was really an
incredibly complex business situation. The truth of Chrysler's situation was more shades of gray than black and white—and since this is
my book (and since I believe that the ultimate key to success in business is truly understanding complex situations by using more of your
gray *matter*), I'm going to give it to you straight (or at least as straight
as my admittedly skewed personality will allow!).

Some of the seeds of Chrysler's second unraveling were, undoubtedly, sown in the headiness of the company's remarkable comeback
from the brink in Turnaround #1. And I, for one, can almost under-

stand why. In 1979, even the pro-business *Wall Street Journal* had told Chrysler to "die with dignity." But the plucky band of survivors at Detroit's number three automaker, led by Lee Iacocca and his rough-and-tumble gang of refugees (and castoffs) from the buttoned-down Ford Motor Company, would have none of it. Sure, they'd bent the rules of free enterprise a bit in wrangling $1.2 billion in loan guarantees out of the Carter Administration (something that I myself, from my perch at Ford at the time, had a tough time sympathizing with), but the company had also gone through hell and back in terms of coughing up additional billions in pay cuts and concessions—not to mention having to go to the mat to wrestle concessions from its bankers, suppliers, and dealers. All in all, Chrysler in the early '80s was like a heart-attack victim that had undergone an emergency transplant right by the side of the road for all to see—and had *survived!* And if nothing else, you had to give them credit for their sheer spunk.

This was, after all, the company that, in the midst of all its travail, brought to market the cheap, fuel-efficient "K-car"—badged the Dodge Aries and Plymouth Reliant—laughable underachievers by today's standards, but exactly the right cars for those recessionary, post-oil-embargo, stagflation times. The K-cars were America's first front-wheel-drive, transverse-engine, six-passenger cars, and they sold like hotcakes. Even more important, they served as the basis for a true automotive sensation—the minivan. Introduced in the fall of 1983, the Dodge Caravan and Plymouth Voyager (and later the Chrysler Town & Country) not only created an all-new segment in the American auto market (arguably the first all-new segment since the Ford Mustang defined the "pony car" segment in the '60s), but they became a cash cow of almost unbelievable proportions. In 1984, Chrysler earned a then-record $2.4 billion—adding another $3 billion in earnings over the next two years.

It was at that point in time, 1986, that one Robert A. Lutz, age 54, decided to jump ship at Ford and cast his fortunes with the swashbuckling crew at Chrysler.

Why, exactly, did I come to Chrysler? One reason, quite honestly, was that it had become obvious to me that I had risen about as high as I would go at Ford. After stints earlier in my career with General Motors (mostly in Europe) and with BMW in Munich, and after serving as chairman of Ford of Europe (a huge company in its own right), I had risen to executive vice president of all of Ford's international operations and been elected to Ford's board of directors. For a while, there was even speculation in the press that I was a dark-horse candidate to succeed Phil Caldwell as chairman of Ford. Throughout my career, I guess I was what you'd call, in today's parlance, a "change agent," and that active, sometimes exacting temperament had certainly served me well. However, change agents, by definition, stir things up—and it's one of the ironies of modern business that while companies all say they *want* positive change, they very often get uneasy about anybody in the organization feeling "uncomfortable" (which of course is how change often makes people feel).

And so it was for me at Ford. Don't get me wrong: I didn't leave Ford "one step ahead of the sheriff"; I could have finished out my career there. But a gnawing feeling had descended upon me—a feeling that I'd started running in place.

Meanwhile, there was a lot about Chrysler that I found very appealing. Chrysler was seen in those days as sort of the last refuge of automotive malcontents, and I guess I pretty much fit that description. In fact, throughout my life, I've never really fit into the standard mold too well.

For starters, unlike what seemed to be true of virtually all American automobile executives at the time, I was not born in that small, bucolic town in the Midwest called "Humble Origins." Quite the contrary. I was born in cosmopolitan Zurich, Switzerland, into the family of one of those Swiss bankers you hear so much about, and I grew up sort of a "mid-Atlanticer," as my father's bank, Credit Suisse, kept transferring him back and forth between Zurich and Wall Street. In fact, by the time I was eight years old, I'd crossed the Atlantic five times and, by age 11, held both Swiss and U.S. citizenship.

It was certainly a privileged life, but it also contained a lot of upheaval for me, as I was regularly held back a grade whenever I returned to school in Europe following a stint in the United States. Even though the U.S. public school system in those days was absolutely stellar compared with today, and even though I always had a rigorous course load that included Latin, literature, higher mathematics, and all of the other subjects of a traditional liberal education, invariably I'd be hopelessly behind my Swiss counterparts. ("Okay, Bobby, we see here you've had a little Latin; would you now please *conjugate these verbs* for us?")

Plus, as is so often the case, privilege in my young life (combined with all these upheavals and setbacks) had a way of leading to a certain amount of restlessness and even outright rebellion. The worst example of this is when my family finally settled down for good in the Zurich area following World War II, and I managed to get myself booted out of high school. Official reason: "Academic and disciplinary problems." Translation: At the same time I was showing little interest in my assigned studies, I was showing a little *too much* interest in the daughter of the biggest industrialist in town.

Luckily for me, six months of manual labor in a leather warehouse taught me that maybe buckling down in school wasn't such a bad idea after all. But my father, in his infinite wisdom, wasn't going to let me off with just that. In exchange for his promise to fund one more chance for me at education (at a public school in French-speaking Lausanne, Switzerland, where I eventually picked up that language in addition to my German and English), he made me promise to return to the United States immediately upon graduation and enlist in the U.S. Marine Corps. (Why the Marines? Well, I think at least part of it had to do with the fact that during one of his stints in New York my father had gotten to know a very impressive former Marine colonel, and, in addition to being a great guy, the colonel used to walk around the office on his hands—and I think maybe my father thought that *all* Marines walked on their hands, and that any breed of people who can do that must be pretty neat!)

At the time, I thought my father's deal might be a Faustian pact—especially since the Korean War was in full swing at the time, and the survival rate of enlisted Marines in Korea was none too high! Instead, it turned out to be a godsend: After graduating from high school (at, yes, the ripe old age of *22*—I was so old the other kids had taken to calling me "Dad"), I went through boot camp at Parris Island, South Carolina, and acquired a sense of discipline (including *self*-discipline) to temper my heretofore unbridled bent.

I was also, eventually, able to fulfill one of my (and probably just about every other boy's) lifelong dreams: to become a fighter pilot.

Because I didn't have a college degree and wasn't an officer, I entered the Naval Aviation Cadet Program (NAVCAD), which was then open to promising enlisted men from either the Navy or the Marine Corps (and even civilians). As events would have it, the Korean War ended before I got my wings; however, I did serve in Korea for a time as the Air Liaison Officer of the 2nd Battalion, 3rd Marines, based on Okinawa. All told, I served five years as an active-duty Marine aviator from 1954 to 1959 and received my commission as an officer.

I *loved* the Corps, and I loved what it did for me in turning around my life. In fact, I loved it so much I intended to make it my career. But to advance as an officer, I would have to get that college degree. So, following my tour in the Far East, I returned to the site of one of my earlier assignments (northern California) to become a Reserve aviator, flying out of the Alameda Naval Air Station, and to finally pursue a degree at the University of California at Berkeley.

But at Berkeley, a funny thing happened *to me:* While pursuing my degree, I became just totally fascinated with the world of business, particularly the whole bundle of human psychological constructs involved in marketing; and I started to think seriously about combining my second burning passion in life—*cars*—with a career in business. So, after obtaining my bachelor's degree (at age 29), I went on to get an MBA at Berkeley, and soon thereafter got into the auto industry with a series of marketing and, later, management jobs at General Motors, BMW, and Ford.

When I finally landed at Chrysler, two decades and three car companies later, I found a place where (at the top of the company, at least) a nonconformist like me seemed to fit right in. Moreover, I saw Chrysler's smaller size (at least in comparison with Ford and General Motors) to be a tremendous potential advantage for the company. In the Marine Corps, and later, when I oversaw the disparate departments that would someday be the motorcycle division at BMW, I'd seen the power of small, dynamic organizations firsthand—organizations that through vision, wile, and, yes, just plain guts were able not only to *overcome* their size and resource deficiencies, but to turn them into *advantages.* And I was anxious to work again in an organization that wasn't too large (or to be more exact, too lethargic) to get out of its own way.

There was one other thing, however, that I quickly discovered on joining Chrysler: that the company, despite its bold demeanor and strong profits, was basically following a *defeatist* strategy in its core car and truck business.

Some of the rationale for this strategy was perfectly understandable. From time immemorial, the auto industry has been one of the most cyclical industries anywhere in the business world—"Every time the American economy catches cold, Detroit gets pneumonia," goes the old adage. And a lot of people, including the money managers on Wall Street, had long pressured us to try to minimize this cyclicality by diversifying our risk—or else pay hell for it in stock prices, credit ratings, even our jobs. Now, though, there was an additional dynamic: Japanese competition. To be more exact, the challenge was Washington's growing reluctance to do anything about the plainly unfair advantages that Japanese automakers then enjoyed over their American counterparts.

It was Washington, to begin with, that in the 1970s had saddled Detroit with a stringent array of fuel-economy regulations to combat an "energy shortage" that, in reality, turned out to be a mirage. (Case in point: A gallon of gasoline in the United States today costs less than a gallon of bottled water!) And in this respect, Chrysler's smaller size was *not* an advantage, because in not having the resources to place two bets at once (one on fuel-sipping four-cylinder cars and a hedge on larger cars and V-6 and V-8 engines, as GM and Ford had done), the company found itself with its chips stacked on the wrong color when the energy crisis turned out to be a false alarm. As a result, the company also found itself—to a greater degree than GM or Ford— right in the teeth of the full-fledged Japanese onslaught of the mid- to late '80s.

Meanwhile, on another front, in the recession of the early '80s— which was really a *depression* for autos—Japanese automakers, under pressure from Washington, had agreed to "voluntarily" limit the number of cars they imported into the United States to 1.68 million per year. This was called the Voluntary Restraint Agreement, or VRA— and it made sense because Japan's own auto market was (and is) locked up tighter than a drum to foreign competition. For example, in the year the VRA was enacted the Big Three American automakers sold a grand total of 4,219 vehicles in Japan, and by 1997 that number had climbed to just 25,000 vehicles.

In 1985, however, Washington decided to let the Japanese lift the VRA (in essence, to eliminate it). On the face of it, this seemed like a sensible decision—after all, the Big Three were all making money once again. However, with foreign nameplates already taking more than a quarter of the U.S. market that year (and now threatening to take a lot more), and with autos accounting for more than half of the nation's all-time record $130 billion trade deficit, it wasn't inconceivable to consider the future for American auto producers, especially those whose products competed so directly against the Japanese, a little bleak.

Moreover, there were a few other Japanese-related factors at work as well: The original imposition of the VRA had given the Japanese an incentive both to sell a higher mix of upscale cars in the United States (just as gasoline prices were falling) and to build what turned out to be a bevy of "transplant" assembly plants in the United States (just as the yen had finally strengthened against the dollar)—proving, much to Detroit's chagrin, the old saw, "Be careful what you ask for, because you just might get it!" Adding insult to injury, as the yen rose from its previous absurdly weak (read *rigged*) levels, the Japanese complemented their growing U.S. transplant production by selling many of their Japan-built products for less in the United States than what they sold for in Japan (which they could get away with because they had a sanctuary market at home, peopled by consumers who had no other choice but to pay high prices to help offset the cost of their market-share grab in the United States).

This is, of course, by definition, *dumping*—an illegal practice in the United States and also against the rules of the World Trade Organization (then the General Agreement on Tariffs and Trade). Whenever anyone from Chrysler pointed out this or any other Japanese transgression, however, the Washington (and media) response was, "Stop whining—it's not trade practices; it's that the Japanese just build better cars!" The fact of the matter is, *both* statements were true: The Japanese *did* generally build better cars, and they *did,* at the same time, routinely engage in unfair trade (which, by the way, in turn helped give them the *resources* to build better cars!). And while I, for one, readily conceded the former point, hardly anyone in Washington or in the media would concede the latter. It seemed almost as if the American mind was incapable of grasping both propositions simultaneously. (And, yes, I know history has proved that the Japanese economic model was ultimately no match for American-style free enterprise; but, really, that's the main point we were trying to make all along!)

Against this general backdrop, the minds at Chrysler, prior to my arrival, had decided to pursue what was internally known as "Plan B." The strategy was partly "If you can't beat 'em, join 'em," and partly "See ya later, Alligator." It called for the concurrent phaseout of North American production of all but our highest-profit-margin vehicles, leaving our smaller vehicles to be built by partners in Asia (and possibly Eastern Europe), and for the accelerated diversification of the corporation at large into areas such as aerospace and financial services. Toward that latter goal, by 1989 Chrysler had acquired Gulfstream Aerospace, Electrospace Systems, FinanceAmerica, E.F. Hutton Credit, and, just for good measure, the exotic Italian supercar builder, Lamborghini, plus four U.S. rental-car companies (not to mention our partnerships and joint ventures with Maserati in Italy and with Mitsubishi Motors in Japan).

We also made one other acquisition—a big one—in 1987: the American Motors Corporation. We bought AMC to get the world-renowned Jeep brand, something that certainly fit in with our "go upscale" plan. It was a risky move—in some ways, *too* risky for my tastes—but in the fullness of time, one that has turned out to be a gold mine (for a number of reasons, as you'll read about in Chapter 2).

The central problem, by the late '80s, with Chrysler's strategic retreat-cum-diversification plan (at least as it related to our remaining auto business) wasn't so much that it left our auto operations without enough capital, but that, in all the "hubbub," the money wasn't being spent as well as it could have been. We just didn't have the right focus or, to be honest, the right kind of passion for cars and trucks. Our minivans were still a smash hit, and the Jeep Cherokee four-door compact sport utility was a nice incremental addition to our lineup. But in the high-volume, high-profit pickup truck market, our entry was, in the words of Lee Iacocca, "old enough to vote." And on the passenger-car side, customers quickly saw through our attempts to puff up higher profit margins by simply stretching and gussying up the original K-car platform. (For example, under the sheet metal, the basic underpinnings and mechanicals of the 1991 Chrysler Imperial, priced at $27,000, were virtually identical to that of the 1991 Plymouth Acclaim, priced at $13,000—and with the exception of a slightly more powerful engine, neither one of them was a whole lot different from the $7,000 Dodge Aries of just a couple of years earlier.)

The K-cars—boxy, narrow, and humble—may have been ideal for the market of the early '80s and ideally suited for the world of higher fuel costs and tightening fuel-economy standards that we'd been led to anticipate. But by the late '80s and early '90s, that wasn't the kind of quality customers were asking for anymore—nor were gasoline prices or fuel economy of much concern to anyone. And, unfortunately, virtually all our passenger cars (save the even *more* "salesproof" sedans we picked up in the AMC acquisition, the Renault-designed Eagle Premier and Eagle Medallion) were derivatives of the original 1982 Aries and Reliant, prompting one wag in the press to remark that our lineup looked as if we'd fallen asleep at the typewriter with our finger stuck on the K key. (Ouch!)

We did, of course, ultimately sell every vehicle we built—but to do so took massive sales incentives. In fact, in many ways, Chrysler was a marketing company without peer. We were the company that, in the '70s, had literally invented the automotive rebate (popularized by Joe Garagiola's famous "Get-a-car/Get-a-check" TV commercials), and in the '80s we perfected this practice to an art form. We'd also pioneered the modern "5/50" (five-year, 50,000-mile) warranty (later upgraded to "7/70") as a "dealer closing tool" to help move the iron. And in what, for me, was a real zenith (or perhaps *nadir* is a better term) of marketing, we once trumped all our competitors by coming out with the industry's first *0.0* percent new-car financing plan—in other words, free money!

As sure as night follows day, however, all these "spiffs" were bound to have an effect on the bottom line. And they did. Chrysler's net earnings dropped to $359 million in 1989, and as recession hit the U.S. economy in 1990, our profits dropped to just $68 million. In 1991 we finally slipped underwater, reporting a $795 million loss (so much for countercyclicality). But equally as troubling as our erosion in profitability was the fact that our pension fund in '91 was underfunded to the tune of $4.3 billion (the largest such deficit in all of American industry), our credit rating was shot (some of our debt was selling at junk-bond levels), and our stock price had plummeted from its 1989 peak of just under $30 a share to just over $10.

In 1979, *Newsweek* ran a cover illustration of a very sick-looking car with a thermometer in its mouth and an ice pack on its head under the headline, "Can Chrysler Be Saved?" Back then, this question was a topic of conversation for all of America—so much so that the U.S. Congress passed a special law to award Chrysler loan guarantees. In September of 1990, *Financial World* magazine ran a stern-looking, arms-folded picture of *me* on their cover (not unlike the gruff-looking shot on the cover of this book, by the way) under the headline, "Can This Man Save Chrysler?" Certainly the magnitude of Chrysler's predicament in the early '90s, while bleak, wasn't *quite* as dire as it was in 1979. But just as certain was the fact that this time there'd be no red-white-and-blue EMS unit standing by to help us out. This time the patient who a decade before had so miraculously survived emergency open-heart surgery, only to get sick once again, would have to *heal himself.*

CHAPTER 2

The Patient Heals Himself: Bringing Platform Teams to Chrysler

THOUGH THE WORST OF CHRYSLER'S SECOND CRUNCH DIDN'T COME UNTIL 1991, the elements of our second comeback were being put in place even as the company's flight path was still on a downward trajectory. In fact, about the same time the whole world was watching the fall of the Berlin Wall in the autumn of 1989, there was a change going on inside Chrysler that was, in its own way, no less revolutionary—but the outside world knew nothing about it. And, just as the fall of the Berlin Wall had been precipitated in large part by the former Soviet Union's adoption a few years earlier of the policies of *glasnost* ("openness") and *perestroika* ("restructuring"), so, too, you might say, were those two principles behind our little revolution within Chrysler.

But, I'm getting a bit ahead of myself. Before I tell you about the *perestroika* at Chrysler, I ought to explain the equally revolutionary new outlook that was emerging at our company toward another *P* word—*product*. That's because the purpose of our *perestroika* was, first and foremost, to build a whole different type of product than Chrysler (and, for that matter, most of the American auto industry) had heretofore been building.

Throughout my career in the auto industry, I've been called, in industry lingo, a "car guy." That hasn't always been a *positive* label (as I'll explain later), but at least I come by it honestly. Back in my youth in Switzerland, I had a couple of rich (literally!) uncles who always drove great, crazy cars—for example, a '34 Alfa Romeo Zagato, a '38 Talbot Lago Pourtout, and a '48 Delahaye. And my father would never have a dull car in our family, either—even though, in those more chauvinistic times, he had a different standard for the cars that *he* drove and the ones my mother got to drive. For instance, when I was about six, Dad bought a 3.5-liter SS Jaguar, and because he felt it was "too much car" for Mom's everyday needs, he bought her a '37 Czechoslovakian-built Skoda. The Skoda was actually a great little car, but the clutch and brake pedals were on flimsy castings that came up through the floorboard, and I remember many trips to downtown Zurich when Mom would have to stand on the brake pedal, and it'd snap off! (At least when it was the brake pedal, we could still get home; when it was the *clutch,* we were out of luck!)

Later, in 1952, after the Labour Government had been ousted in Britain, Dad decided it was time to celebrate by buying himself an Aston Martin, so he got a beautiful DB2 (of which, by the way, I'm now the proud owner, having spotted the exact car—totally by luck—at the premises of a Swiss Aston Martin dealer in 1997). But, once again, my father didn't think my mother could handle such a nice car, so he got her a Volkswagen Beetle, with its four-speed "crash box" (i.e., lacking in synchronizers to aid in shifting) transmission. As things turned out, however, it was my mother who had the last laugh. One day my father's bank happened to be hosting American financier and famed race-car driver Charles Moran, teammate of the legendary Briggs Cunningham (who, by coincidence vis-à-vis my own later career, was at the time immersed in building and racing a series of very successful sports cars powered by Chrysler "Hemi" engines—a Chrysler-powered Cunningham C5R, for instance, would place third overall in the 1953 "24 Hours of LeMans" race). Somehow, Mom was pressed into service to drive ol' Charles around Zurich—and he wound up standing in awe of her ability to double-clutch, heel-and-toe, and whiz through that Bug's gearbox with nary a grind!

So I guess you could say my love of interesting cars, no matter what their price or pedigree, is something I learned at my mother's knee. And it's a passion I indulged throughout my youth by constantly sketching pictures of cars during school (yet another part of my early scholastic undoing!) and, later, by doing some regional racing (in an MG-TD and an MGA) with the Sports Car Club of America. In fact, for a while there in my 20s I thought semiseriously about maybe trying to become a race-car driver and builder like Briggs Cunningham. In any event, once I'd decided at Berkeley to work toward a career in business, there was no doubt at all in my mind that the field I wanted to be in was the *car* business—for the simple reason that, first and foremost, I did indeed like cars.

That may seem kind of axiomatic for an auto executive. But the truth is, it's not. In fact, throughout my automotive career I've never ceased to be amazed at the number of highly placed people in the auto industry who aren't, in fact, "car guys" (or, in some ways even worse, those who *pretend* to be car people when in fact they really aren't). True, to a certain degree business is business, and you don't necessarily have to have high-octane ethyl in your veins to be an effective automotive executive—any more than it's mandatory that you be a computer geek to run a computer company. But I maintain that it *helps*.

In my own career, one of the big reasons I left General Motors for BMW in 1971 (other than an eightfold increase in pay) is that I'd grown increasingly frustrated with the kind of direction that GM was giving to its Opel division in Europe (where I was then the head of sales and marketing). In essence, GM was behaving as if Europe were merely a retarded version of the U.S. market. I recall, for instance, a trip I once made to GM's New York office to meet with a very senior executive of GM Overseas Operations, after I'd been peppering the system for months with memos about how we desperately needed brakes that could actually stop a car at high European speeds (often more than 100 mph), as opposed to the undersized, heat-prone (and therefore fade-prone) U.S. drum brakes of that time. After a short discussion during which he urged me to stop writing all those silly memos about disc brakes (and during which he patronized me for obviously being so naive about the superiority of GM technology), he took me to the executive garage and showed me the brake pedal in his Cadillac. "Look at that pedal, boy," he said. "It says 'Power Brakes'! I can be going 35 miles per hour and just *touch* that thing with my toe, and the car stops on a dime! Best damn brakes in the world! You go back and explain to those Europeans that it just doesn't *get* any better than this!"

At BMW—a company that was just then really starting to forge its "driving machines" image—I found that it *did* get better than that. BMW was a company that, in the early '70s, had recovered from its own brush with bankruptcy a decade before and had gone from building a weird mix of vehicles that stretched from the sublime (the Albrecht Goertz–designed 507) to the ridiculous (the Isetta, a car whose only door opened in the front) to building models like the 2002, a car that came to define the term "sports sedan." I became BMW's executive vice president for sales and marketing and a member of the board of management—and I also had the opportunity to indulge my love for two-wheeled transportation by acting as the godfather to the company's organizationally scattered motorcycle operations. In fact, by simply bringing all the cycle people (none of whom actually reported to me) together weekly as a team, we were able to do some great bikes in a very short period of time—a lesson I would put to good use later on at Chrysler.

Of course, like any company, BMW could occasionally get a bit stiff with its own success. I arrived in Munich just as the company was preparing the replacement for the beautiful 3.0CS coupe. One of the problems that the company hoped to rectify in the new car was the relative difficulty of getting in and out of it. (At the time, only the wealthiest Europeans could afford this top-line GT, and the well-heeled folks in that socioeconomic strata were not known for being terribly lithe.) The company's answer was a taller, rather stodgy design, ordered up at an outside styling consultant. I rebelled, and sketched out another, lower design on a piece of notebook paper—which, after passing through BMW's styling department, eventually became the 6-series coupe, considered the worthy successor of the classic 3.0CS.

But I stayed at BMW for only three years—partly because I didn't feel I was really making my mark, partly because I didn't care for the cutthroat politics inside the company at that time, and partly because, quite frankly, I was once again lured away, in 1974, by a better offer: to become chairman of Ford of Germany. At Ford, however, we tried to emulate a lot of what BMW was doing, from tasteful design to superb ride and handling. We "de-chromed" our cars, changed the interiors away from the U.S. loose-cushion look, and added BMW-style instrument clusters and other features that German buyers found attractive. The results were dramatic: We went from a 7 percent share of the market to 15 percent in under a year! And we'd done it, not by the usual route of cutting prices, but simply by paying attention to our gut feeling about the market and the products in it and then adding (at a relatively low cost to us) value to the product in places where the intuitive, car-loving, right side of our brains told us it would be most appreciated.

Right-brained thinking, for a good period of time, served me very well in the otherwise left-brained world of Ford Motor in the mid-'70s to mid-'80s. From my Ford of Germany post, I was promoted to vice president of Ford Europe; a year later to president; a year after that to chairman—a period during which we developed what became Europe's best-selling midsized sedan, the Ford Sierra, whose then-radical "jellybean" design also set the pattern for the smash-hit Ford Taurus and Mercury Sable in the United States. Then, in 1982, I was named to run all of Ford's international operations and was moved to Detroit as an executive vice president of the company and a member of its board of directors.

By the time I finally landed at Chrysler in 1986, I'd become totally convinced that "right-brain cars" were not only the kind of vehicles that I myself preferred, but the *only* kind of products that stood a prayer of truly standing out in a supersaturated auto market that today is crowded with more than 300 nameplates (and that's just in the United States alone!). I'm talking about the kind of cars (and trucks) that make the pulse quicken—and the pocketbook open. Or, to look at it from the opposite perspective, *not* the kind of vehicles that my good friend and editor of *Automobile* magazine, David E. Davis, once described in summing up the woes then besetting General Motors. The problem with GM, he said, is that nowhere in America is there a 14-year-old boy with tears in his eyes saying, "Please, Dad, buy a Lumina."

The problem with Chrysler was that we didn't have any right-brain vehicles, either—save perhaps the minivan. But, luckily, we *did* have a design team, and we also had a built-in industry forum for market-testing all-new ideas—wintertime auto shows and their displays of "concept cars."

While some concept cars genuinely presage the future of car design, the auto industry has historically more often viewed them merely as attention-grabbing flights of fancy by the industry's designers—fantastical visions in steel (or, in many cases, fiberglass) meant to draw in the general public to an individual automaker's show stand, and little else. Most show cars are conceived of as novelties that don't even imply a pretense of production. One of my own less-than-great ideas was a far-out car-within-a-car concept—a Chrysler minivan whose back half detached, giving birth to a microcommuter car. (The idea was that families would leave the "highway cruiser" part in a peripheral parking zone, then drive the tiny "urban module" into the inner city.) Chrysler's then-head of sales and marketing (and resident wag), Ben Bidwell, said at the time, "We'll never build it. We wouldn't know which end to put the rebate on."

But concept cars have always held a lot of latent potential: Since only *one* actual car has to be built (and since it doesn't really have to be roadworthy), show cars can be designed, engineered, and manufactured much more quickly than bona fide production cars—simultaneously giving their builders the opportunity, if they care to use it, to quickly test out *real* designs (if somewhat disguised and sometimes accompanied by a little disinformation!) on the public and, maybe more important, on the opinion-leading auto press, while at the same time softening up the outside world to what might be a bold new idea.

Sometime around 1986 to 1987, Chrysler's design team, led by Chrysler veteran Tom Gale, had a bold new idea. It was called "cab-forward design"—a new kind of vehicle architecture in which the vehicle's cabin is extended forward to create an absolutely cavernous interior vis-à-vis the exterior silhouette. Other carmakers had done cab-forward designs before, but no one had gone as far with it as Chrysler was about to.

In Frankfurt (then-West) Germany, in September of '87, and then again at the Detroit auto show in January of '88, Chrysler displayed a four-door concept car called the Portofino. Some of Portofino's disinformational features included a midmounted Lamborghini V-8 engine, clamshell hood and deck-lid openings, and rotational front doors that pivoted up and out of the way like the eyepiece cover on a telescope. But the most salient feature of the Portofino was its swoopy, curvaceous (and, at that time, intentionally extreme) cab-forward design, a look so aggressive that it made the car look like a two-door sports car even though it offered more interior room (75 percent of the car's total volume was devoted to the passenger compartment, compared with 65 percent for the average car) than most four-door sedans then on the market.

Industry observers were impressed, some stunned, by the Portofino. They didn't know for sure if its design and vehicle-packaging scheme were merely yet another flight of fancy from Chrysler or something that was for real. But in either case, the mere fact that "the K-car company" was able to even *think about* something this innovative (and this gorgeous!) said to them, "Watch this space!"

And those who kept watching saw that Chrysler's thinking about cab-forward continued to deepen and evolve. A year later, we debuted the Millennium, a concept that showed off futuristic safety devices and, more important to us, displayed a somewhat more road-ready version of the design and packaging cues pioneered in the Portofino. And then a year after that, in January of 1990, we premiered the Optima concept car, a by-then very thinly disguised version of what was to become perhaps the most important symbol of Chrysler's bold new product philosophy—our original Chrysler Concorde, Dodge Intrepid, and Eagle Vision family sedans . . . or, as they were perhaps even better known at the time (thanks to our sometimes-too-liberal use of their internal code names!), our "LH" cars.

So, with the idea of the LH and cab-forward design, Chrysler now had a tangible vision—not just of survival, but, if we could somehow muddle through the interim, of a promising and exciting new future. It was a future to be based on not just better products, but *astonishingly* better products—products that would excite the right side of the cranium for their verve and, we hoped, the more rational left side for their tremendous value.

The problem was, how to get from here to there?

.   .   .

To a lot of people who don't know me very well (and to some who do!), I'm the *last* person you'd expect to be a champion of teamwork.

For instance, the trade journal *Automotive Industries* once said of me, "Lutz is outspoken. He is opinionated. He perfectly embodies the symbol of the rugged individualist, the loner, the one who is not afraid to tell anyone exactly what he thinks no matter what the consequences. He never was a 'team player.' And he knows it."

Well . . . maybe. But then again, I guess I've always been a walking contradiction. That, in a phrase of songwriter and former Army helicopter pilot Kris Kristofferson, is "partly fact and partly fiction"—and there have been times when *that's* applied to me as well, I'm afraid!

The truth is, going all the way back to my earliest days in the auto industry, I was surprised (and a bit appalled) at the lack of functional integration in the companies I worked for. In particular, I just couldn't understand why there was so little real communication between the operational units of the companies—the design, engineering, manufacturing, and procurement organizations. This was very unlike my experience in the U.S. Marine Corps, where there was always lots of open, honest, and free-flowing communication across—and up and down—the ranks. People who've never been in the military and/or those who get their view of the military solely from John Wayne movies like *The Sands of Iwo Jima,* tend not to believe this; but they're mistaken. True, boot camp is not exactly an exercise in participative management, nor are life-and-death battlefield situations where split-second, top-down decisions are clearly necessary. But all one has to do is pick up a copy of the *Marine Corps Gazette* to see the degree to which the USMC version of middle management feels free to challenge conventional wisdom and to offer up—often in the form of long, eloquently written essays—constructive dissent that would be unheard of in the corporate world. I believe it's this openness and willingness to be honest, in fact, that has allowed the U.S. military, despite a few setbacks over the years, to maintain a degree of unit cohesion that American society at large might envy.

Chrysler itself had tried several stabs at more open, teamwork-based organizations over the years. Like everybody else in the Western world, the company tried Japanese-style quality circles in the early '80s—and, like everybody else, it found that that concept didn't translate too well. In the mid-'80s, the corporation formed what it called "business groups" within its engineering organization, hoping to turn its engineers into "entrepreneurs"—but that didn't work, either. Then, in the late '80s came Chrysler's version of "brand management," whereby the company's *marketing* managers—à la Procter & Gamble's successful formula in the packaged-goods industry—were put in charge of product development (on the partly plausible theory that those responsible for moving the widgets *off* the shelf ought to have some say over what goes *on* the shelf to begin with). The problem was, Chrysler wasn't a packaged-goods company—cars being significantly more complex to conceive and to manufacture than bars of soap—and, in time, that idea was abandoned as well.

But for all its experiments at alternative ways of organizing—and for all its outward appearances as a swashbuckling company—Chrysler remained, under the surface, a very bureaucratic, very hidebound organization. Like so many patients with a heart condition, we'd survived emergency surgery several years before only to revert to our old, unhealthy lifestyle.

The way, in reality, we operated looked pretty much like the graphic on the bottom of this page. (By the way, I've labeled this graphic "traditional" vehicle development because it represents the way not just Chrysler but virtually all Western automakers—and for that matter, much of Western industry—operated from time immemorial. Most companies today, of course, call their old, vertically oriented,

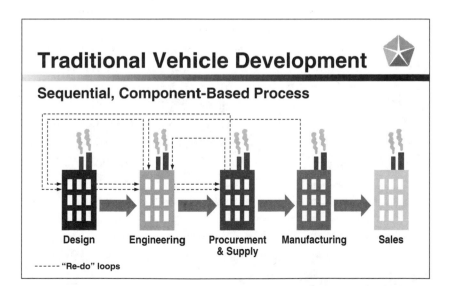

Traditional Vehicle Development

Sequential, Component-Based Process

Design　　　Engineering　　　Procurement　　Manufacturing　　　Sales
　　　　　　　　　　　　　　　& Supply

------ "Re-do" loops

functional departments *silos*—but, hey, since autos are supposedly a smokestack industry, we called ours *chimneys!*)

Typically a new car would begin life as a series of sketches, then a clay model, in the design (a.k.a. "styling") department. This phase usually engaged the attention of only the designers and senior management. Once a design had been sufficiently "improved" by the bosses' input, it was thrown over the wall to the next chimney: engineering. There, engineers, working in their own balkanized world, would inevitably find dozens of ways in which the design was either impractical, too costly, or even impossible for mass production. Discovery of these shortcomings would trigger what I call "re-do loops," with the car's design being sent back to the design department, which would (grudgingly) make the necessary changes, only to have to then submit another, modified, clay model to management for its approval.

After a countless number of re-do loops, the now-engineered design and all the blueprints would be thrown over the wall again—this time to the procurement (a.k.a. "purchasing") chimney. Only in this case, the chimney functioned more like a feudal castle up on a hill, with the company's outside suppliers playing the role of so many industrial vassals offering up their meager wares to the lords of this particular chimney/castle. Or, to put it another way, because of arrogance and because of the usually rampant "not invented here" (NIH) factor at the automaker, we always thought that *we* knew better how to design the suppliers' parts than they did. So, what we would do, in essence, was hold up our design in front of a bunch of suppliers and ask, "How much?" The lowest bidder got the business. The problem was, the lowest bidder was, in reality, seldom that—as yet more necessary changes would drive up the total cost of the component in question to well beyond the bid price.

Next came the toss over the wall to manufacturing. Invariably, even more problems would come to light, either ones affecting cost or ones bearing on the car's unsuitability for mass production. And, once again, there would be yet more re-do loops—enough so that, when all was said and done, an actual graphic of this whole process would look more like a fur ball!

That's for the changes in a vehicle's design that were possible to make. At this late stage, many of the worst blunders sometimes just had to be accepted. Most car companies, for instance, have tales of finding out too late that a fully engineered car was a little too wide or a little too long to pass through the manufacturer's paint tunnels in the assembly plant. In these drastic cases, the solution was either to start all over again (resulting in a huge, costly delay) or to spend millions for new equipment (e.g., new paint tunnels).

At the very end of this painful gestation process stood the chimney with SALES & MARKETING stenciled on its side. This is where the re-do loops stopped and where reality set in. Often, by this time, the new model was late to the market (because this process routinely took four to five years) and was priced higher than either the designers had envisioned or the sales force had ever wanted (because the project wound up being so costly). This did, however, lead to a certain esprit de corps among the sales force, albeit a twisted one: They came to view themselves as macho cowboys whose mission in life was to "move the iron," no matter how ill suited to the market that iron might be.

Obviously, the chimney system wasn't *all* bad—it had, after all, served the Western auto industry pretty well for a number of decades. It was, in fact, merely a variant of the time-tested division-of-labor principles that go all the way back to Adam Smith's celebrated pin factory. The problem was, "division of labor" had devolved into "suboptimization at the expense of the whole." Plus, the system had simply become ossified with age—and the Japanese had figured out ways to run circles around it, developing new products in a lot less time and for a lot less money. Clearly, if Chrysler hoped to survive (much less prosper by building great right-brain vehicles), an all-new paradigm was needed.

Some might say it's ironic that, for all of Chrysler's denunciations of Japanese trade practices in the '80s, Japan was, in fact, one of the places we looked for ideas about how to construct a new product-development paradigm. Maybe it is ironic, but no more, I submit, than Japan's looking to America after World War II (and to the teachings of people like W. Edwards Deming) for their own ideas about efficiency and "lean production." And so it was that, first of all, we learned everything we could from our Japanese partner at that time, Mitsubishi Motors. Falling in line with the transplant craze of the day, we and

Mitsubishi had built a 50-50 joint venture plant in Bloomington-Normal, Illinois; and it's not for nothing that the senior Chrysler representative in that venture, a very able veteran engineer named Glenn Gardner, later became chief of our LH program.

But the really hot Japanese car company in the mid- to late '80s wasn't Mitsubishi (or even Toyota); it was Honda. Honda was then the poster child for Japanese competitiveness, and with breakthrough products like the Honda Accord, the Acura Legend, and the Compound Vortex Combustion Chamber (CVCC) engine, the first automotive engine to meet U.S. air-quality standards without the need of a catalytic converter, they were proving that efficiency and innovation really can go hand in hand.

Probably every car company in the world was doing a "Honda study" of some sort at that time. The difference at Chrysler was that we in senior management actually paid attention to ours! The study had been commissioned by my boss at the time (and now CEO of United Airlines), Jerry Greenwald, and it was carried out by about a dozen young staffers from different functions throughout the company.

Like a lot of reports done by junior staffers, the Honda study done at Chrysler contained more than a few naive recommendations—like "bulldozing down all executive offices." However, for all its naïveté, it simultaneously displayed an honest and passionate concern for our company that hit most of us in senior management right between the eyes. In short, these junior staffers were telling us, candidly and in no uncertain terms, just how screwed up we really were!

They pointed out, for instance, that the Honda system was based on mutual trust throughout the enterprise, whereas Chrysler was based on *mistrust*—of suppliers, of dealers, of other departments. Honda's senior management empowered employees, allowing them considerable autonomy and coaching them in how to make quick, sound decisions on their own. We, by contrast, micromanaged. Honda worked in partnership with its suppliers; we dictated. Perhaps most important, going all the way back to its fabled founder, Soichiro "Pops" Honda, that company advocated a collegial style of management that, while demanding, also put a high premium on teamwork and cooperation.

True, we'd heard all this type of thing before. (The press, for instance, had never been shy about pointing out our shortcomings!) But the fact that it was coming from our own people really resonated. Still, however, there's a big difference between merely reading about somebody else's better way of operating and actually implementing a better way yourself. For one thing, Honda was a Japanese company—and there was certainly no guarantee whatsoever that a "Honda solution" would translate any better to Chrysler than quality circles had. What we really needed, then, was a working model that was maybe a little less foreign—something that would help get our minds unstuck and thinking beyond the old paradigms that we all were so familiar with.

Voilà! Enter American Motors!

If the Honda study helped reinforce to us the "what" of our needed transformation, then Chrysler's August 1987 acquisition of AMC (in one of the all-time great moments in corporate serendipity) most definitely played a key role in demonstrating the "how."

To the outside world, American Motors had long been the Big Three's weak little sister, the perpetually money-losing company that happened to own Jeep but whose product line otherwise was as quirky and undistinguished as the angular turn-signal stalks on the cars supplied to it by its French parent, Renault. True, AMC had more than a few problems (which is the reason I myself was lukewarm about the acquisition to begin with). However, what we soon found is that, far from being a bunch of brain-dead losers, the troops at AMC were more like Wake Island Marines: With almost no resources, and fighting a vastly superior enemy, they had in recent years rolled out an impressive succession of new products—namely, a new Jeep Wrangler, the all-new Jeep Cherokee, the all-new Premier sedan, plus an all-new 4-liter, 6-cylinder engine and an all-new 2.5-liter, 4-cylinder engine.

When we acquired AMC, a large percentage of Chrysler's technical community reacted first with anger (because they felt, as I had at first felt, that we had enough on our plates already) and then with almost gleeful anticipation—as in, "Hot dog! We're finally going to get all those extra engineers we've been asking for!" To his eternal credit, however, Lee Iacocca agreed to keep the former AMC engineering unit intact, expanding its scope to work on Chrysler's pickup trucks as well as Jeep vehicles in order to get a closer look at how they were able to get so much done with so little.

Also to his credit, he later allowed me to elevate the leader of AMC's engineering unit, François Castaing, to head up all engineering at Chrysler. Born in France and a former employee of Renault itself, François had spent all of the 1970s working on (and being in charge of) Renault's very successful Formula One racing team—where he learned all about cross-functional teamwork. (It wasn't at all unusual, for instance, for François—even though he was chief engineer of the whole program—to be changing tires in the pits during a race, nor was it unusual for a member of the pit crew to give him engineering suggestions to improve the car once the race was finished.) A lot of people give me the credit for instituting teamwork-based product development at Chrysler—what came to be known as our "platform teams"—but the truth is, François was the human linchpin who, from his post in the engineering department, helped us to turn the lessons of the Honda study into action.

I mentioned earlier that our engineering department itself was very balkanized, and that was true. Body engineering, chassis engineering, power-train engineering, electrical engineering, and so on were all not-so-little chimneys unto themselves, replete with their own re-do loops. And, as a result, no program inside engineering could move any faster than the organization's slowest-moving part. For instance, if the door locks, handles, and mechanisms department got swamped with work at any given time, then the whole system bogged down waiting for them to catch up.

François did the heretofore unthinkable: He completely dismantled each of these entrenched, component-specific engineering groups. In their place we formed units that were responsible not just for components, but for a *whole vehicle* (or "platform," in industry jargon). Lots of companies today have organizations they call "platform teams," but they're just half measures compared to this—little tugboats off to the side of the still-existing corporate battleship, attempting (often without much success) to nudge the bigger boat a few degrees to port or starboard. What we did was to get rid of the battleship altogether!

The ship didn't go down without a fight, however. Many engineers and executives who held positions of power in the old, compartmentalized structure felt cheated—and, to a degree, I can understand why. For a good period of time, harkening all the way back to the days of railroad-man-turned-auto-tycoon Walter P. Chrysler, Chrysler Corporation had been known as "the engineering company." As a reminder of that, Lee Iacocca received literally hundreds of anonymous letters expressing righteous indignation that "the evil Frenchman and his Swiss buddy [me!] are screwing up the finest engineering organization in the world." Suffice it to say that this was not an easy period for either François or me. In fact, it was probably during this period that I lost all hope of someday becoming CEO of Chrysler—even though, I'm convinced, we were laying the groundwork for saving the company in the process. (And I have no regrets whatsoever; in fact, I'd do it all over again in a heartbeat!) The truth was, poison-pen letters or not, by the late 1980s Chrysler's reputation for engineering (along with our reputation for a lot of other things) was totally shot—and only dramatic action was going to change that.

So, we persevered.

And we also turned our attention to the all-important LH cars.

By 1988, the LH project had already been kicking around inside Chrysler for a couple of years. And, like a lot of Pentagon weapons systems, it was trapped in the classical "more is more" planning maze, bedeviled by requests for more and more body styles, for both front- and rear-wheel drive, and for exotic features like active suspension and rear-wheel steer (then-fashionable technologies, which ultimately went out of fashion as fast as they'd come in). It was an awful situation: Our LH cars, our best hope for the future (some in the press were saying "LH" stood for "last hope"), were poised to consume upward of $2.5 billion in scarce investment capital. Worse, the variable cost per car had ballooned more than $1,500 over target, severely compromising the cars' marketability. (This same phenomenon had, in fact, bedeviled Chrysler for years. Indeed, one of the reasons Chrysler sought to take its existing cars upscale as part of Plan B is that we had to: It was the only way we could ever hope to recoup our all-too-frequent cost overruns!)

François stopped the LH program cold. With Glenn Gardner as his point man, he assembled our first major platform team within engineering and told them to work together to make the necessary cost and functional trade-offs as they saw fit. The "how" of the program was to be totally their responsibility. But first, I stepped in as well: Throughout my career I'd seen product programs mushroom in cost simply because senior managements weren't clear about defining the absolute parameters of the program to those below them—or, more often, weren't in tune enough with the product itself to have a clear idea of just what those parameters should be. I was bound and determined that wasn't going to happen this time.

So we assembled the team and laid down the law as to the "what" of the LH program: the timing envelope, the maximum investment by the corporation, the targeted variable cost, the fact that we were going to be using cab-forward design, and, perhaps most important, the LH's mission—*not* to be all things to all people, but to be a highly affordable family sedan that hit "the sweet spot" in terms of features the way the best Japanese and European cars had been doing for years. In short, we wanted these cars to be "the imports from Detroit." To focus the team, we also gave them a benchmark to work from: the Renault-designed Premier sedan. The car may have been a little off-beat, but under the sheet metal it was a thoroughly modern vehicle, and, just as it's always easier to totally rewrite someone else's piece of writing than it is to start from scratch all on your own, so, too, was it easier for the team to rewrite the cost, weight, and performance of the LH cars by using the Premier as a takeoff point.

About this same time, we also began to implement a costing system in the company that would help the teams keep track of their actual costs and to stay within budget. As a "car guy," I've never enjoyed the full trust of the auto industry's finance staffs. Going all the way back to Henry Ford I (who purportedly resorted to estimating his company's costs by *weighing* his bills and invoices) and to Billy Durant (the hot-headed founder of General Motors who was twice ousted from that company), there's been a mistrust on the part of the auto industry's green-eyeshade crowd toward those seen as less buttoned-down than they. From their perspective, trusting a car guy to take the lead in managing a vehicle program's finances was like trusting an alcoholic to manage your bar.

But in this case, as well, we proved that teamwork and empowerment really do work—and work better than the alternative. François's finance director in engineering at that time was Tom Sidlik, now an executive vice president in charge of all purchasing activities. Knowing that Tom had once worked in finance at Ford, I asked him if he could implement a version of Ford's industry-famous (some might say infamous!) Red Book system of product costing—so-called purportedly because when the program was first implemented at Ford by Robert McNamara, the most notable of the former U.S. Air Force Office of Statistical Control "Whiz Kids" whose financial-control methods came to dominate Ford from the '50s onward, the numbers were kept in red three-ring binders. I asked Tom, however, if he could please apply one of my own tried-and-true favorite rules of business to his mission: the "80/20" rule—80 percent of net benefit, but with only 20 percent of the BS and red tape.

Prior to this time, not only did Chrysler have frequent variable-cost overruns on product programs, we also had very little idea of exactly how much those costs would be until *after* the car was built. It was sort of like navigating via the rearview mirror. Every year, just after the launch of the new models, we'd have an October surprise as the actual bills for parts and components came in. And, consequently, at the beginning of each year we'd have to book hundreds of millions of dollars in contingency fees "just in case"—money that obviously could have been put to much better uses, including, perhaps, in improving the product itself.

Our central problem was that we were managing the *variances* instead of managing the *absolute* costs of components or systems. In other words, when it was time to do a new model, we'd look only at the parts of the car that were obviously changing vis-à-vis its still-in-production predecessor model, and we'd say, "Well, the grille this year is going to be bigger than on the old model, so that part can cost a little more; but the fascia is going to be smaller, so it had better cost less." What we never took into account, however, is that there were lots of other parts connected to and/or affected by the part in question, and we were paying virtually no attention whatsoever to the costs of those parts (even though they would all have to be changed or updated as well). Plus, over the four or five years it was then taking us to develop a new vehicle, the costs of *all* the parts had most likely changed from their original price—so the only honest response to the command "Make this part 50 cents cheaper!" was "Cheaper than *what?*"

Most problematic of all, however, was that by overly focusing on the predecessor model, we were condemning ourselves to that model's cost paradigm rather than thinking out of the box about quantum-leap improvements in costs. For instance, instead of thinking about how we could cut the piece cost of bodyside cladding for a car, maybe we should have been thinking about getting rid of the cladding altogether—and perhaps thus making the car more attractive in the bargain! But, of course, to make those kinds of decisions intelligently, you'd want to have more than just the "bean counters" involved; it was mandatory that the *car people* be an integral part of the system as well—and, in fact, that they take a leadership role in the whole costing process.

And that's just what happened. Within no time, we had our "20 percent solution" working, not just in engineering, but throughout the whole company and, importantly, in the company's interfaces with its suppliers. And, thanks simply to the fact that our finance people and our product people were now on the same team, we were finally able to start estimating with precision what the absolute cost of a part or system should be, instead of merely measuring the after-the-fact variances. (And, by the way, one big reason this works is the kind of finance people we had. Led in recent years by CFO Gary Valade and controller Jim Donlon, our finance staff shucked the traditional "numbers Nazi" role played by finance people the world over and instead became a true partner with the operations people.)

In very much this same vein, there's one other big thing that we were able to accomplish in the area of finance: erasing the increasingly artificial distinction between variable and fixed costs. Throughout my career in the auto industry, I was always perplexed by what I call the "two-meeting syndrome." You'd go into a meeting to discuss the *variable* costs of a product program, and everybody would agree that in order to get the variable costs under control, something had to be done—and that something was usually increasing the investment in the program for things like new plant tooling (which would, of course, give you higher efficiencies for the parts produced). But then, right after that, you'd go into another meeting, and everybody would want to know how the *fixed* costs got so out of control!

Today, the whole company is focused as much as possible on all-in, fully accounted profits and losses. The overriding question: "Is this program making money for the shareholder even *after* its fair share of the company's overhead is assigned to it?" It's a great question to ask, because, after all, costs are costs—sooner or later, whether fixed or variable, they *all* make their way to the bottom line. I'm not saying that Chrysler makes a fully accounted profit on every vehicle that it sells, but just by asking the question—and by working together as a team to try to find the answer—I think we made a big step in the right direction.

Meanwhile, concurrent with all these other actions, we also began spreading the platform-team gospel out through the company at large—including our heretofore macho-to-the-extreme manufacturing group, now headed up by a gentle giant named Dennis Pawley, a natural-born leader who'd seen Japanese-style production from the inside, during a stint as head of Mazda's U.S. manufacturing operations. The gospel also spread to our procurement and supply organization. Suppliers are arguably more important to Chrysler than to its domestic competitors, because around 70 percent of the dollar value of Chrysler's finished product comes from suppliers, compared with about 50 percent at that time for Ford and only about 30 percent then for General Motors. So, adopting all-new ways of doing business with what we came to call our "Extended Enterprise" (a term we even trademarked!) was absolutely critical to our success.

Under the leadership of Tom Stallkamp, our procurement group invented a whole new paradigm for OEM-supplier teamwork—one that the *Harvard Business Review* has called "an American *keiretsu*" in reference to the term for the famously close supplier relationships in Japan. And the vehicle they used for this task was, ironically, a cost-reduction program—the SCORE program, which stands for Supplier Cost-Reduction Effort.

The core philosophy behind SCORE was that we and our suppliers were really both links in the same value-added chain—and that we could demand price cuts from suppliers till the cows came home, but if we didn't work together to get total costs out of our common chain, we'd just be fooling ourselves in the end. To that end, Tom and his people did away with the age-old practice of sending suppliers a letter every couple of years demanding a 2 or a 5 percent price cut. Instead, they invited suppliers simply to come in and talk to us about how, together, we could eliminate waste from the value chain—including waste that Chrysler itself might be causing at the supplier. (Something we would never have been able to accomplish, by the way, if we hadn't first eliminated the "NIH factor" in our engineering group, the source of most of the prior rigidity.) And, as an incentive to root out the waste, Tom and his people let suppliers keep half the cost savings for themselves. That's what you call an incentive!

At the same time, we also took a cue from the Honda study and began to source our business to fewer "supplier-partners"—making the business "theirs to lose" instead of "theirs to beg for." In the old days, we'd fooled ourselves into thinking that because we were maximizing competition, we were ipso facto maximizing efficiency. Of course, to a certain degree, that's usually the case. But we'd taken it to such an extreme that even our better suppliers were practicing what I like to call "malicious obedience"—as in, "I know this isn't how this part should be built, and I know that I could give them a better design at less cost, but if this is what they're insisting on, hey, I'll build it now, charge 'em through the nose for all the necessary changes later, and laugh all the way to the bank." I myself had had several supplier CEOs confide in me over the years things like, "You know, Bob, we could have given you that part for half the price if only your people had been willing to change their design just a little bit."

Today, Chrysler has just three suppliers for instrument panels. And the company has just two suppliers for its multi-million-dollar-a-month tire buy: Goodyear and Michelin. Similar to the system inside the company today between senior management and the platform teams, the procurement group negotiates a target cost with the supplier, leaving the "how" part of the program totally up to the supplier—who is, after all, more of an expert in its own field than Chrysler could ever hope to be. And in almost every case, the final component is of a better design than it otherwise would be and its total cost far less than it would have been under the old auction system.

All told, Tom Stallkamp's SCORE program saved Chrysler more than $5 billion between 1989 and 1998—which, I suspect, is one of the big reasons why, in 1997, he wound up succeeding me as president of the company!

Five years before that, of course, is when Bob Eaton appeared on the scene to become Chrysler's CEO, arriving from his previous post as chairman of GM-Europe. When Bob was brought into Chrysler in 1992, the betting in Detroit was that he and I would never get along—that his presence would somehow upset the apple cart at the company, either by my doing my best to torpedo him or else his doing his best to change things just for the sake of change (and ego gratification). But people who thought that don't know me—and they certainly don't know Bob Eaton.

Bob has an uncanny, almost Zenlike understanding of cars and of the car business—something that I came to appreciate immediately. And he did, in fact, bring a lot of changes to Chrysler—constructive ones. Instead of caution, he urged speed. Instead of drawing in our horns on product, he urged us to be even bolder.

Finally, while he certainly has an ego, he's able to submerge his ego for the good of the enterprise—something a lot of executives just aren't able to do. It's this very trait, in fact, that ultimately made possible the recent historic merger between Daimler-Benz and Chrysler. Most mergers of this sort either never happen or wind up not working because, in reality, neither CEO wants to sacrifice personal position and power for the good of the whole. Not so Bob Eaton. At the time the merger was announced, it was also announced that Bob and Daimler-Benz chief Jürgen Schrempp would serve as cochairmen of the new company during a three-year transition period; Bob also made it clear that at the end of the transition period he would then step aside, thus paving the way for a peaceful transition into a whole new era—both for Chrysler and for global business.

It is, as well, because of Bob Eaton that "the two Bobs" (Eaton and Lutz) worked at Chrysler—and why our revolution not only continued, but accelerated.

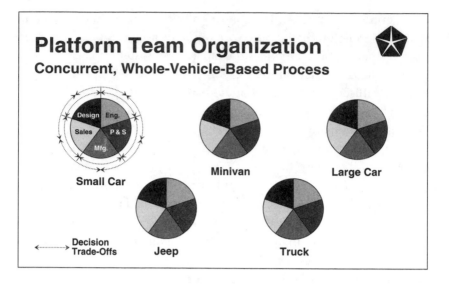

Before long, the chimneys that once characterized the company had started to metamorphose into something more resembling the pie charts you see on this page. Where Chrysler had once been highly compartmentalized and focused mainly on functions, the whole company was now moving toward a cross-functional "platform" setup—centered, not around individual disciplines, but around our major product types: the small-car team, the large-car team, the minivan team, the Jeep team, the (pickup) truck team. The focus was *holistic* (bye-bye suboptimization!), and the information flows were *concurrent* and *two-way* (bye-bye re-do loops!).

And, importantly, one key reason our teams at Chrysler worked (while so many other experiments in team-based management in the business world have failed) is indeed the fact that we sank the battleship. Platform teams, in essence, *are* the company today. (In fact, even the finance and public relations staffs are now "platformized.") The old mother ship exists only as a secondary support function, and in its place are five nimble cruisers, each able to operate in different waters simultaneously. Moreover, and perhaps just as important, we made sure the cruisers didn't fire at each other by having most of our corporate officers wear two hats—one relating to their functional discipline and the other as a "godfather" of a platform organization. For instance, early on, Tom Stallkamp, in addition to heading up procurement, was also general manager of large-car operations; and Tom Gale, in addition to heading up product design, was general manager of minivan operations. This setup provided a natural system of checks and balances (e.g., Tom Gale knew that if he wanted to get supplier parts for his minivans, he'd better make sure Tom Stallkamp had great designs for his large cars), but more important, the genuinely collegial atmosphere at the top of the company permeated down through the ranks, sending a strong message that internecine warfare was out.

Don't get me wrong; *platform teams* is not a synonym for *love-in*. Sure, trade-offs over things like "Should we spend the money on providing leather seats or should we spend it instead on beefed-up suspension?" are now made at much lower levels of the organization, where the best information is to begin with. But the very term *trade-off* means that somebody (or, often, everybody) doesn't quite get what he or she wants. That's just simple reality.

By the same token, however, that's often when the most creative thinking of all kicks in—thinking by the individuals who make up the team. And that, I think, was one of the pleasant paradoxes of Chrysler's platform teams: Though their very name implies group-based teamwork, we found the real value to be in the freeing up of individual initiative throughout the organization. The individual mind, after all, is more powerful than any computer. (Or, as I used to say back in the Marines whenever somebody would talk about remote-control aircraft replacing human pilots, "Don't forget: The human being is the most complex, easily programmable, nonlinear servomechanism ever devised—plus it can be cheaply and easily reproduced by unskilled labor!") Unlocking that power was where the real magic lay.

And the magic was working: In the case of the LH cars, investment had dropped from $2.5 to $1.5 billion; development time shrank (once we'd restarted the clock to reflect the massive change in the program) to 39 months from the usual four to five years; and variable cost ultimately came in at several hundred dollars *under* target!

Meanwhile, other projects were simultaneously progressing through the other platform-team organizations, one of which certainly deserves special mention (for its very creation drove a stake into the heart of Chrysler's Plan B forever): the Neon.

As I pointed out in the previous chapter, conventional wisdom in the auto industry in the late '80s and early '90s was that it was crazy to try to build small cars in the United States—that the Japanese had cornered that market forever, and that it was utterly impossible for an American company to either (1) design a competitive small car to begin with or (2) make money on it. But conventional wisdom had a couple of things wrong: For one thing, the Japanese yen had finally strengthened against the U.S. dollar, making production in the United States significantly more attractive than it had been up to that point. And, frankly, conventional wisdom also didn't take into account the guts or the ingenuity at Chrysler!

At the Detroit auto show in January 1991, Chrysler displayed a cute, bug-eyed, cab-forward subcompact concept car. It was called the Neon. Again, a lot of industry observers probably thought the car was just so much disinformation. But the fact was, we had already begun work on cost and investment studies to see if, in fact, we could achieve the elusive goal of designing and building a small car in the United States that would actually *not* drag down corporate profitability while still helping the company meet the federal law for corporate average fuel economy (CAFE).

There was, to say the least, a lot of skepticism from some quarters in the company about our ability to produce a small car without a foreign partner—and without losing a ton of money on it. At the very least, the line of thinking went, we should use a foreign partner's small-car design.

But again, we persevered. And in this particular case, what I like to call a "significant emotional event" played a big role.

A veteran Chrysler engineer named Bob Marcell was the leader of the small-car platform team working on the Neon, and in the summer of 1990 his team was holding a rally (to which all of Chrysler's senior management was also invited) in a drab conference room in the garage of the company's engineering building (a former 1920s-era Maxwell Motors factory) at Chrysler's old headquarters in Highland Park, Michigan, an enclave of inner-city Detroit. Bob is a soft-spoken, self-effacing native of a once-proud mining town, called Iron River, in Michigan's upper peninsula. In a 10-minute slide show that kicked off a series of presentations on the Neon, he used what had happened to

Iron River over the years as both a cautionary tale and a battle cry. And, though he was ostensibly speaking to his own troops, his message was for the senior managers in the room as well.

Bob opened up his talk with a series of slides of the prosperous, beautiful community that Iron River had been when he was growing up there, and then he showed another series of bleak, dust bowl–like pictures of what Iron River had become: shuttered mines, boarded-up businesses, downtrodden people. Bob's father was one of those who had lost his job; in fact, he was the last man out of Hiawatha Number Two, the deepest iron mine in North America, before he himself flooded it shut. "The ground in Iron River shook at three and eleven every day," Bob said, referring to the daily charges in the mines signifying new exploration. "But now the ground doesn't shake anymore." In Russia, he said, Chernobyl had been a nuclear disaster; but Iron River, which had failed to stay competitive with low-cost iron-ore pellets now coming out of Brazil and Canada, was an economic disaster. Seventy-five percent of the people in the town were now below the poverty level, and most of the schools in town had vanished.

Bob concluded his presentation by asking, softly and rhetorically, "Is *this* what we want to have happen to the automobile business in this country? Or are we going to fight back?"

I glanced over at Lee Iacocca. His eyes, like mine, were brimming with genuine tears (and I'd seen this presentation once before!). From that moment forward, "Remember Iron River" became a rallying cry throughout the corporation, the Neon was a go (with the small-car team viewing their mission as a holy war to save America's industrial base), and Plan B was deader than a doornail!

Throughout this entire period, however, the press continued to write about the "beleaguered" Chrysler. (In fact, that term was used so often that for a while there, we thought maybe "beleaguered" had somehow become the company's new first name!) Wall Street, too, had very little confidence in us. With our pension fund about to go bust, we went to the market in the fall of '91 to try to raise some badly needed cash via a stock offering. Barely two weeks before the offering, one of our big syndicate underwriters got cold feet and withdrew from the deal. As it was, the $400 million we raised came at a very steep price: We had to price the stock at just 10⅛ a share, which was indeed only about a third of our share price just a couple of years earlier.

But what the outside world didn't see was what was going on *inside* Chrysler. As I told anyone at the time who would listen, Chrysler was like a submarine-launched missile. The outside world kept saying, "Missile? Missile? What are you talking about? I don't see any missile." That's because nothing had yet broken through the surface of the water. But, down in the sub, we knew that the payload had already left the silo.

In 1994, the missile broke through the surface of the water, and success began to follow our revolution at Chrysler like a juggernaut: Instead of being our last hope, the LH cars had been named "Automobile of the Year" by *Automobile* magazine, while, aptly, the trade publication *AutoWeek* had featured them on their cover under a banner headline reading "The Cure!" The Neon, profitable to Chrysler though originally priced at just $8,975, made even the Japanese sit up and take notice—in fact, in Tokyo there were headlines reading, "Japan Car Killer?" (The Neon didn't quite live up to that billing, but it was a great little car nonetheless.) Our Jeep Grand Cherokee—a vehicle that I introduced at the Detroit auto show by driving up the front steps and through a plate-glass window—caught the wave of America's love affair with sport utility vehicles just as it was starting to swell, and it's still riding that wave today.

Our bold, "baby-Kenworth" Dodge Ram pickup, developed by our Truck platform team (under the very able leadership of Bernard Robertson, another long-time Chrysler veteran who's been responsible for Chrysler's dramatic success in recent years in both Jeep vehicles and light trucks) deserves, I believe, to be a business-school casebook study all by itself. In its last month of production, in 1994, the Ram's predecessor captured just 3.8 percent of the U.S. full-sized pickup truck market. Three years later, the new Ram took *18* percent of that market! And then, in '95, came our family of all-new minivans—America's first minivans with four doors. While the competition had dithered by slavishly following its market research that seemed to imply that a fourth, left-side sliding door on a minivan might be "unsafe" for passengers exiting near the flow of traffic, we'd simply asked ourselves,

"How many *three*-door sedans do you see on the road?" The result: Chrysler continues to "own" that market segment.

And our juggernaut made itself felt in the numbers as well. Chrysler earned $3.7 billion in 1994 and a cumulative $8.5 billion over the next three years, paving the way for the company's first full "A" credit rating in 22 years and allowing it to actually overfund its once grotesquely underfunded pension plan. Along the way, our worldwide sales increased from 1.9 million cars and trucks in 1991 to more than 3 million in 1998; our overall North American market share increased by three percentage points; and, I believe, we also managed to build an impressive amount of "equity" in our brands (i.e., measurable financial value due to reputation alone). (One way, I believe, we helped that latter process along: A couple of years back, we resurrected Walter P. Chrysler's original "gold ribbon" logo from the '20s for the hoods and grilles of our Chrysler-brand vehicles. We wouldn't have dared to do that five years before. But on that day, I believe, ol' Walter P. was smiling down on us!)

The great movie mogul Sam Goldwyn once said, "There's nothing wrong with Hollywood that good movies wouldn't fix." I think Chrysler's success in its second turnaround proved that there was nothing (or at least almost nothing) wrong with Detroit that good cars and trucks couldn't fix. Similarly, I think it also proved that of the famous "four Ps" of marketing (price, place, promotion, and product), the most critical element is the product itself. With great, bold, right-brain products—and with the right system in place to bring them to market—you may not be able to raise the dead, but you can, as we proved, heal the sick!

The kind of products we started building at Chrysler were, in reality, the kind of products that we ourselves wanted to drive—cars and trucks that oozed passion, the same kind of passion that we didn't mind wearing on our sleeves. The buying public bought into that passion: While our new products weren't perfect, they produced a fierce "gotta-have-it" impulse in the market. But no single product of ours produced a fiercer response—or struck a more visceral chord with automotive enthusiasts around the world—than the car that deserves its very own chapter (the next one): *Viper!*

CHAPTER 3
"WE JUST DID IT": THE STORY OF THE VIPER

A SINGLE SWALLOW, WE ARE TOLD, DOES NOT A SUMMER MAKE. BUT A single snake—the Dodge Viper—effected Chrysler's second turnaround. This wasn't because Viper sold in large quantities or, by itself, generated huge profits. Instead, it gave us a high-torque boost at the very moment we most needed it, while at the same time affording us a test bed for our platform team approach to production. If ever there was a right (and right-brained) product at the right time, the Viper was it!

To understand how "right" Viper really was—and how great a change a single product can make to a company's public image—one has to understand just how precarious Chrysler's health really was back in the late '80s and early '90s.

Chrysler's product line, as noted in the previous two chapters, still depended heavily on our K-car platform, which had been stretched and shortened, "luxurified" and luxurified again in an attempt to create vehicles of different sizes, price classes, and brands. These sold passably well, but not without the self-defeating lubricant of rebates.

The nation's automotive press had collectively made up its mind that our cars and trucks—with the exception of our minivans and recently acquired Jeep vehicles—were technologically dated (one of their favorite terms for describing us: "yester-tech"), uninspired, and generally not up to the standards of GM, Ford (then riding high with its hugely successful Taurus), or the Japanese. The view commonly held of the latter was that they were inherently superior in corporate culture, engineering, supplier relationships, and manufacturing—everything that determined success. Conventional wisdom among business scribes (and their related species, financial analysts) was not just that the Japanese soon would dominate the auto industry, but that Chrysler, as the weakest and most uninspired of the Big Three, would—*this* time—surely die. Our employees daily saw headlines predicting our demise or otherwise attesting to our gloomy future.

The irony, of course, was that this cloudburst of pessimism hit us after we had already started changing for the better. We were instituting our soon-to-be-famous platform teams. We knew we possessed both the human and financial resources needed to overhaul our product line. And we had agreed internally on a bold, break-the-mold design strategy that was to set new standards for styling, not just in the United States but abroad. We inside the company knew all this ferment was at work, but none of it was visible yet to the outside world. We despaired of ever getting our good news out—news crucial to investor and customer confidence. In the media's eyes we remained laggards, a technologically (and stylistically) benighted company riding a tired, one-trick, K-car pony.

We did what we could in terms of conventional public relations. We displayed exciting concept cars at auto shows, demonstrating (we hoped) that we had "gotten it" so far as contemporary design was concerned. Lee Iacocca proved, as always, a skilled and tireless promoter. But his upholding of our strengths was complicated by the fact that he was trying at the same time to tell the truth about Japan's mercantilistic trade practices. Result: Much of what we said, institutionally, was dismissed by the media as "Chrysler's whining about its inability to compete."

At this delicate juncture, with the future of the company hardly assured, what we most needed was some event, some symbol, some proof that Chrysler was not dead, that within our company there bubbled the optimism, creativity, and sense of outrage necessary for us to fight our way back to health. While we needed such proof for the press and for analysts, we needed it most of all for ourselves. We were tired of being treated with the same dismissiveness shown to the terminally ill, tired of being patronized at cocktail parties by executives from other car companies.

Finally, what we needed came. As with so many right-brain-inspired breakthroughs, this one owed its origin to serendipity. For Newton, the precipitating agent was an apple. For me, it was a black roadster.

I was blasting my 1985 Autokraft Mk IV Cobra (a splendid re-creation of the Shelby Cobra of the 1960s) around some of southeastern Michigan's more interesting roads one day in the warm-weather months of 1988, pondering Chrysler's situation and reflecting on how the original Cobra, with its lightweight, two-seat aluminum body and its outrageously powerful Ford V-8 engine had become the single most imitated sports car in history. And for good reason: The brainchild of Carroll Shelby, a self-described Texas chicken farmer who was one of America's best racing drivers in the '50s (and who frequently competed in his trademark bib overalls), the Cobra blended the sheer muscle of Ford's thin-wall V-8s with gorgeous bodywork unabashedly inspired by Ferrari *barchetta* (Italian for "little boat") roadsters. Cobras earned a fearsome reputation on the racetrack, effectively unseating the Corvette as America's most potent race car, and they also made an indelible impression on just about every enthusiast in the world—not to mention adding a high luster to the image of the Ford Motor Company! I reflected sadly that this era had passed. What was more pathetic, I couldn't even demonstrate good corporate loyalty by powering my Cobra with a Chrysler engine, since I would have had to give up half the horsepower in the process: We just didn't make a big-block V-8 anymore.

Then came a sort of blinding flash of inspiration: In our future product plan, we had identified a big, new pickup (what was later to become the highly successful all-new Ram pickup, introduced in 1994) to be powered by an equally monstrous cast-iron V-10 engine. Also planned for the truck was a new five-speed, heavy-duty, manual transmission. Why not, I thought, combine a prototype of that new truck power train, wrap it in an exciting two-seat body only slightly less voluptuous than Raquel Welch's, and display it at auto shows? That we were shamelessly lunching off Ford's heritage did not trouble me overmuch; the Cobra's mystique transcended any one company's ownership. (Plus, Carroll Shelby himself now worked as an exclusive consultant for Chrysler!)

The next morning I talked over the idea with Tom Gale in our design shop and François Castaing, who was then heading Jeep/truck engineering (the potential source for the prototype parts). It took the three of us about 10 minutes to decide to do at least some initial design sketches and preliminary mechanical layouts.

The legendary Carroll Shelby, having transferred his allegiance to Chrysler along with Lee Iacocca, was brought into the picture next. Carroll had lent his name to, and actually produced, some limited-volume high-performance derivatives of Chrysler production cars, including the Dodge Omni "GLH" (short for "goes like hell"). But his heart's desire was to make, as he termed it, a real "kick-ass," big-engined, high-performance two-seater. We were delighted to have his help, since as a certified "friend of Lee," he could help convince a possibly skeptical chairman that we should at least create a show car.

We soon had design sketches and the assurance that we could make all the parts fit. The early drawings, very close to the final Viper, were (to tell the whole truth) initially disappointing to me. My personal vision had been of a car much closer to the original Cobra, though somewhat modernized. But Tom Gale and a tiny handful of designers had (wisely, as it turns out) decided instead to embark on an all-new look, an interpretation of the character and feel, the aesthetic impact, of the Cobra, but bearing no direct Cobra-derived visual cues.

Over the years, I have learned not to react too quickly when shocked by a design proposal. The very best designs, the freshest and most audacious, are often hard for a nondesigner to integrate. Appreciating them takes "soak time." (At Ford, earlier in my career, my then-superior Don Petersen was equally shocked when I showed him the proposed design for the new Sierra, Ford's first radically aerodynamically styled sedan. I gave him a small sketch to put in his pocket on his return to the United States and inscribed on it the words, "View daily until familiarity is achieved." It worked!)

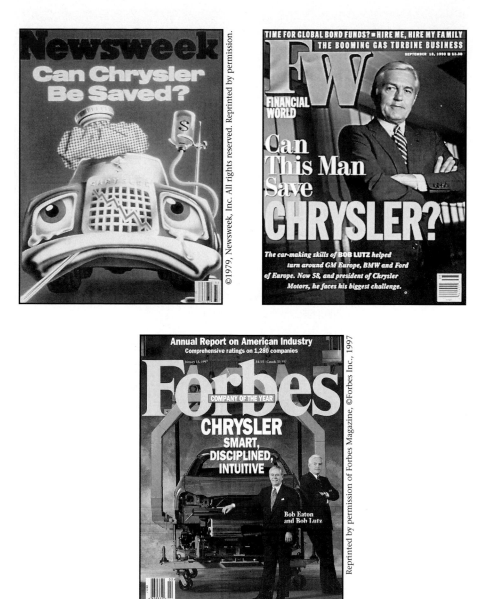

The "Chrysler story" in press clippings: First heart attack, from 1979 (upper left); second heart attack, from 1990 (upper right); a clean bill of health (and then some!), from 1997. (I especially like the "Smart" part of the headline!)

The embodiment of our cab-forward design concept: The 1993 Dodge Intrepid, the best-selling "LH" sedan (top), and its subcompact cousin, the 1994 Neon.

My "smashing introduction" of the Jeep Grand Cherokee at the Detroit auto show (top) and me "hamming it up" again for the Dodge Ram "Quad Cab" intro at the Chicago auto show.

"Lutz's loves" (and inspirations): My black Autokraft Cobra beside the original Viper concept car (top), and my ultimate "speed machine," my Aero L-39 "Albatros."

The pace car at the 1996 Indianapolis 500 (top) was the "GTS" model of the Viper, and I got to drive it! Bob Eaton and I don "cruising shades" at the 1996 Detroit auto show to introduce yet another car that no one else would do: The Plymouth Prowler.

The genesis of "cab-forward design" at Chrysler: The 1988 "Portofino" concept car (top). Definitely *not* cab-forward: The 1998 "Chronos" concept car, whose interior includes a built-in cigar humidor!

The juggernaut continues: The *second-generation* 1998 Chrysler Concorde (top) and 1999 Chrysler 300M, a car for world markets as well as for America.

Daimler-Benz CEO Jürgen Schrempp (left) and Bob Eaton announcing the largest industrial merger in history: "DaimlerChrysler."

So I deliberately gave myself soak time with the Viper. Later, when I saw it as a full-size clay model, I was overwhelmed by its impact. I was immediately sold, and the "gang of three" (plus Carroll Shelby as our "Cobra conscience") decided we should execute it as a concept car for the Detroit auto show in 1989.

Work was begun in Newport Beach, California, by Metalcrafters, a highly skilled and oft-used source of concept cars. On a visit with Lee Iacocca, we saw it semicompleted as a real car for the first time. It was stunning—much more dramatic in shiny metal and fresh paint than in dull-brown modeling clay. Lee Iacocca became a fervent supporter on the spot. Skilled promoter that he was, he perhaps had an inkling already of what the car would do for us when unveiled to the public. Already in place was our very first handmade prototype of the V-10 engine—created by welding six cylinders of one V-8 block to four cylinders of another! It ran not well but adequately: After all, all this car would ever have to do was start, be loud, and demonstrate that it could actually move under its own power!

Now to name it. We'd decided already it should be a Dodge (too big for Plymouth, too outrageous for the Chrysler brand). Dodge marketing, to be honest, was eager to tie it to some heroic but semiforgotten Dodge icon like Challenger or Avenger. The four fathers didn't like that idea, however, because it didn't make the clear statement that this was "son of Cobra." (We couldn't use the Cobra name itself, although we would have liked to, because Ford owned and occasionally used it, despite Shelby's association with Chrysler.) But we knew it had to be some kind of snake.

"Asp" was out, since the serpent in question was tiny. "Boa Constrictor" and "Anaconda" sounded too fat and too lethargic. "Rattlesnake" didn't seem to suggest sound construction.

Finally, on the corporate airplane taking us from California back to Michigan, François Castaing, Tom Gale, and I agreed on "Viper." The marketing folks caved; the name was instantly assimilated; and one of our designers was sufficiently muse-kissed to generate, spontaneously, the now-famous emblem of the slyly grinning reptile, seemingly sharing some intimate joke with the viewer.

When we unveiled the car in January of 1989 at the Detroit auto show, it blew the roof off. The "fathers" had to pose for picture after picture; television coverage was incessant; and the bright-red Viper wound up being on the cover of virtually every automotive publication in the country (if not the world). Nothing remotely like it had ever been displayed by an American or foreign volume producer.

Everything about it screamed performance: Viper sat on the widest wheels and tires anyone had ever seen. Its voluptuous, sweeping curves and endless hood promised power—an unprecedented 400 hp, to be precise.

It was blatant ("subtle" was its polar opposite). It defiantly made no excuses for lacking many basic creature comforts, being not just windowless and topless, but door-handle-less (like many roadsters of yesteryear). We suspected (correctly) that Viper customers couldn't care less about such lapses. To them, the presence of glass side windows or of a proper top did not denote quality. They wanted excitement and exhilaration. "Zero to jail in four seconds" was this car's message! (Actually, the final car could go from zero to 60 in four seconds—and perhaps even more impressive, from zero to 100 and then *back again to zero* in under 14 seconds!)

When they saw it, even executives from competitors privately congratulated us, though we also heard via journalists that Ford was tossing sour grapes our way, saying, in effect, that Viper was nothing more than a vulgar, testosterone-laden expression of a teenage fantasy by a bunch of middle-aged men. Actually, that assessment wasn't far wrong! We soon discovered, though, that we had touched a huge neural network that reached far beyond the four of us.

Cards and letters came pouring in from all the states of the Union and from all walks of life. Investment bankers, airline pilots, real estate investors, doctors, lawyers, plumbers, physicists, authors, hourly workers, people who owned old muscle-cars, and people who had never before owned an American vehicle sent us wheedling, pleading letters, many with unsolicited deposit checks (one in the amount of $70,000 from someone who wanted to reserve *two*) and many others with hundred-dollar bills stapled to them. Some requests were eloquently composed on impressive corporate letterhead; others were primitively scrawled, displaying questionable grammar and spelling. But their bottom line was always the same: *I need that car!*

These letters contained another, unexpected, emotion: patriotism. The writers rejoiced that America could still "kick butt." Viper, to their eyes, had thrown down a stinging gauntlet to the Japanese: "Don't take us on when it comes to muscle-cars, pal," Viper seemed to be saying. "We're talking, here, about a sacred American tradition!" Had Mitsubishi recently introduced a 300-horsepower, technologically sophisticated, all-wheel-drive, twin-turbo, four-cam coupe? "Fine," said Viper. "We'll see that and *raise you* 100 hp." Thanks to the boldness, exuberance, and self-assertion of our designers, Chrysler—the "dull, stodgy, beleaguered" K-car company—was suddenly a flag-waving champion of high performance.

Much to the chagrin of the guardians of Chrysler's purse, we proceeded to explore the possibility of actually manufacturing the car.

We knew the project would have to be lean in terms of investment. We knew it would have to be done fast, before the public forgot the show car's impact (and before Chevrolet's Corvette corps or some other competitor could counter it with a muscle-car of their own). And we knew that to execute it quickly we needed a small, agile, highly motivated cadre of commando-type car buffs, not a docile herd of plodding, business-as-usual engineers. To that end we called a meeting during which anyone, regardless of rank or function, could come forward and volunteer for the Viper team. And come they did! The meeting was packed with eager faces, spanning the age spectrum from recent college graduates to combat-hardened veterans on the brink of retirement.

From these, François Castaing picked 80 shock troops. At their head we put a strong and capable leader—Roy Sjoberg, an experienced engineer who had been an instrumental member of the Corvette team when at GM.

We housed the Viper group in old facilities in the former AMC engineering center on the west side of Detroit. The building had been erected by Nash and had also been the old Kelvinator refrigerator factory. The only good thing about the "Snake Pit" (as it was soon to be called) was that almost the whole team could be brought together under one gigantic roof. Hourly UAW members fabricating and assembling prototype parts worked side by side with technicians and engineers. Semiassembled prototypes vied for space with desks, drawing boards, and workstations. Whenever a problem arose requiring input from several team members, Roy Sjoberg would ring a big hand-held school bell, the signal for everyone to drop what they were doing, gather round, and hammer out a solution. This was real-time, right-now problem solving, with no reports or focus groups to slow its progress. Communication was instantaneous, since all parties were trapped within the same four walls. Whoever could not be reached by e-mail could be reached by shouting across the room!

In retrospect, it's clear that the Viper team really was confronting two challenges at once. One was building the car. The other, no less imortant, was testing in microcosm our thinking about how platform teams should work. Progress on both of these parallel paths moved along at breathtaking speed.

The team soon had a running "mule"—a full-scale mock-up made of fiberglass laid up by hand. It had a Chrysler 360-cubic-inch V-8 truck engine heavily modified to simulate the performance of our not-yet-available V-10. On a blustery winter afternoon at our old Highland Park headquarters, I had the privilege (and thrill!) of being the first person outside the Viper team itself to drive the car, which, even in so crude a form, demonstrated the power and handling that would characterize the finished car. With the entire team gathered round, we took pictures of our baby snake. It was an emotional, right-brained moment.

We knew, however, that if Viper were to stand a chance of getting a green light from all of senior management, we would need to show the car had more going for it than our own right-brained passion and gut instinct. We subjected Viper to an unflinching, left-brained analy-sis: For how little cost could we build it? How many enthusiasts might buy it? Where in the market should it be priced? The preliminary results were encouraging: Chrysler might not ever get rich on the Viper, but the risk of our going broke on it looked even smaller, assuming we could keep costs down.

Even so, our financial people argued, we shouldn't spend the money. Strictly speaking, they had a point. The $50-or-so million we were requesting could certainly have been spent in ways less venture-some and less dramatic. We could have used the money to (at least in some very small way) pay down debt and refurbish plants. Other doubters worried that suppliers, already busy supporting Chrysler's more conventional products, would be distracted by Viper's "boutique" needs. They, too, were right. Next, sales weighed in. They fretted that no American producer had ever successfully sold a $50,000 car. (Back in 1989, $50,000 was Mercedes S-Class territory!) In fact, Dodge dealers, whose clientele was largely blue-collar, had never sold anything priced over $20,000—let alone something without door handles. Finally, there came the left-brained trump card: Hadn't Mazda, with its popular Miata, already met the market's demand for a two-seated sports car? How was I to explain that, yes, a household kitty and a lion are both cats—but that's where the similarity ends?

I didn't criticize these dissidents, since I had learned to expect legitimate disagreements over radically new products. But I must confess I was disappointed that sales, who stood to benefit most from a rejuvenation of the Dodge brand, proved so difficult to bring along.

Luckily for the Viper (and Chrysler!), senior management ultimately sided with the enthusiasts—but only because we'd done our homework and had marshaled a persuasive left-brained case to go along with our right-brained instincts. At long last, in mid-'89, Lee Iacocca, in a nicely staged bit of showmanship during a West Coast financial analysts' meeting, tossed me a set of Viper keys. "Go build it, Lutz," he barked. He didn't have to tell me twice!

Viper was now an officially approved, full-fledged program, with the right to sign up suppliers and spend serious money. Its cost had increased somewhat (but still to only about $80 million—mere pocket change by auto industry standards for an all-new car), because the Viper team had insisted (and François agreed), that the V-10 cast-iron truck engine should be recast in aluminum, saving about 150 pounds, and that only a six-speed transmission (rather than the original five-speed) would be able to take full advantage of the eight-liter engine's power. I wasn't happy about the extra cost; but I was overjoyed that the program was now a go, since it represented a victory for the project's nonquantifiable attributes: for Viper's heart, its excitement, and for what that excitement might do for our external image and our internal morale. It just as surely represented a defeat for the overly analytical, risk-averse, business-as-usual approach that too often prevails in institutions.

Though the car had won out over the objections of our own finan-cial naysayers, I still worried about what Wall Street would think of it. After all, we were spending scarce funds (and devoting precious exec-utive attention) on what they might well view as a frivolous project.

During a road show for our 1991 stock offering (now two years into the Viper project), an institutional-investor analyst asked me what projects Chrysler might have to cut if we started running out of money. Putting on my most sober, fiscally responsible face, I told him we might have to cut the Viper. The buttoned-up East Coaster recoiled in horror. "My God," he said, "You can't do *that!* This car's changing everyone's perception of the company. It's reestablishing confidence. It's the *last thing* you should cut." I never made that mistake again!

On another occasion we were seeking support from international banks for renewal of Chrysler's worldwide revolving-credit agree-ment—never an easy task, even under the happiest economic circum-stances. We were performing our customary dog and pony show for a group of German bankers whose mien, to say the least, was somewhat dour and indifferent. That is, it was until we started showing slides of the Viper. When we uncaged our snake, the meeting came to life, and the executives grew more and more supportive. The bank's chairman for the first time became totally engaged.

We got our renewal.

After our presentation, as I was preparing to leave, the chairman approached and asked if he could see me privately. *Ah,* I said to myself, *I knew it was too easy; he wants to stipulate new terms.* When we were alone he slipped me his business card. "Look," he said, "I want you to contact me when that red sports car comes out. I don't care what it costs. *I want it bad.*"

So it goes with many a felicitously right-brained project: In its wake come benefits that defy left-brained analysis. Viper—our "crazy, preposterous, childish" investment (as a competitor had called it)—was now helping to tip bankers' and investors' sympathies in our favor. Even the most analytical financiers recognized it as a potent symbol of our new spirit, our unconventional thinking, our daring, and of the speed with which we were regaining our strength. The Viper, in brief, was becoming profitable in ways impossible to quantify.

Plus, there was one other group that was wowed by the Viper—or perhaps *mystified* is a better word: Japanese automakers. To this day, I have Japanese car executives coming up to me and saying, "Tell me, Mr. Lutz, exactly what market research led you to build the Viper? That research must certainly have been quite in depth." My response: "We didn't do any research at all—we just did it!"

I wish, having said all this, I could report that Viper was a smooth program, but that wouldn't be true. As with any radically new endeavor, this one was, in its own way, fraught with problems. The technical ones I had anticipated, since these reasonably might have been expected from a program requiring us to perfect so many firsts: our first aluminum engine, our first tubular space-frame chassis, our first use of plastic-molding technology for the body. But these paled in comparison to the human problems we encountered.

We who formed the Viper Technical Committee, a group of senior executives who oversaw the project's financial and technical progress, had expected that so select and highly motivated a team would attack their task with gusto, bulldozing all obstacles aside. Alas, we forgot that over many years we had trained these employees to behave entirely differently. Commando action did not come naturally to them. Despite the fact we told them to *forget* corporate bureaucracy, to *forget* traditional approval paths, to *forget* belt-and-suspenders sign-offs and just do whatever they had to do to get the job done (providing, of course, that it did not violate the triple test of being legal, moral, and not in clear violation of corporate policies), these human hamsters refused, at first, to quit their cage.

Years of fearing failure and of seeking safety in collective decision making had taken their toll. Team members sought guidance where they needed none, asked permission when they'd been told they already had it, and dutifully followed old, hoary, wasteful administrative procedures when they'd been told to throw these out the window. The familiar exerted too strong a hold for them to break free overnight.

From this, we in management learned a less-than-obvious lesson: Employees must be *led* to empowerment; they must be taught and coached. They cannot be declared "empowered" by executive fiat. As Team Viper learned from our coaching that error-free *in*action would be frowned upon more than action risking error, its autonomy grew. As the team gained self-confidence, more and more program milestones were met successfully and on time. It became a joy to see the group turn into a highly motivated, self-assured, fast-moving entity.

Our other problems concerned suppliers. The Viper program proved to be our first experiment in having suppliers do the core engineering for a new model's components. Curiously, it wasn't that tough a goal to reach for those suppliers who'd already agreed to sign on. Most of Chrysler's suppliers had caught Viper fever and wanted to participate. (The fact that many of their CEOs lusted after having their own Viper probably didn't hurt.)

But some of our most trusted partners simply refused to join, contending that the low volume didn't justify the effort. From a narrowly left-brained viewpoint, they were right. Had they engaged their whole brain, however, and considered the project's potential total benefits, most, I suspect, would have chosen differently. A German supplier whom we had asked to produce Viper's new six-speed transmission really let us down. When we were already well into the program (and when it seemed too late to change something as fundamental as the transmission), he told us the deal was off unless we could cough up several million dollars not previously discussed (and not available in our budget).

What to do? Knuckle under to prevent delay? Or tell the supplier, "Thank you; it's been semi-nice working with you, but forget it"? Bravely, the team picked the latter course. Working quickly and creatively, they found an excellent alternative in the all-new Borg-Warner T-6 transmission, which was then under development for GM's Camaro, Firebird, and Corvette models. Viper remained on track, while the German transmission company won an empty victory: To achieve a trivial savings, they sacrificed their opportunity to become a supplier for Chrysler's more mainstream products and, more important, the unquantifiable but undeniable luster they would have enjoyed from being associated with, perhaps, the most publicized car in modern times.

Undeterred by such surprises, Team Viper marched on: Our aluminum V-10 more than lived up to its promise, the myriad problems with the plastic body ground toward a solution, and by Christmas

1992, three years after presenting the original Viper concept to the car world, two and a half years after program approval, we had the first cars ready for customer delivery. Were they perfect? No. But our first owners were such fervent, thankful enthusiasts that they forgave the car its teething problems and worked right alongside Viper engineers to find solutions. (To give those engineers their due, it was not unheard of for a Viper team member to fly across the country with a part under his arm in order to repair an owner's early-build Viper on the spot.)

The Viper met its cost and investment targets, and it has sold at more than its production capacity. Its price never posed any obstacle: The car was half the price (or less) of Europe's supercars, yet it outperformed them. To this day, its fanged face continues to smile out from more magazine covers than anyone can count. One can even say it has burrowed deep into popular culture, since so many companies want to produce scale models and toy Vipers that, to ensure good quality, we have to police the use of Viper's trademark.

The very same Dodge dealers who, early in the program, urged Lee Iacocca and me to cancel the car ("Use the money to get us a new pickup sooner") now speak of the car with reverence. Enthusiasts' Viper Owner Clubs have sprung up all over the globe, even in Japan, and it is difficult to imagine a more loyal, fanatical, and fun-loving group of consumers than these members. When the original Viper roadster was joined in 1996 by its sibling serpent, the GTS coupe, many original owners decided they needed to own both! The racing version of the GTS coupe—the Viper GTS-R—is built right in the same plant as the production car. In 1997, under the leadership of Hugues de Chaunac and his French ORECA Viper team, the GTS-R won the Federation Internationale de L'Automobile GT-2 world championship, the first time any American producer has achieved this feat with an in-house, production-based automobile.

So Viper was, and continues to be, a huge success—including for its role in having proved, dramatically and effectively, the merit of the platform team concept. And not incidentally, Viper has cast a halo over Chrysler's other products. Some Viper owners who had never previously bought a Chrysler now own small fleets of the company's trucks, sedans, sport utilities, and minivans. Externally, Viper created confidence among investors and earned respect from journalists. Internally, it boosted our morale and pride. And, yes, it taught us about teams—and about leadership, working with suppliers, and the limits of empowerment. It was a dress rehearsal for Chrysler's renaissance—a lasting one this time!

Who'd have expected so much from a snake?

In the pages that follow, I've tried to codify a bit of the unconventional wisdom (plus some of the insights, perceptions, realizations, epiphanies, and other cognitive miscellany) I have gained not just from Chrysler's second turnaround (and from being snake-bit by the Viper), but from my 30-some years in industry. How does an organization manage two different kinds of people—the left-brained and the right? How does a leader decide which type of thinking is best used where in an organization? And how does he or she maintain the dynamic tension between two elemental forces: creative change on the one hand and predictable dependability on the other? I feel sufficiently confident about my answers that I've called the first seven of them (with characteristic panache) "Lutz's Laws."

GUTS

PART II

LUTZ'S IMMUTABLE LAWS OF BUSINESS

Promulgated here in the spirit of my longtime personal motto: "Often wrong but never in doubt!"

INTRODUCTION TO THE LAWS

Far be it from me to borrow Moses' mantle. While my own credentials as lawgiver may be unique, they do not extend to my ever having chatted up a burning bush or been given ready-made laws atop a mountain. (Plus, as a purely practical consideration, I think Charlton Heston has the Moses thing pretty well sewn up!)

Having noted that, however, I do think I've got a thing or two to say!

My own philosophy I've fashioned while in transit, moving from one continent to another, one stage of life to another, one company to another. For that reason, you'll find my laws are formulated from the perspective of someone in-between.

As I bounced between Europe and America in my adolescence, I learned to straddle two cultures. Later, when I enlisted in the U.S. Marine Corps, I had to find a middle ground between my natural bent toward creative independence and the military's ethic of disciplined teamwork. It was my luck (good? bad?) to have been at U.C. Berkeley (as a Marine Reservist) during the frenzy of the free-speech movement. In a tie-dyed world, Bob Lutz was the guy with the buzz-cut hair and polished shoes!

Through all this straddling, I've acquired an ability to live between two camps and borrow what I think are the best elements from both. For instance, I was a cigar smoker and martini drinker long before either of those activities was fashionable, and I remain vegetarian long after that's become unfashionable. I'm a free spirit who deplores the self-indulgence of casual dress, whether in the office or in fine restaurants. Attention to detail? I've mastered it well enough to have logged hundreds of hours in my military jet (a Czech-built Aero L-39 "Albatros"), and on the whole, I fly it rather well—though one time, on landing, I forgot to put the wheels down!

That was in 1995, when I was president of Chrysler. Reporters asked me when they heard I'd belly flopped: "Gee, Mr. Lutz, how does it feel to make a landing like that?"

"It feels bad," I said. "Not as bad as running over your dog, but bad."
Two weeks later I ran over my dog.

She was sleeping under my car's front wheel, where I couldn't see her. I felt awful about it, of course. But $10,000 in vet bills later, she's fine and insists that she's forgiven me.

My point, I guess, is that I indeed possess a certain duality of mind. And I think I've imparted enough of this same quality to Chrysler that today the company has what amounts to two different but complementary personalities.

Where financial matters are concerned (things like maintaining a strong balance sheet and controlling costs), the company is like Dr. Jekyll—about as conservative, buttoned-up, and left-brained as you can get. The goal is to be the kind of company that any mother's son (or any banker) would be proud to bring to dinner. But where products are concerned, Chrysler is delighted to have a touch of right-brained wildness show through—a little Mr. Hyde, if you will (minus the mayhem, of course!). In fact, Chrysler's success in the last few years has been predicated on the belief that you deliberately have to be a little wild with products—even at the risk of polarizing consumers—if you want them to stand out in a crowded market.

This in-between approach, borrowing a little from left and right, causes what I call "corporate schizophrenia." It's been an extremely advantageous illness for Chrysler to have, and I hope to communicate it to you in the heretical Laws that follow.

CHAPTER 4

The Customer Isn't Always Right

BLASPHEMY! I CAN SEE A LIGHTNING BOLT MARKED "LUTZ" SPEEDING ON ITS way already, and we've only just begun.

Honestly, though, who in his or her right mind believes the customer is always right? Not I. I've seen too many customers who hadn't a clue about what they wanted, or worse, who deliberately fibbed when the nice survey taker with the clipboard asked them what they'd like: "Mrs. Ferguson, would you like your next car better if it had a heated cup holder?"

The Mrs. (and Mr.) Fergusons of our great land *always* want a better cup holder, gearshift, trunk, rearview mirror, hood ornament—whatever it might be. We didn't get to be a consumer society by not consuming everything we could lay our hands on, and in ever bigger, ever better shapes and sizes.

"And would that larger, roomier, more contemporary cup holder, Mrs. Ferguson, be worth to you, say, an extra $40 the next time you buy a car?"

I can guarantee she'll answer yes. It's possible, of course, that she really does want a heated cup holder and is prepared to pay for it. But more often than not, the respondent simply wants to avoid any appearance of being a cheapskate. Heated cup holder? Sure, why not? Gimme two!

Ford ruined the Thunderbird by taking such responses too seriously. The original Thunderbird was a sleek, zippy, tightly designed two-seater. Ford asked T-bird customers what they'd like more of: Would they like, say, a little extra room? They would. How about a backseat? You bet. So Ford introduced an "improved" four-seater (and later, a four-door). The restyled car was no longer the sleek sportster that had first attracted drivers. Its mystique paled, and what had been a unique addition to Ford's line was now just another car. (There's a rumor afoot now that Ford may bring back a modernized Thunderbird, in more or less its original configuration. If so, congratulations! The design will have come full circle.)

Perhaps the ultimate folly of oversensitivity to consumers' wishes occurred at Chrysler in the late '80s. The Dodge Shadow and Plymouth Sundance, Chrysler's subcompact cars, had been on the market for about two years and were selling reasonably well. Even in strong months, though, they had trouble attaining half the market share of the then-best-selling Ford Escort.

Some of our folks decided to ascertain why the little cars weren't selling better.

After conducting some research, the returns were in: By a vast majority, respondents said they would like the car much better if it were just a little bigger—say, four inches longer on its wheelbase. Now, anyone even passingly familiar with the U.S. auto market knows that most people buy subcompacts because that's all they can afford, not because they have some warped desire to sit with their knees up around their chest. Thus, when asked what they'd like changed about their cars, it's axiomatic that subcompact owners would like them *bigger*.

On the strength of this self-evident response, a crash campaign was launched to achieve a four-inch wheelbase stretch, at a cost (if memory serves) of at least $170 million in scarce capital. It apparently occurred to no one that the resultant vehicle would, in its dimensions, exactly match the existing Dodge Aries and Plymouth Reliant compacts that Chrysler was already selling (albeit with a lot of incentives) at higher prices. (Not to mention the fact that the Shadow and Sundance would have also been the same size as the soon-to-arrive Dodge Spirit and Plymouth Acclaim.)

So fixated were the marketing people on solving the customers' "problem" that when the ludicrousness of this solution was at last pointed out (creating a car we'd already created, then selling it for less than we were already getting) their riposte was: "But we've *got* to listen to the customer!

In exasperation, I followed the precept of one of America's more famous First Ladies and finally just said *no!*

See what trouble comes of listening to consumers? And that's assuming consumers are giving survey takers truthful answers. In fact, consumers often lie—albeit for the noblest of reasons.

By virtue of having been asked a question, a respondent ceases to be a real person. He's so proud of being one of "the chosen" that answering the survey becomes his big chance to represent with honor all of his consumer brethren. Time for him to cast away childish things—whims, emotions, his own eccentric taste—and instead uphold the honor of his class by giving serious, mature, eminently left-brained answers.

"Would you prefer the sports car or the battery-powered station wagon?"

With more than a little twinge of regret, he checks off *wagon,* knowing full well it's a lie, but knowing, too, that he's doing the ecologically sound, fiscally responsible, family-oriented, politically correct thing by opting for the wagon. Only later, in the showroom, when poll time is done and nobody's looking (figuratively speaking) does he succumb to the message being pounded out as if by tom-tom in his right brain: *Buy the V-10! Buy the V-10!*

It's this Jekyll-and-Hyde duality that accounts for the perennial failure of the "safe car" consumers so often say in surveys they want: a perfectly rational car whose sole design criteria would be crash resistance and efficiency.

You've never seen this car, and I contend you never will. It's not that consumers don't want or deserve cars with these two attributes. It's that they want so much more. They want to be delighted, surprised, even challenged. They want to be seduced by a product (though few would admit it to a survey taker). Sometimes they want something they can't yet express. When they see it, though, they buy it.

Anyone who doubts the power of the right brain to settle purchasing questions has only to ask, "Pardon me, sir or madam, but why did you buy that all-alligator briefcase, that $300 pair of custom shoes, that $75-a-pot wrinkle cream?"

You'll get the flimsiest of left-brained rationalizations: "Oh, well, gee . . . you know it wears longer, holds better, keeps me warmer—my face can *really* feel the difference." Believe such dissembling at your peril.

When I was in military flight school in Pensacola, Florida, back in the '50s, I fell in love with a used Mark 7 Jaguar sedan. I remember sitting in that car with its wonderful, British, burled-walnut dash and all its beautiful round gauges and great little aircraft-style, up-down toggle switches. And I remember thinking to myself: *I don't have much money, and I know I can't afford this car, but I simply must have these instruments!*

Was I right to lust for switches? Maybe not, but left-brained people err if they think consumers make buying decisions any other way.

In the late '70s, when oil-producing nations had just hiked gasoline prices and I was working at Ford of Europe, I watched Ford sit idly by while competitors, responding to the gas crisis, brought out fuel-saving diesel engines and five-speed transmissions. Why didn't Ford? It "knew" the public wouldn't go for them. Ford's product planners had run some numbers and established that neither feature could be justified on the basis of its cost savings. True, diesel fuel was priced less than gasoline. But a driver had to drive three years before the savings made up for having bought the more expensive engine.

Same with transmissions: Research showed the fifth gear was useless in stop-and-go city driving; fuel savings showed up only on long trips.

So what happened?

The public went *crazy* for diesels and for five-speed transmissions. Ford had to play an abrupt (and humbling and costly and ultimately ineffectual) game of catch-up.

It didn't matter to consumers that diesel engines were more expensive. Every time they filled their tank, they felt they'd made a smart decision: Diesel fuel was cheaper, wasn't it? As for the transmissions, the only time most drivers ever check their mileage is on long trips, where the fifth gear does makes a difference.

There's another way customers aren't right: They can't see the future. Nobody in 1940, listening to a furniture-sized radio, ever said, "Gosh, this is nice; but what I think I'd like instead would be a Sony Walkman." Today's shoppers are at best a rearview mirror, offering perspective on products that already exist. They can't supply you with ideas for tomorrow's breakthrough. For those, you or somebody on your team has got to be a right-brained visionary.

When manufacturers run up against this predisposition of consumers to be wrong—to fib, to not foresee the future, to not even know their own minds—they throw up their hands in frustration. What to do? Sometimes they decide the safest course is to devise a one-size-fits-all hybrid, an Everyman product, which, by offering a multiplicity of options, can customize itself to each buyer's individual taste.

There's a word for this strategy: *doomed.*

That didn't stop Lincoln-Mercury from bringing out an all-new Continental sedan in 1996 that offered not just something for everybody, but something for everybody's brother and sister.

It featured a high-tech, high-performance V-8, which put the car on a par, enginewise, with the Cadillac Seville, Lexus LS 400, and the BMW 540 and 740. So far, so good. But Lincoln, fearing American drivers might not like the "Euro-feel" of the car's sport steering, decided to make steering programmable: Customers could select any feel they liked, from pinky-finger-blue-haired-little-old-lady effortlessness to NASCAR-tattooed-ham-fisted bubba.

Suspension posed a similar problem. The Europeans (Mercedes-Benz and BMW) had garnered a loyal following by offering crisp suspension. But what of the traditional, all-American, 55-year-old lard-butted luxury-car driver? Did not his more delicate posterior deserve a plusher, cushier, more spring-assisted ride? The same solution presented itself: programmable suspension! Everything from "floating on clouds" to a ride guaranteed to loosen fillings. Most other features of the car were programmable as well.

Yet buyers failed to flock to the chameleon Continental.

Its fatal flaw, I think, was best summed up in Lincoln's own brochure: "If you experience difficulty in selecting the modes that best suit you, your local Lincoln-Mercury dealer will be happy to tailor your Continental to the characteristics of your choice" (or words to that effect). Words, I contend, that spoke eloquently of the manufacturer's total lack of conviction, of its unwillingness to take an uncompromising stand and design a car for a single set of owners, of its desperate confusion as to the car's mission. "Heck," Lincoln was saying, "we don't know what you want. *You* decide!"

It's the *manufacturer* who's supposed to do the heavy lifting. What a cop-out (and an expensive one, at that) to leave the creative work to the consumer!

Drive a BMW, and people look at you and say, "There's a person who likes a sporty feel, crisp responses, and a feeling of oneness with the vehicle." Drive a Cadillac, and people likewise feel they know your taste. But drivers of that confused Continental were . . . what? Who knew? Who cared? Customers turned up their noses at a car that stood for nothing. And perhaps on some intuitive level they felt annoyed at Lincoln's leaving it to them to do the creative work.

I had originally learned of the chameleon's advent when, quite by accident, I saw some of its parts at a supplier's plant. I asked the supplier what volume Ford expected him to tool up for, and he replied 100,000 units per year. "If that car ever reaches half that volume," I said, "I'll eat my hat." A year after its debut, he phoned me: "Your hat," he said, "is safe."

It's my pleasure to report that Ford, in its most recent iteration of the Continental, has returned it to what it used to be: a great automobile. How? They did it by exercising courage. They hitched up their pants and made some dramatic styling choices, which the buying public likes. Perhaps more important, Ford dispensed with much of the car's "weird science" programmability, freeing the car's previously buried character and thoughtful engineering. The latest reviews have been flattering.

It's not easy to take a stand on a multi-million-dollar product like a mass-production automobile. When, in the 1994 model year, Chrysler introduced the original five-passenger LHS sedan, the flagship of our cab-forward revolution with its vintage Jaguar-inspired roofline, our own lack of conviction caused us to build a six-passenger, fluff-suspensioned New Yorker version as well. Research indicated that not everyone would like the sporty, Europe-inspired LHS. Well, not everybody did—just the overwhelming majority. New Yorkers languished on dealers' lots while we scrambled to keep up with LHS demand. No one is immune from the tendency to let the consumer do the work, and the disease is catching. So one must watch vigilantly for its symptoms.

If you're going to base important decisions on consumer research (and if you're reasonably certain the questions were asked in such a way as to keep respondents truthful), make sure you understand what the numbers are *really* telling you. It's easy to be snookered by your own horrendously false conclusions.

For instance, in determining which model of a product survey participants find most visually appealing, scores typically run from 1 (lowest) to 10 (highest). Thus, a model that after evaluation by 500 respondents in a product clinic has an average score of 7.5 would be picked as the winner over one that scored only 5.0, right?

Actually, no. Here's where it's important to understand the story that the underlying numbers really tell. The proposal scoring only 5 might be the average result of half of the respondents awarding it 9s and 10s, and the other half giving it 1s or 0s. Obviously this is a sharply polarizing model that divides respondents into those who love it and those who hate it, with very little middle ground. There's no ambivalence here. It's a case of passionate fans who can hardly wait to buy it being offset by complete rejecters. In a crowded market, it's those people with the 9s and 10s you want—those whose enthusiasm will cause the product to be noticed and sought after. They have the power to make this a breakthrough product for you.

When we showed the early prototype for the new "big rig–inspired" Dodge Ram pickup to consumer focus groups in the early '90s, the reaction was so polarized that the room practically vibrated with magnetism. A whopping 80 percent of the respondents disliked the bold new drop-fendered design. A lot even hated it! They wanted their pickups to keep on resembling the horizontal cornflakes boxes they were used to, not to be striking or bold. According to traditional consumer-research strategy, we should have thrown that design out on its ear, or at least toned it down to placate the hatemongers. But that would have been looking through the wrong end of the telescope, for the remaining 20 percent of the clinic participants were saying that they were truly, madly, deeply in love with the design! And since the old Ram had only about 4 percent of the market at the time, we figured, what the hell, even if only half of those positive respondents actually buy, we'll more than double our share! The result? Our share of the pickup market shot up to 20 percent on the radical new design, and Ford and Chevy owners gawked in envy!

What if we had gone ahead with a prototype that scored 7.5? Examine the underlying data: If the 7.5 is a result of almost everyone scoring it a 7 or an 8 (with few or no 9s and 10s), it means that you've got a guaranteed, inoffensive, uncontroversial, bland, everybody's-second-choice loser! Nobody, in today's market, has to settle any more for second choice.

The Primary Purpose of Business Is Not to Make Money

I CAN SENSE THE CELESTIAL PITCHER WARMING UP BOLT NUMBER TWO.

"Not make money? That's ridiculous," you say. And of course you're right. A business must make money. What I mean to suggest with this Law, however, is that companies that *do* make a lot of money almost never have as their goal "making a lot of money."

They tend to be run by enthusiasts who, in the normal course of gratifying their *own* tastes and curiosities, come up with products or services so startling, so compelling, and so exciting that customers practically rip their trouser pockets reaching for their wallets.

Robert McNamara (I don't think I'm letting any cats out of the bag here) was not such a man. When he was president of Ford, he reportedly arrived in the office one Monday morning with some calculations he had jotted on the back of an envelope during church. These specified the financial performance he expected could be had from a new car of such and such a weight and size. He told his designers to get busy on it. "Gee, Mr. McNamara," they asked, "what should the car look like?" That didn't matter, said McNamara, so long as it met his financial stipulations.

People of this stripe regard product as nothing more than a conduit: In one end they pour as little money as they can get away with; out of the other end they expect a munificent return.

Business doesn't work like this. Great profits are produced only one way—by great products. And great products derive from enthusiasm turned loose, which is a fair description of how we at Chrysler arrived at the original Viper concept car—the kind of machine that sets car buffs drooling, but that hardly anyone ever sees outside auto shows.

As I mentioned in the previous chapter, I'm frequently asked—especially by the Japanese, who worship research—what process of market analysis led us to Viper's design. There was none. I'd love to say we did a careful survey and found that a huge segment of the American (and European and Japanese and Middle Eastern) public was just dying for a $50,000 car with no door handles, no real top, no windows, a big gas-guzzler tax, no factory air, no C/D player, no automatic transmission, a steering column borrowed from the Jeep Cherokee, room for barely two people, and next to no luggage space. But we didn't *do* a survey.

We just decided it might be nice, for a change, to let our most impassioned car buffs design a car to suit *their* tastes.

The result is a beautiful example of what can happen when the whole brain is engaged. The car owed its birth to an act of almost pure, spontaneous creativity: the proverbial "eureka!" or "aha!" when a designer is smitten by inspiration. That was quickly followed, however, by more than a little left-brained analysis: Could we actually *build* the car? How much would it cost? How badly might the expenditure imperil Chrysler's finances if the experiment went wrong? What price could we sell it for? Who'd buy it? How many buyers might there be? All left-brained questions—all highly necessary!

Was our primary goal with Viper to make money? No. It was to see if we could, in one fell swoop, design and build the world's most unique and desirable sports car. As the car's cult has grown, Chrysler has indeed made money on it. But Viper's role in *rehabilitating Chrysler's image* has been the car's far more valuable contribution. In a stroke, Viper erased two of the three words everyone had grown thoroughly sick of hearing: "stodgy old Chrysler." Now Chrysler wasn't stodgy. It was the company with the breakthrough product.

It's hard to predict with certainty which products will succeed. Indeed, some of the most unlikely ones become the biggest hits. The very same idea that causes a Mr. McNamara nothing but a derisive chuckle may, when it gets to market, sell better than he or anyone else could have predicted. Look at *Cigar Aficionado* magazine.

In case you are not acquainted with this sterling publication, it is dedicated to the proposition that cigars, cigar smoking, cigar bands, cigar humidors, cigar cutters, women who like the smell of cigars, and all adjuncts to and appurtenances of cigars are either good, very good, or better.

Now that a large segment of the U.S. public has rediscovered (rekindled?) an affection for cigars, this proposition may not seem revolutionary. Yet in 1991, when the *Aficionado* was but a smoky gleam in the eye of its publisher, Marvin Shanken, the idea of a pro-cigar magazine seemed outrageous if not daft. Shanken might as well have been singing the praises of cholera. "Health Nazis" were then at their most puissant.

It was Shanken's peculiarity, however, to love cigars. And it was his genius to apprehend that huddled masses of would-be libertines were chafing under Healthdom's iron heel. He decided he would offer them a pro-smoking, pro-drinking, pro-steak-eating magazine whose ethic might be expressed as, "Eh, so what if it kills you—*live a little*." He published the first issue with his own money, and the rest, as they say, is publishing history. *Cigar Aficionado* caught fire.

So popular have cigars become that retailers have experienced shortages. Some have imposed rationing—only-three-to-a-customer-type limits on how many cigars a customer may buy of certain heavily sought-after brands. I myself have experienced sticker shock. As demand has driven prices skyward, I have seen the cost of one of my favorite cigars, La Gloria Cubana (of course, I smoke only the U.S.-legal ones!), waft upward from a not unreasonable $1.75 to $2.25, then $4, then $5 and then all the way up to as high as $14!

All of which proves what? That great products are unpredictable. That most, in their infancy, seem indefensible (at least to left-brained people). That the best are expressions of quirky tastes and squirrelly passions, irreducible to neat formulas on the backs of envelopes. Tom Peters states succinctly: "Whether we're talking about art, science, or

Apple computers, the signature products and services of our time will continue to come from some kinky mind somewhere." It's fine (necessary!) to test the brainchildren of that kinky mind for soundness, strength, and viability, just as Chrysler subjected Viper to a cost and sales analysis. But these ideas must not be dismissed out of hand simply because, on first hearing, they *sound* batty. Dismiss them, in fact, and you risk parboiling a golden-egg-laying goose.

Forbes magazine, during a recent ebb in Disney's business, asked, "When did the magic start to ooze from the Magic Kingdom?"

Box office returns for the company's animated features, it seemed, had fallen steadily since the release of *The Lion King*. *Forbes* fingered Disney's "battalions of MBAs [who] too often win over the more creative types." Every time creatives suggested a premise they thought might make for a hit, they were asked: How can you prove that? (One can imagine the meetings: Why *seven* dwarves, exactly? Wouldn't six be cheaper? Wouldn't 1,000 be bigger box office? Can't we get a computer analysis of dwarf configurations?) Yet, concluded *Forbes* sagely, "The computer hasn't been invented—and probably never will be—that can predict how many tickets a movie will sell."

You usually can tell how well a company understands Law 2 by seeing how they go about formulating a five-year business plan: Do they start with the numbers (e.g., so much investment will generate so much return)? Worse, do they start with a specific return, then figure their way back to the minimum amount of money they think they'll have to invest in order to attain it?

Or do they instead start with a passionate, all-consuming vision of an idiosyncratic product or service? Do they themselves find the idea for it exciting? Do they go to work each morning because they love the challenge of creation and wouldn't switch vocations even if they were offered marginally higher pay? If so, then hock your kid's retainer and buy stock in this second company! It's certain to outperform the first in every way, including profits.

Much of business devolves, it's true, to a mastery of disciplines and science. Running a successful restaurant requires an understanding of food science. Making movies takes accounting. But technical proficiency by itself is not enough—especially today, when competitors are apt to be every bit as adept as you. To make money, a business must generate products that *demand* attention—ones so compelling that they push the consumer's "gotta have it" button, rather than the one marked "hmmm, that's nice."

To get such products, foster a corporate culture where right-brained visionaries feel safe suggesting "gotta have it" ideas. Then, only after giving your enthusiasts a respectful hearing should you ask the necessary left-brained questions.

CHAPTER 6

When Everybody Else Is Doing It, Don't!

THE MANAGEMENT PROFESSION, I SUBMIT, IS DRIVEN BY FASHION EVERY BIT as much as . . . if I say "women's hemlines," I know I'll get hate mail, so . . . microbrewed beers.

In the '60s and '70s, when conglomeration was all the rage, corporations diversified into countercyclical businesses and blimped out. They grew still bigger thanks to merger mania in the '80s. Then came the inevitable crash diet: shedding all but one's core business was the epitome of hipness in the '90s.

In my own corner of the world—the auto industry—we saw a rush to embrace such questionable innovations as talking cars. You remember talking cars: Every time the driver's door was left ajar, a disembodied voice like Hal's in *2001* reminded you to close it. ("A door is ajar, Dave. When is a door ajar, Dave? When is a jar a door?") Then there was the vogue of digital speedometers. For one brief and shining moment, you had the satisfaction of knowing you were going exactly 62 miles an hour, not 61 or 63. The numeral displayed on the dash was luminous, huge, and very fidgety: 62, 63, 62, 63, 64, 63, 62. . . .

Allow me, as a veteran of these and many other fads, to say, *Enough!*

Why do people subscribe to such foolishness? Because, literally, they subscribe—to the *Wall Street Journal,* to *Fortune,* to *Forbes,* to *Business Week,* and other leading journals of enlightenment whose pages would be left dangerously blank were it not for journalists constantly discovering new reasons apples fall from trees.

Gravity, do you think?

"Yes," say the business journals sagely, stroking their collective chin and smoking their collective pipe. "You could call it that. But a recent study by the Harvard Business School at Stanford-on-Avon suggests that what we call *gravity* may actually be an empowerment of fruit downward. Managers who understand this—and few do—are poised to harvest rich rewards. So read this article. And, by the way, did you notice we're hosting a corporate seminar next month on this very topic ($1,500 per person)? Reserve now, and you'll get an extremely handsome drink coaster that says *Empowered Downward.*"

The fad spin cycle fomented by the business press goes like this:

1. An article appears: "More and more companies, it seems, are doing X." (There follows a long list of the benefits of doing X.)

2. A CEO sees the article and sends it to his or her subordinates with a petulantly scribbled note: "Why aren't *we* doing X?" The note implies the company wouldn't be in the fix it's in today if only they'd done X three years ago.

3. Analysts, asked why the company's stock is languishing, explain: "They're not doing X."

4. The company does X. It makes a big announcement; it invests heavily in coffee mugs that say, "Yesiree, we're doing X."

5. The first article appears questioning the wisdom of corporate America's headlong rush toward X.

6. The business press openly criticizes managers who were too quick to embrace X.

7. Huge piles of coffee mugs go begging.

8. The first article appears advocating bold new strategy Y.

By all means read the business press. Keep abreast of fads and buzz-words, and you'll at least have some vague understanding of what a colleague means when he sidles up to you by the water cooler and says, "You know, Jim, as hierarchy has flattened, the trust gap actually has widened." But keep your skepticism well oiled. There's frequently no better, cheaper, or more effective way to skirt disaster than by avoiding whatever "-ism" may be hot. Is everybody opening a factory in some new market? Maybe you should, too—but not because every-body else is doing it.

Several years ago, Chrysler considered embarking on a major ven-ture in China. After due deliberation, we decided against it. At the time, we felt our resources were better used in other ways. People would ask, "Why aren't you in China?" (I'm pretty sure they meant Chrysler and not me, personally.) Analysts pointedly observed that everybody else in the auto industry had either headed off to China already or was busy packing.

Perhaps someday Chrysler will reconsider this decision. But I must say I don't regret it when I pick up the morning's paper to see that yet another car company, after having invested $100 million there, is pulling out.

Another choice I don't regret—though it was painful at the time—was our decision not to go ahead with a world-class, rear-wheel-drive luxury car, code-named LX, that was to have been a unique flagship iteration of the LH platform. It would have been a beautiful car, no question. But by 1994 to 1995, it seemed, every one of Chrysler's com-petitors had already piled into this same segment. Margins shrank. Deals being offered to consumers became cutthroat.

Just *how* cutthroat I found out one day when my tailor showed up driving a Cadillac Seville STS. I asked him, "Have I been paying too much for my suits?" No, he said. He hadn't set out to buy a Cadillac. He'd set out to get a Saab, but found the payments were too high. The Cadillac was $100 a month cheaper. So here you had a curious situa-tion: A guy tries to buy a $35,000 car, finds he can't afford it, and drives off with a $55,000 car! One must ask, "Who's subsidizing this lease?" The maker of the $55,000 car, that's who. Much as we would have liked to have made the LX, we decided that that class of expense-is-no-object luxury car, at least for Chrysler, had become a trip to nowhere.

I've here expressed what might be called the negative case for fad avoidance. But there's a strong positive case as well.

Picture a white carpet. It's absolutely pristine, white as snow. When a catsup spot appears on it one day, the world is thunderstruck: "Gracious—look at that spot!" It's all anyone can talk about. Then some days later a second spot appears, eliciting much the same reaction. A third appears, a fourth, and so on. A week later, the carpet looks more red than white, and nobody much notices or cares when catsup spot number 46 comes calling.

So it is with products (and services and entering new markets). You don't want to be just another late-arriving spot. You want to get noticed. You want to be the first spot of something entirely new: Time to get out the mustard!

We might call this Lutz's ABC Law: "Anything But Catsup"!

Let me cite an example of it, as applied to advertising. From day one, Chrysler's ads for our new Dodge Ram pickup have intentionally ignored the truck's most obvious and appealing trait—its solid, in-your-face design. I call it the Cindy Crawford school of advertising: If you have Cindy Crawford in an ad, you don't have to *tell* people she's beautiful; folks can see that for themselves. With the Ram, we flattered ourselves to think we had an automotive Cindy Crawford (or maybe Arnold Schwarzenegger is a more apt comparison). So rather than *tell* the consumer that this truck was tough—with the obligatory run-it-through-the-mud footage—we decided to put the brute, in Dodge red, by itself on a stage and to let a calm, intelligent-sounding, disembodied voice (that of urbane actor Edward Herrmann) describe, not the Ram's biceps, but rather just one or two of its less salient features in each commercial. The idea was, as they say, to focus on the grain of sand that proves the whole desert—as in, "Boy, if they put this much thought into the bumper, just think how good the whole truck must be!"

Thanks in part to our willingness to break the mold for truck commercials, the Ram's North American sales have risen from 78,000 units a year in 1993 to 400,000 today.

Consider, too, the hugely positive reception given Volkswagen's new Beetle. Now, you could say that VW broke no new ground in bringing back the Beetle. Except that this car isn't the old Beetle. Mechanically, it bears no resemblance to it. More to the point, the market into which the new Beetle has been hatched has nothing comparable to it in styling. Did I say *comparable?* There's nothing even close. The car's a standout—a spot of a new and startling color. It's the kind of breakthrough product I think of as a category-buster—or better yet, a chart-buster.

You're familiar, I'm sure, with pie charts—those handy graphic devices representing 100 percent of a particular market and all the various segments into which it can be divided. The only problem with thinking of real markets in pie-chart terms, however, is that all the existing slices, taken together, may *not* represent the whole pie. The whole is always bigger.

Thus a pie chart of the U.S. nonalcoholic beverage market prior to the advent of carbonated drinks might well have shown three segments: coffee, tea, and milk. As far as marketers at the time were concerned, that was it! If you weren't in coffee, tea, or milk, you weren't selling drinks. Happily, Coca-Cola failed to get the word, and a whole new category was born. My point: Those willing to think *outside* the confines of existing segments can serve themselves a double helping of sales. VW, I predict, will sell every single Beetle made.

Instead of looking at the automotive pie and saying, "Well, let's see now. . . . There's small coupes, there's large coupes, there's small sedans, and there's large sedans. In which one of these will we put our new car?" VW instead said, "We're defining a new slice!" They stepped outside the pie altogether and created a new type of vehicle. Let's call it a "Heritage two-door."

Chrysler, in the early '80s, did the same thing—in spades—with the invention of the minivan. And American Motors, for its part, also invented an all-new automotive segment—the compact sport utility vehicle—with the original Jeep Cherokee in the mid-'80s. And after the Viper proved that new niches in the specialty car market were not mere fantasy, we challenged the conventional wisdom again, and came up in 1997 with the Plymouth Prowler, our homage to the street rods of the '50s and '60s. Of course there were a lot of skeptics who complained that the Prowler was impractical to build and even more impractical to drive. But we and our suppliers came up with revolutionary manufacturing techniques to mass-produce a thoroughly modern car (not bad for a car whose basic shape harkens back to

1934!). I'll tell you what I said when we first hatched the idea (and what became the credo for the whole program): "Those who don't like it, or don't get it, never will. And that's fine with us!"

But frankly, we also had an instance or two of what we thought was "out-of-the-pie-chart" thinking that turned, instead, into pie-in-the-face reality. One was a car called "Chrysler's TC by Maserati." The year before I joined Chrysler, the company announced that, in addition to taking a 15 percent ownership in Maserati, we and Maserati were going to work together on a limited-production "image" car—to be assembled in Italy using mostly Chrysler parts—that combined "the best of the Old World with the best of the New." Four years later, the coupe-cum-convertible TC finally came to market. And, true, it did feature a higher-performance, 16-valve version of Chrysler's then-ubiquitous 2.2-liter turbo engine, a five-speed manual transmission, a sumptuous leather interior, and the revered Maserati "trident" emblem on the deck lid. However, even though most of the TC's major exterior body stampings were supplied by Maserati, to all but the most astute observer the car looked like a mass-production (and K-derivative) Chrysler LeBaron convertible! In fact, one Detroit-area car dealer was caught displaying the $30,000 TC on the showroom floor right next to a look-alike Chrysler convertible priced at about $12,000. When asked, by a Chrysler executive, why he would do such a seemingly foolhardy thing, the dealer's reply was, "Hey, I'm trying to *move LeBarons!*"

Betting on a category-buster takes guts. And since guts are in perennially short supply, marketers often settle for what seems a safer course: making incremental changes in existing products.

A bad idea? No. But it's no substitute for category-busting; and, like anything else, it can be overdone. My own personal bête noire is Crest toothpaste. It used to be just Crest—a greenish paste that, with regular use, promised to reduce cavities. Over the decades, it has pro-liferated into a contentious, multigenerational tooth-cleansing family. There's the venerable pater, wearing its years proudly and calling itself Original Flavor. There's Mint. There's Normal Crest, as opposed to Tartar Control Formula. And, sadly, there has come most recently that inevitable consequence of inbreeding, Crest Gel—a greenish blue translucence that I personally find revolting.

As the *Detroit Free Press* said (with what I thought was almost British understatement) in a story last year noting there are now some 130 varieties of paste on the market, "Toothpaste options are multiplying."

Presumably (but maybe not) these many permutations of Crest have added significant amounts of volume and market share; and the extra revenue and profitability, one hopes, have more than offset the added costs of production, scheduling distribution, and advertising. But does this proliferation of choice really enhance customer satisfaction? How much time does the customer waste in front of the Crest display, turning boxes over to make sure the right subspecies is in hand? How often has the family shopper returned with the requested tube only to be told "I said paste, dummy! tooth*paste!* You got *gel!*"

Is there not, perhaps, a case to be made for *focus?*

I say "less is more." Keep it simple. Let your brand or product stand for something *specific*. The more you try to broaden appeal by attempting to please every whim of every consumer, the less you pinpoint the area in which your product, and *only* your product, can be of service. Don't fall prey to "the dilution solution" when, with the same investment of time and effort, you could be hatching yourself a category-busting Beetle!

CHAPTER 7

Too Much Quality Can Ruin You

QUALITY HAS BECOME A KIND OF HOLY GRAIL, CHASED AFTER BY ALMOST everyone. Yet few of the chasers, I think, really know what they are chasing.

They assume their idea of quality is synonymous with the customer's. It may not be. And when it's not, consumers are bombarded with quality they never asked for, didn't want, and aren't about to pay for (let alone pay a premium for).

Such surplus quality sometimes results from the best intentions, as author John Jerome recounts in one of my all-time favorite books, *Truck,* a hugely entertaining account of his efforts, over the course of a long New England winter, to rebuild a 1950 Dodge pickup. (Being a car restorer myself, I really relate to, among other things, his description of utter helplessness at having a vehicle torn apart, the parts all lying before you, and not knowing for sure how to put the damn thing back together again!) Jerome, brought "simultaneously to the edge of hernia and despair" by his inability to unscrew the truck's left-side wheel bolts, eventually discovers why:

Back in the Mesozoic period of automobiles, some Chrysler engineer decided that since the wheels on the left-hand side of the car were turning in a direction that corresponded to the loosening, rather than the tightening, of standard bolt threads, it therefore would be safer to have reverse-thread, or left-handed bolts holding the wheels on the left-hand side of the car. [Voilà, better quality!] In 1970, Chrysler abandoned reverse-thread lug bolts. One of those engineers must have realized, after about fifty years of close observation, that, sure enough, none of the wheels were falling off the competition's cars, which had your ordinary, right-hand-thread wheel fastenings.

Lest you get the idea such excesses are a thing of the past, Ford recently had to recall 1.7 million trucks when it was discovered that Ford's having put too much anticorrosion coating on their lug nuts was creating a small problem: The overcoated nuts were coming loose, causing wheels to drop off. One imagines conversations with accident investigators that begin, "Well, ma'am, the good news is your wheels are entirely corrosion-free. The bad news, though, is that they're no longer on your car."

An overzealous pursuit of quality has even, on occasion, jeopardized the reputations of brands already synonymous with excellence.

Rolls-Royce in the 1960s, like many other smaller manufacturers of cars, wanted to offer its customers the option of an automatic transmission, but lacked the resources to develop one on its own. So Rolls turned to GM, who made the best-matured, best-performing automatic then available—the Hydra-Matic.

Despite the transmission's reputation for flawless operation, Rolls found its Hydra-Matics experiencing harsh shifts, erratic shifts, and slippage. GM was unable to account for this, since the units being used were identical to ones used in Cadillacs, where they performed perfectly.

A teardown of a recalcitrant Rolls Hydra-Matic revealed the problem: At the bottom of almost all automatics sits an aluminum die-cast plate, called a *valve body,* containing an array of channels that route hydraulic fluid this way and that as valves in the transmission open and close during shifting. The surfaces of these channels, being die-cast, aren't especially pretty. Quite the opposite, in fact. They look dull, gray, and rough.

It was this appearance that had led Rolls astray. If the channels were to carry fluids in a Rolls, by George, they would have to be shined and made gleaming to a fare-thee-well. The worldwide reputation of Rolls-Royce could tolerate no less! This quality-driven change was what had caused the Hydra-Matic's troubles. The rough, disreputable-looking channels in fact offered just the right resistance to hydraulic fluid, ensuring that it flowed in a stable fashion. Prettying up the channels made them too slick, speeding up fluid flow and causing shifting to happen out of sequence.

The fix? Rolls, at GM's behest, stopped trying to improve the inner looks of the Hydra-Matics and instead just bolted them in, same as Cadillac did. Drivers in the British Empire could once more shift with confidence.

As this happy ending may suggest, quality is not always what it's popularly believed to be: an absence of "things gone wrong" (or TGW, as it's quantified in all those J.D. Power & Associates quality surveys out there in the world today). "Wrong" may not always be *wrong*.

If quality were only an absence of TGW, then the most desirable restaurant in the world would be the one with the lowest incidence of food poisoning per calorie (not exactly the definition one thinks of when remembering that charming little bistro you fell in love with on your last trip to Paris).

If quality were to be defined as "zero TGW," then the hottest show on Broadway—the ticket that inspires the sort of scalping not seen since Little Bighorn—would be for the performance where no actors forget lines, no scenery falls, and seat bottoms are admirably free from gum.

Get the idea?

Quality has less to do with the removal of negatives than it does the addition of strong positives: The four-star bistro makes a *tarte tatin* so delicious it's worth the trip to Paris all by itself. The greatest Broadway show makes you laugh till you cry, or (in the case of a tragedy) cry until everyone points to you and laughs.

Products perceived as high-quality needn't be useful. They needn't be practical. The women's shoes showcased in *Vogue* have little to do with walking. But what they may lack in arch support they more than make up for in a power to startle and delight. And in a world where all products are being manufactured to pretty much uniform technical standards, that ineffable, impractical, extra delight is what *real* quality is all about. You don't see delight sitting dusty on the shelf. It's back-ordered and in perpetuity.

Given two extremes—"zero defects with no delight" and "delight with a few squeaks in it"—the public will always buy the latter.

Case in point: convertibles, for which *squeaky delight* might once have been a synonym. Compared with their hardtop cousins, convertibles expose drivers to more rattles, squeaks, leaks, and noise. Yet convertible owners keep coming back for more. Asked, "Do you love your car? Would you recommend your car to a friend? Would you buy another one yourself?" they answer, "Yes," "yes," and "yes!"

I once worked for a carmaker that wanted to kill its convertible because the car generated more customer complaints than any other car the manufacturer made. I argued that this was only natural. From an engineering standpoint, convertibles are like shoe boxes with the lids off. They're looser structurally than a hardtop, thus more prone to squeaks and leaks. What the company had overlooked was that this car, despite (or maybe because of) its defects was the most popular convertible in all of Europe. People who owned it loved it. Its positive ratings far surpassed its negative ones. In the end, the car survived—as it deserved to. You don't love a baby less because it burps. (BMW drivers used to carry a toolbox in their trunks as a badge of honor!)

Today, no matter what the product—convertibles or hardtops, transmissions or *tarte tatin*—the market has become so competitive that few if any "squeaks" are tolerated. Consumers expect—and get—technical proficiency *and* delight. Neither attribute alone will cut it. Consumers demand both, and they'll go to the company that gives them this combo most dependably.

Still, it remains easy for some executives to forget that attributes like charm, romance, and fun matter. To define quality independent of them is to define it far too narrowly.

Financial Controls Are Bad!

CHAPTER 8

EVEN THOUGH I'M KNOWN AS A "PRODUCT GUY," I HAVE GREAT RESPECT for finance—contrary to what the title of this chapter may imply. After all, my father was a Swiss banker, so you could say I grew up with a little finance in my blood (though I didn't possess sufficient conservatism to be a banker, especially not a Swiss one). Yet I feel strongly that the function needs to reinvent itself. As constituted now, it's much too much obsessed with imposing tight controls.

Wall Street loves companies with tight controls—the tighter the better. Is this because (as I've long suspected) financial analysts are secretly masochists? ("Just a minute, darling, while I slip into something less comfortable.") Or is it because they believe tight controls invariably cut waste? If it's the latter, they're wrong.

Tight controls do harm in two ways. First, they can jeopardize an organization's ability to exploit big opportunities. While I was at Ford of Europe, for example, one of our products was getting murdered in the market because it lacked a then high-tech cassette tape deck. It was a matter of our spending $40,000 (the cost of engineering and tooling for the tape deck) in order to protect an $8 million business. Finance balked!

The second way is more subtle: Because measurements are based on past performance, controls tend to sanctify the status quo. They promote a false sense of orderliness and predictability. The future seems only a matter of extrapolation, prompting managers to say such daft, left-brained things as, "That can't happen; it's not in the five-year plan."

With financial controls, looser frequently is better—as we found at Chrysler when we instituted a cost-savings drive. Departments had wide leeway in deciding how to cut their spending by 10 percent.

In what has to be my favorite example of creative thinking, some very junior people at one of our facilities looked at the amount of money spent for what we euphemistically term "hygienic paper"— toilet paper and hand towels.

A control-mad, left-brained cost cutter would simply have cut the paper budget 10 percent.

The response from employees is easy to imagine: *What am I supposed to do, go to the bathroom 10 percent less often?*

Our junior people had an inspiration: They looked at Chrysler's hygienic-paper purchases corporatewide, not just in their own facility, and discovered that by consolidating purchasing and using one supplier, we could cut our collective cost not by 10 percent but by 50 percent. (Best of all, people can still go to the john whenever they want!)

Make controls too loose, of course, and you pay a price in chaos. But screw them down too tight and you pay a different price: stasis. When nonfinancial costs are factored in, the "savings" attributed to tight controls quickly disappear.

At Ford of Europe in the '70s, we had an organization that, unfortunately, was a little *too* buttoned-down. I recall having to sit through monthly meetings where all requests for capital expenditures from all over Ford's empire were consolidated into huge black binders festooned with tabs. One by one, the requests went under a financial microscope, to be approved, denied, or consigned to that terrifying limbo called, "We'd like to have a little more information on this before we decide."

No request was too trivial to escape maximum scrutiny.

Exhibit A: A $25 Polaroid Swinger camera was stolen from the car of a Ford service rep. The question before the court: Should it be replaced? The following interrogation ensued:

Q: Why does the company provide cameras in the first place?

A: So when the warranty people are at the dealership, they can verify that a part actually was broken or a seat torn, thereby reducing fraud.

Q: Who pays for the film?

A: The company does, because this system costs less than shipping the broken parts back to headquarters.

Q: How do we know the reps don't use the cameras on the weekends to photograph their family?

A: We don't. We tell them not to, and we don't think it's a problem.

Q: Do we have controls? Do we count films? Why not? How many packs are allocated per week to each service rep? Who checks? Who keeps the books on films?

Wilting under this barrage of questions, the executive who'd requested the expenditure withdrew, promising to come back in a few months with all the details, plus a plan for a comprehensive film-per-camera-per-week monitoring system.

Need I add that this entire exercise was idiotic?

Some of the questions someone should have asked were: How much of senior management's time is being wasted arguing the merits of a $25 camera? Why are senior managers of the world's second-largest car company, men in charge of a (then) $10 billion operation, squandering their resources on such trivia? How much clerical time will be consumed writing and distributing the new proposal? And what of the poor employee who'd suggested the idea of using cameras in the first place? That had been an inspiration. But will Ford ever hear a peep from him again? Not likely.

Does this mean management should forgo controls? How much control can you relinquish without losing the *essence* of control? Where does the benefit of enhanced personal initiative end and the specter of waste and employee abuse start? There's no recipe, alas, and the truth is that most organizations merely oscillate between the extremes of too much and too little control.

May I suggest a parable to illustrate?

Our tableau: a nice, suburban home with swimming pool; a mom, a dad, and son Johnny, nine, whom mom and dad are teaching how to swim.

Johnny's making all of the appropriate motions, and he's completing circuits of the pool. But he's doing it only because mom and dad are helping. Did I say *helping?* They've got him tethered by his ankles and his wrists. There's a strap around his tummy with a wire on it. Johnny looks like he's in traction. Mom and dad are walking him from one end of the pool to the other, as if trolling for some bigger child. It's not a perfect system, but it's theirs.

One day dad looks over the fence. Lo and behold, there's the neighbor's kid, and he's swimming without help: no belts, no hooks, no tethers—nothing. Plus he's doing flips and pirouettes that dad hasn't seen since the last airing of *Million Dollar Mermaid.*

How does the neighbor's kid do it? Mom and dad don't know; but they decide to risk an experiment. They unbuckle Johnny, take him to the deep end, and drop him in. He sinks.

Horrified, they quickly haul him back up and hook him up again, this time redoubling the belts and straps. "Well," they say to one another sadly, "that didn't work. We are officially unable to say how the neighbor's kid does it. All we know is, it doesn't work in our culture!"

If mom and dad plumbed deeper, they would no doubt discover that the much-envied neighbor kid manages to swim without constraints because he has been taught both skills and rules (e.g., "Don't dive off the shallow end."). If it weren't for his training, he couldn't be trusted; he'd still need a harness.

The path to financial autonomy (or to mastery of any discipline or business goal) can only be taken in measured steps. As subordinates absorb a company's mission and its goals, they internalize management's own sense of limits. And as management gives them opportunities (small at first, then bigger) to operate with autonomy, they learn to swim—first 10 feet, then 30, then 50, and eventually the length of the pool. They may need some minor floatation devices at first (financial controls), but in time these shackles fall away. Management becomes just a supervising coach, providing encouragement and incentives.

This ideal of leanness, consisting only of swimmer and coach, requires a dynamic balancing of the left and right brain: Lean systems, lacking the heavy prop of supervision, appear fragile. The left brain yearns to heap on supporting controls (a few floats here, a tether there). Right-brained management must then resist, instead championing their original vision: a kid slicing cleanly through the water, swimming powerfully, gracefully, and (most important) on his own.

CHAPTER 9

Disruptive People Are an Asset

TODAY WE LIKE A CALM, GENTLE CORPORATE CULTURE:

No cynicism.

No disagreements.

No stars or heroes (and no villains, God forbid).

No dissenting theories to gum up the works.

In this climate, people who argue a bit too vehemently, who "die hard" in meetings when they're overruled, who voice doubt about the direction in which the organization is heading, or who praise the competition (thereby suggesting we're not the best) aren't liked—to put it mildly.

They're not liked by senior management. They're not liked by peers. Some, probably, aren't liked by their mothers.

The reason isn't hard to find: Such people sometimes are disrespectful, cynical, critical of higher-ups, impatient, frustrated, angry. A small but significant number of them actually are nuts.

Yet you ignore disruptive people at your peril, and not just because one of them might someday bop you over the head with a stapler.

These people are "change agents" (that's the polite term). And change agents aren't supposed to be liked. They're supposed to effect change, which never is an easy or attractive undertaking. Their ranks include many illustrious figures whose rough edges have been smoothed by history: Henry Ford the Elder, Thomas Edison, Admiral Rickover, Billy Mitchell, and, if we were to reach still further back, a fair number of the Founding Fathers (a.k.a. revolutionaries).

Though conversant with rule books, such persons aren't prisoners of them. They arrive quickly at solutions that the tractable and hidebound never see. For this reason, by the way, these people tend to make great fighter pilots—at least in military establishments smart enough to let them exercise their own judgment. The United States does; the Soviets didn't.

The difference became clear in comparisons between the dogfighting techniques of Top Gun U.S. fighter pilots and their MiG-flying East German counterparts during the Cold War. The Russian-trained pilots were all highly analytical, left-brain trained, not the least disruptive. Their mechanical ability was flawless. But what they didn't have—and what the Top Guns did—was the ability to use their airplanes creatively, even artistically. Borrowing the language of ice-skating, the East Germans were great at performing a set program. But since neat and tidy choreography tends to be war's first casualty, it's the "free" program that matters more. For that, you want pilots who are glad, when circumstances dictate, to throw the rule book away—in short, you want disruptive types.

This isn't to say you ought to canonize mere orneriness. It's to say that some (repeat, *some*) disruptive people are very much worth keeping. They're more asset than cost.

They're the irritating grains of sand that, in the case of oysters, every now and then produce a pearl. Disruptive people precipitate breakthroughs, sometimes by forcing an uncomfortable reexamination of comfortable assumptions. Their favorite question is, "Why?" When everybody else is too afraid (or too lazy) to ask it, they ask.

As you may already have surmised, I feel a particular affinity for such people, being one myself. For as long as I can remember, "Why?" has come easily to the Lutz lips.

Even I, however, sometimes have trouble distinguishing *creative* disruptives (harbingers of needed, beneficial change) from *crackpot* disruptives who spread negativity and accomplish little else. How can you develop finely tuned BS radar so you can tell one from the other?

There's no foolproof way, except to supplement your own judgment with that of others. If you like a disruptive person (or like what he or she has to say), ask the person's current or former colleagues for their perspective. If what you hear is, "I like that guy, but he blows it every time we try to implement an initiative," or "That person's demoralizing—always negative and critical, without a single positive thought," then chances are he's more trouble than he's worth. Often, how the person talks about others proves to be a useful litmus test. Does he give realistic assessments, praising where praise is due? Or are his comments always negative—an unremitting tirade against fools and incompetents? The latter should warn you that you're dealing with a nut.

I've dealt with what sometimes seems like more than my share. There was the guy, early in my career, who believed all automatic transmission engineers were charlatans—simply because he didn't believe in automatic transmissions! The system was correct when it branded this disruptive-creative guy plain old disruptive. He was! I'm reminded of people like him whenever I turn on the TV news and see someone demonstrating an engine that runs on "molecularly realigned, water-based fuel," usually to the delight of local TV anchors in California.

Sometimes the temptation to fire *all* disruptives can be keen. Resist it. Removing irritants feels good, but only in the same way that changing doctors feels good when your old one has been needling you to lose weight. Switch doctors however much you like, you're still fat.

Observe and listen to disruptive people. When you discover one to be merely disagreeable, ignore him. Dr. Ernst Fuhrmann, CEO of Porsche in the 1970s, put it very well: "Great employees are often the most difficult employees. But not all of the most difficult are great employees." Collectively, however, they're a pool from which pearls emerge.

Are you perhaps an irritant yourself? Then take a tip, please, from a veteran: Even the greatest change agents—those who, if given free rein, could take the organization to great heights—must learn to temper their behavior or they will self-destruct. You need to be just irritating enough to set change in motion, not so irritating that superiors and colleagues conclude they're better off without you. (See Chapter 14 for further thoughts on how to effect change with the least cost to you personally.) I'm not advising conformity. I'm simply suggesting you'll be happier and more effective if you exercise self-discipline.

CHAPTER 10

Teamwork Isn't Always Good

I'LL REPHRASE THAT: TEAMWORK *CAN* BE GOOD—AND THE PEOPLE AT Chrysler know just how good. Harnessed properly, teams work miracles. A team of just 80 people took the Viper from show car to show room in just 36 months—a record at that time. And a cross-functional team of 50 Chrysler employees studied what had been our 68-day order-to-delivery cycle (the time it takes from receipt of an order for a new vehicle to the vehicle's being delivered to a dealer). They reduced that time to *20 days,* putting us a whole month closer to the market. That ain't hay!

Teams more typically are *not* being harnessed properly, though; and the evidence of this is as close as your nearest movie theater.

Did you go to the movies this summer? Did you happen to notice that what was offered you was just a warmed-over hash of movies that you'd seen before? Oh sure, the disaster movies were 10 percent more disastrous. The action movies had an extra (pick one): midair collision, crash, skid, fireball, or beheading. But they differed only slightly from the genre of movies that preceded them. They're mere extensions of existing brands—Hollywood's answer to Tartar Control Crest.

Who's responsible for these banalities? Are these the offspring of an original and kinky mind? Obviously not. So what entity, then, brought its fist crashing down decisively on some desktop and declared, "Yes, by thunder, we've got to get *Honey I Shrank the Dog III* into production *immediately*"?

Teams. Me-too movies, like most other mediocre products that stumble gracelessly to market, are the fruit (mealy fruit, I might add) of *too much* teamwork. Teams prefer the safe, the familiar, the middle of the road, the well-researched. They fear originality.

Can you imagine a team of executives coming out of a huddle at a major studio and saying to their boss, "J.B., we think we've got next summer's blockbuster right here. It's about this disabled guy, see? And he can only use his right foot. Maybe it's his left—we're still working out details. Anyway, he's some kind of an artist, and . . ." Or, "J.B., the story's set in a concentration camp, see? And there's this really noble guy . . . some kinda businessman . . . a metal fabricator, maybe . . . and he saves Jews by having them make pots and pans in his factory. It'll be smash-ola!"

An individual—a Steven Spielberg or a Jim Sheridan—may possess the vision and courage to suggest a *Schindler's List* or *My Left Foot*. But a team? Not likely. Teamwork demands compromise; and compromise is not a soil friendly to the growth of extreme, yeasty blossoms. A breakthrough film? A segment-buster? A daring what-if scenario that defies the rules yet sells a million tickets? Don't look for these from teams.

And yet you'd be surprised how many CEOs believe, thanks to what they've read in the business press (vive la fad cycle!), that the best way to generate breakthrough ideas is to stick a group of employees in a room, give them sodas, and let "consensus" be their only guide.

In truth, most groups, left to their own devices, devote far more time and effort to the practice of teamsmanship (promoting group harmony, smoothing and protecting everybody's ego) than they do to *working*. As John Katzenbach of McKinsey & Co. wrote so refreshingly recently in the *Harvard Business Review*, "Spending time together seeking consensus is not the same thing as doing real work." (And this, by the way, is from a person who's hardly a Neanderthal—in fact, he's coauthor of the highly acclaimed book *The Wisdom of Teams!*) His observation recalled to me the "Marty" school of management.

You remember *Marty*—the classic movie starring Ernest Borgnine. In it, two protagonists sit around, endlessly tossing back and forth the same question—"I dunno, Marty . . . what do *you* want to do?" (As Marty figures out, this is no way to get a date for Saturday night!)

Teams aren't just bad at coming up with provocative ideas. (It's not for nothing that, as the old saw says, "A camel is a horse designed by a committee.") When entrusted with somebody *else's* brainstorm, they too often mess it up. In fact, teamwork nearly defanged Viper.

As originally envisioned, Viper was supposed to be extreme: a V-10 monster with six-speed manual transmission, no real top, and curtains where driver's and passenger's side windows ordinarily would be. Not for everybody, of course—but that's exactly the quality that we wanted.

So strongly did we feel that Viper shouldn't be a car for everybody that, at the car's introduction to our retail dealers in Las Vegas, I went so far as to write a little poem singing the praises of what we fully believed would be the Viper's power to repel certain types of drivers, most especially those who liked cars so easy to drive, so slick and silent, that you might as well be sitting in your La-Z-Boy watching a videotape of the road go by you.

Walt Whitman I admit I'm not, but the dealers seemed to like "Ode to Viper," of which I immodestly submit this sample:

> Viper is the perfect toy
> For grown-up people to enjoy;
> Viper's there for wind-in-hair,
> For those whom big-blocks do not scare,
> For those who love the lure of speed,
> Who traffic laws do *usually* heed,
> For those who like a manual tranny,
> And passengers who don't look like granny;
> But Viper's not for timid souls
> Who like to play more passive roles;
> So if your hobby's hugging trees,
> Don't consider this one, please.

Viper salesmen! Please take note
Of Chairman Lee's immortal quote:
"If Viper doesn't turn your head,
Check your pulse . . .
You may be dead!"

There were, as well, a few expurgated verses, whose composition owed something to my having consumed, in the hot Vegas sun, a gin and tonic or two before dashing them off:

Now, other sports cars *are* on sale,
But theirs won't be a happy tale;
Mazda's Miata may well be cute,
But Viper is a nasty brute.
Porsche may have lots of class,
But Viper's made for haulin' . . . a-a-at most two people and a bit
    of luggage.
300 ZX is made by Nissan,
Which Viper owners will gladly . . . p-p-pit their cars against.

(I had another verse about Corvette being Chevy's "techno-truck" . . . but discretion and sobriety prevent my repeating it!)

As Viper grew from inspiration to reality, we at one juncture passed the project to a "car marketing plans" team to get marketing input, telling them the project could absolutely cost no more than $80 million.

Time passed. Eventually the team reported back to senior management with a modified proposal: Chrysler should build *several* Vipers.

There'd be the one we'd asked for—the monster—but there would also be an automatic version and a tame V-8 that would offer power seats, power windows (real glass this time), and a top. Viper could now please everyone, albeit for a cost of $350 million.

Senior management abruptly yanked back the wheel, reassuming command of the project; and Viper as originally conceived went on to stardom.

How had Viper so nearly gone astray? Simple. Absent a strong leader who tells a team, "Look . . . pick either A or B; you can't have both," a team will often pick A *and* B. No member has the gumption (or authority) to veto suggestions of his or her peers, so an easy out becomes, "Let's do both!" It's an opportunity for a team to do what teams do: compromise.

The ability to compromise is, of course, a wonderful thing. And the promotion of team members' self-esteem is, of course, a noble goal. But neither is an end in itself. We're not running major corporations in order to perform social experiments. We are attempting to get work done. Remember work? It's what's required of us if we are to create the breakthrough products our shareholders expect and the public demands. And if that means, every so often, that we have to let some of the steam out of someone's self-esteem, I say fine; so be it. The entire business community in general seems to have grown far too concerned with sparing the feelings of those who've made peace with shoddiness and imperfection. It's become somehow tacky now to demand originality and excellence because, don'tcha know, that just might inconvenience someone. Risking an unpleasant confrontation in defense of excellence is a risk, I believe, that is eminently worth taking. Why? In today's hypercompetitive world, with dozens of nations eager to press their particular advantage, even a slight aversion to confrontation can prove crippling.

Teamwork without strong leadership leads to waste, to bad decisions, to failed products and services. We can all love one another, but what good is that if the amorous lemmings are all running off the same cliff together?

And what happens if love sours? Levi Strauss is finding out. In 1992, the company switched from its traditional way of compensating employees, based on each individual's piecework productivity, to a team system where groups of 10 to 35 workers each were rewarded according to their collective productivity. Levi's overall productivity fell. Fast workers resented being lumped with slowpokes who, they felt, were dragging down their pay. Since the groups received only limited supervision from coaches, resentments were allowed to fester.

But give a team a leader willing to insist that hard choices be made— a man or woman who doesn't mistake collaboration for democracy—and most problems I've here ascribed to teamwork disappear.

Most, but not *all*. There's one other problem endemic to teams— to any aggregation of humanity, really—that I've never seen discussed in business schools, in books, in military training, or anywhere else.

Yet it's so demonstrably true that it qualifies almost as a mini-Law unto itself: *"The percentage of idiots remains constant."*

This holds true in all fields of human endeavor and at every level. I discovered it as I moved through life, from school to school, company to company, level to level. Sometime in the last 10 years, it suddenly dawned on me that I had perhaps stumbled on a powerful truth about the natural order of things.

As far back as grade school, I noticed that roughly 20 percent of the class didn't really belong there, being either intellectually impaired or personality challenged. (*I* should know, for at the time I fit that very profile!) Surely, I told myself, when I get to junior high school, all the kids will be wonderful, bright, intelligent. Imagine my disappointment when I found 20 percent again hopelessly over their heads, thoroughly uninspired, or worse yet, unpleasant to be around.

Well, thought I, the Boy Scouts are an elite unit, with highly motivated, self-selected young men. In the Boy Scouts *everyone* will be great, just like in the comic books. Why was I not surprised to find that roughly 20 percent of my fellow Scouts were lads I would rather not share a pup tent with?

So, on to a prestigious boarding school in Switzerland for my high school years (that is, until I got booted out of it). The Swiss, I assumed, were highly selective about who they let into their premium private schools. So how did my nonfavorite 20 percent get in? Beats me. But there they were again! Was this nature's perverse randomness at work?

By now, the Korean War was on, and I was going to join the U.S. Marines, which, as every moviegoer knows, are just cram-packed full of the finest physical and mental specimens known to humankind. But, in boot camp at Parris Island, that 20 percent had somehow managed to creep right in there with me! The only difference was that here, for once, the 20 percent were under heavy pressure to shape up or ship out. And a huge portion of them did just that, quitting the program.

Well, if USMC boot camp had the "infestation of the 20 percent," surely U.S. Navy flight training—where only one in every 3,000 young Americans was considered qualified (according to the propaganda of that day) and where exactly $1 million of taxpayer money would be spent helping each one of us earn the coveted Navy Wings of Gold—would have to be, at long last, my idiot-free Valhalla. And yet the 20 percent had risen again, like an improperly staked Count Dracula! Was I never to be free of them?

No, as it turns out. They're everywhere—especially in giant corporations (and especially, it seems, in management). They're 20 percent of every team ever put together, be it a brain trust, a blue-ribbon panel, or a team competing in a sack race. The natural statistical scatter seems to provide, at any station of life and in any field of human endeavor, 20 percent who are outstanding, about 60 percent who are average, and 20 percent you wish you didn't have.

What can a leader do about this little problem, besides grin and bear it? You can, of course, raise standards, so that the 20 percent at the bottom drops out. But, even more important, you can make sure that the idiots don't, in fact, waft their way into management. The single biggest reason the "Dilbert" comic strip has struck such a chord out there is that all too often the "Dilbert Principle" really is true: Today, idiots don't just rise to their level of incompetence (as the famous old Peter Principle stated); today idiots are being promoted straight into management without being competent *at anything!* And, ironically, one reason is that many of these idiots are quite adept at understanding—or, rather, faking an understanding of—some of the principles just outlined in this section of the book. They've learned all the buzzwords of "change management," all the jargon about "intuitive leadership"—and their real understanding of these types of issues is as shallow as a glass of water.

It's time to stop the madness! It's time to "out" the idiots. It's time to expose fatuous phonies for what they really are . . .

It's time to turn to Part III of this book!

GUTS

PART III

LUTZ'S COROLLARIES, OR "THE *REST* OF THE STORY!"

Having just gone to the barricades in defense of the world's beleaguered creative folk, I now feel compelled to put in a few words in support of the enemy. "Wait a minute," you say, "how can Lutz—Mr. Right-Brained Thinking, Mr. The Goal of Business Is Not to Make Money—turn around here and advocate more left-brained thinking?" As the old Desi Arnaz character Ricky Ricardo used to say, "You've got some 'splainin' to do!" (And, as President Clinton likes to say, "I feel your pain"!)

For almost all of my career, I've argued that my own industry and Western business at large have been too much a slave to centralized control and to quantitative analysis. Whenever I could, I've called for greater empowerment of employees and more openness in thinking—especially thinking of the intuitive, right-brained variety.

Chrysler, I'm proud to say, has benefited greatly from an increased adherence to these principles. Detroit's (and, indeed, much of Western industry's) old chimneys have been toppled; workers feel empowered; fear has been driven out of the system; and cultures dominated by ably led teams have taken root. Best of all, in my view, in the car business, companies have come to be run again by true enthusiasts, the "car guys"—that wonderful, gender-neutral term describing what Walter P. Chrysler once called the "poets" of the industry.

That's the *good* news.

The bad news, I fear, is that this revolution in Western industry is in danger of having succeeded *too* well. In fact, I think in some ways it's gone too far already, to the point where I've begun to sense a countervailing need for greater discipline, better attention to detail, and, yes, greater individual accountability.

The most competitive organizations—the ones that enjoy what we might call the most robust mental health—are those that manage to maintain a careful balance between the right and left brain. They walk a path between chaos or stasis, careful not to veer toward either.

Such organizations, says Laurie Broeding, a former senior vice president at McDonnell Douglas, may *approach* chaos, but they never actually succumb to it. Instead, they live on its edge, which she calls that "constantly shifting battle zone between stagnation and anarchy [where] one set of forces (the need for order and control) pulls every business toward stagnation, while another set of forces (the need for growth and creativity) drives it towards disintegration."

None of us, of course, wants to work for an institution rendered sclerotic by too much autocracy, too much micromanagement, and too little empowerment. Yet who among us prefers chaos? My worry now is that in our holy war against stasis, we may already have overcorrected a bit.

One sees evidence of it not just in the world of business but in U.S. society (and Western society) at large. Traditional standards—whether of workmanship, intellectual achievement, personal deportment, or moral probity—are being flouted or ignored. Our schools are churning out illiterate and "numerically challenged" graduates, ill-equipped to compete in a global economy that puts an ever higher premium on intellectual skills. So-called service industries provide slipshod service. And an increasing number of consumers, uncomfortable, evidently, with past standards of personal responsibility, are subscribing to the idea that they are victims—not, heaven forbid, of their own incompetence or stupidity, but of rapacious and greedy manufacturers. Our national leaders, meantime, seem to lack the heartfelt conviction, let alone the courage, to go to the mat in defense of anything approaching a real, live, bedrock value.

I see a dreaded new disease—FDH—sweeping the land. Fat. Dumb. And happy (i.e., having a sense of personal well-being totally divorced from reality!). Before FDH claims one more victim, before civilization lists any further toward chaos, before the very planet begins to wobble on its axis, I, kindly Dr. Lutz, am going to prescribe an inoculation—three prophylactic postulates designed to revive rigor and stiffen standards. Since they follow from the preceding Laws in a cautionary "yes, *but*" fashion, I suggest we dub them "Lutz's Corollaries."

IT'S OKAY TO BE ANAL SOMETIMES

BEING DETAIL-CONSCIOUS, BEING PUNCTUAL, BEING FASTIDIOUS AND REA-sonably well dressed, being punctilious (even so punctilious as to make sure *punctilious* is spelled right), being, in short, a little anal . . . isn't a bad thing. Quite the opposite. In fact, as Martha Stewart likes to say, it's a *good* thing. What of the big picture—doesn't it matter more than details? It matters, but not more. As the saying goes, "Trifles make perfection, and perfection is no trifle."

Yet where trifles are concerned, we seem to have lost our capacity for outrage. Sloppiness, carelessness, and thoughtlessness go increasingly unchallenged. You see this slacking off in everything from rudeness on the street to a laid-back "Hey-what's-the-big-deal-it-still-works-doesn't-it?" attitude regarding product defects to my personal pet peeve: typos and misused words in national newspapers and magazines.

This insidious drift, far from being trifling, is one of the most fundamental problems now facing the business community and American society. And one of its foremost causes, I think, is modern human-relations theory—the idea that it's bad form to criticize (even when the criticism is constructive); that it's not smart to make waves (especially not in an era of 360-degree performance evaluations!); and that it's somehow tacky to demand perfection, because, don'tcha know, demanding it just might inconvenience someone. Even more unthinkable, it might dent their self-esteem!

I like to think I'm a pretty positive guy. And I also like to think I place a very high value on self-esteem. But by the same token, I don't think that putting feelings ahead of a wholesome regard for workplace performance makes any more sense than putting them ahead of academic performance in the classroom. Why not? Because the self-esteem thus created is, to be blunt, phony and ephemeral. It vanishes the moment the student or the employee hits the real world and can't read a job application or gets laid off because his or her company is no longer competitive.

Nobody better understands the importance of performance and of detail than Japanese carmakers. Take Toyota, whose unflinching commitment to excellence shows itself in the fit and finish of the smallest dashboard control knobs. In addition to our Honda study in the late '80s, Chrysler also did a lot of benchmarking of how Toyota ran its business. We particularly looked at the way it had increased profits and cut costs. Toyota had suffered a humiliating brush with bankruptcy in 1949, and it had sworn ever since to eliminating all waste, however small, as one means of maximizing profits. By the time we studied the company in the late '80s, Toyota's cash position was in excess of $10 billion (and is more than $13 billion today), so what they were doing evidently worked!

Just how detail-conscious was Toyota? The company's cost-control policy decreed that employees extract every bit of use from everything, even pencils: When a pencil became too short to be held between the fingers, employees were instructed to soften the tip of an old pen with a cigarette lighter, then insert the pencil's stub. The stub then was to be used until there was no longer any of it left to sharpen, even manually.

Yours truly caught a fair amount of flak when, emboldened by Toyota's rigor, I urged my colleagues during Chrysler's own humiliating period in the late '80s to be similarly vigilant about cutting out waste. The point I sought to make was that eradicating big, obvious examples of waste would not be enough. If Chrysler were to survive our Crash #2, we'd have to root out waste in every form, however small. Was I being too anal? Decide for yourself. Here are a few examples of what I considered then (and now) to be waste:

9 August 1989
To: Chrysler Motors Officers
From R.A. Lutz
Subject: Avoidance of Waste

As I reread the "Toyota-endaka" document [a document about how Japanese automakers were valiantly and rapidly offsetting the effects of a stronger yen] for the third time, it occurred to me more and more that the core message is: "Cost cannot be reduced as long as waste is tolerated." Only when waste, however minor, is recognized for what it is . . . ([examples of] which, individually, may be small but which, cumulatively, risks our survival) will we be able to make significant progress. . . .

Waste is:

- Needless plaques and in-house commemorative items
- Elaborately produced and framed policies and statements
- New name tags for every event. (I don't know about you, but at any given moment I seem to have a collection of about 50 name tags all saying "Bob Lutz, Chrysler." I suggest executives need only one, which they should be recycling.)
- Late arrival at meetings
- Excessive participants at meetings
- Meetings that run too long
- Elaborate slide presentations for in-house use
- Fat, multitabbed "marketing plans" books
- Back-and-forth memos to either allocate or ward off blame
- Trays and trays of uneaten cookies, Danish, and doughnuts
- Multiple copies of videotapes (when one, circulated, would suffice)
- Missed deadlines
- Lights left on
- Getting photos and certificates framed in-house
- Controlling and explaining variances rather than improving absolutes

- Re-dos
- Anything, anywhere regarded as a neat freebie of working for a big company
- Anything, anywhere not directly tied to the benefit of our customers

Too austere? Maybe, but you have to admit it got my point across. And I think I deserve some small credit for *not* suggesting people melt their old pens to accommodate old pencil stubs! Sure enough, Chrysler, through economies not just big but small, did manage to save billions.

These suggestions of mine did not exactly endear me to everyone who got them, and before long a memo in reply (part parody, part counterblast) made its way to me through the office grapevine. Here are a few examples of "waste" the unnamed author cited:

- Three brand vice presidents with twelve directors reporting to them

- Any corporate resources used to aid employees practicing helicopter maneuvers on company property [a "shot" at a certain fellow who sometimes flew his chopper to work!]

- $2,000 per night hotel rooms for company presidents in Tokyo, when more modest accommodations are available

- Major corporate reorganizations twice a year every year

Regarding the first and last of these: I couldn't have agreed more! In fact, the writer did me a favor by saving me the trouble of having listed them. As for the middle two, these speak to a serious question I mean to tackle later in the book: whether executive privileges do more harm than good. (Not wanting to keep you in suspense, I'll give you a hint: In my upcoming chapter on Leadership, I say hooray for the corporate dining room!) Readers lacking in self-discipline may feel moved to peek at it now. We of sterner stuff, however, will next take on one of the most subtle and pernicious frauds being perpetrated on business today: the forced relaxation of standards of office dress. Yesterday's dictum might have been "dress for success." Today's, apparently, is "dress like a mess!"

REAL CREATIVITY VERSUS "CASUAL DAY"

A misconception has somehow gained currency that if you neglect to bathe before coming to work, if you dress in a turtleneck sweater, and if your overall deportment suggests you aren't quite sure what day it is, this proves you are a card-carrying creative person, exempt from the rules and standards governing more prosaic employees.

What transparent bunk! *Real* creativity has nothing whatsoever to do with such externals. It is the product of courage (an individual's willingness to experiment) and disciplined hard work (his or her determination to keep experimenting until the best solution is found). Yet it's the "turtleneck" conception of creativity, I suspect, that has contributed to the current rage for casual days, dress-down Fridays, or other such exercises in cosmetics. The forced relaxation of standards of dress, so far as I can tell, works but one miracle: It offers new hope to a beleaguered corduroy industry.

Let me revise that. It works *two* miracles. The second is that it allows a certain kind of company to create the appearance of doing something about creativity without actually having to come to grips with any of the fundamentals.

Let's say an organization is having trouble generating new ideas, that it's embarrassed that it's always last at everything. Senior management either hires a consultant or goes on a retreat (or both), and decides, "We're too rigid; we're too isolated; our employees are afraid of us." Somehow the fix amounts to announcing that henceforth casual wear will be appropriate on certain days at Ajax Corp. so as to provide an environment "free from stress or fear in which every employee feels that he or she can contribute to his or her full ability . . ." (you provide the rest of this verbiage).

Exactly *how* eliminating neckties is supposed to promote original thought is a question that never gets close examination, being taken more or less on faith. I've never found anyone willing to claim that a switch to casual dress made them feel more empowered, freer, or more creative. And my own observation of several decades—of offices both civilian and military—suggests just the opposite is true.

Formality of dress—having a "uniform" (literal or figurative)—imbues a group with an extra measure of pride, professionalism, and esprit de corps that is greater than they would have if they dressed every which way. A uniform—whether fatigues or a coat and tie—signifies the wearer is a member of a team, and that the team has special abilities and a special mission. The act of "dressing for duty" causes a subtle shift in a person's attitude. It focuses the wearer on his task; it signifies that he's about to join a body of peers, who together will do battle with the enemy.

Real creativity's first order of business is not the relaxation of standards but the mastery of them; once mastered, they then can be tweaked, flaunted, or otherwise played with. (Isn't that a working description of the creative process?) Being able to think "out of the box" presupposes you were able to think *in* it.

REASSERTING THE THREE R'S

Right now we are raising a generation of kids who cannot think inside, on top of, under, or outside the box. And unless we smarten them up soon, this Generation D (the youngest, dumbest Americans) is going to compromise our country's ability to compete economically somewhere down the road. Too strong a claim? I don't think so.

Though the relationship between a nation's economic performance and the intellectual attainments of its young may be neither simple nor direct, common sense dictates that a global economy that rewards knowledge in its workers is not going to shower its richest and most glittering gifts on a nation of the dim. Moreover, the costs of bad schools aren't waiting for us in some distant future; they're here now, and we're paying them. As IBM chairman Lou Gerstner warns, U.S. business already is paying tens of billions of dollars every year on remedial training for workers wanting basic skills. He cites a National Association of Manufacturers survey in which 30 percent of companies said they could not reorganize work activities because employees could not learn new jobs; 25 percent said they could not upgrade products because their employees could not learn the necessary skills.

Thanks to school offerings in ecology and on social issues, American schoolchildren rank second to none in their sympathy for squirrels, green leafy things, and the downtrodden. But in their ability to read, write, and figure nonvegetable roots (the square kind), they rank among the least-competent young being produced by any warm-blooded species. It's a big world, of course; and maybe there's a place in it for people who can sit around feeling good about themselves but can't write a coherent sentence. But that place is not my office or anybody else's.

As David Letterman once asked, on seeing Don King's hair, "What's the deal?" How did we stray so far from mastery of basic standards? And what's necessary to get us back?

Before I advance my own, peculiarly Lutzian views, let me first state my credentials. They read: "Parent, Citizen, Taxpayer, Employer, and Alumnus." As for my biases, I am an old-fashioned, unreconstructed, un-reengineered mossback who believes that the role of schools is to impart knowledge—period and full stop! I believe schools ought to give students a love of language, a sense of history, a respect for the scientific method, some dexterity with numbers, an appreciation of the arts, confidence in democracy, and the ability to think critically. When it comes to children's self-esteem, I'm all for schools promoting it. But, as I've said earlier, *durable* self-esteem comes from one source only: hard work and personal achievement.

I'm not (nor do I claim to be) any sort of expert on didactics or pedagogy. But the brutally unforgiving arena of the global auto industry, has, I think, given me what amounts to a postdoctoral degree in the one subject that seems invariably to come up when the question of how to fix the schools gets debated. I am a fully accredited expert in competition.

THE TERRIFYING "C" WORD: *COMPETITION!*

I don't know why, but it's a word that seems to strike mortal fear into the hearts of many educators, especially those in public education (and even more particularly, those involved in the administration of public education). I think the fear is largely irrational. You'd think we were talking about the *E. coli* bacteria lurking out there, but we're not. We're talking about something that's as common as breathing.

Competition is the core process in the natural order of things, from evolution to free enterprise. It's why human beings can walk erect and write poetry, and it's why the American economy is able to spend considerably more resources on education than any other nation in the world. Competition, I submit, has the potential to be the best thing that's happened to teaching since chalk.

There are, however, two basic facts to understand about it.

Number one—it's unfair. There is no such thing in the adult world as fair competition. Someone always has the advantage. Fairness is irrelevant.

Let me give you an example of how unfair competition can be: Charter schools are a big issue today. We hear that competition from charter schools could take resources away from established schools. But let's say, for conversation's sake, that you wanted to start one. In order for it to succeed, you'd have to compete with the already established public school in town. You'd have to take some of its students away.

That established school not only has the students already, but it has all the other necessary assets: the schoolhouse, the buses, the teachers, the gyms, the cafeterias, the football fields, the libraries, the labs and the cars for drivers' ed. All you have is a piece of paper called a charter—no building, no books, no buses, nothing.

Can you imagine any kind of competition more unfair than that? The established school has all the advantages, and if it's doing its job to the satisfaction of parents and the community, it has absolutely nothing to fear from competition. It can't lose.

On the other hand, if it's not doing its job, then the second truth about competition comes into play (and this is the part that scares some people). Competition implies there will be a winner and a loser. There's no such thing as "outcome-based competition" to make sure that nobody's feelings get hurt. The real world is not a padded romper room at McDonald's. It has edges to it.

If the established school I just described isn't doing its job, in spite of all the unfair advantages it enjoys, it's going to fail—and be replaced by something better. That's a wholly good thing.

Twenty years ago, the U.S. auto industry was failing. It wasn't entirely our fault. We didn't shut off the industrial world's supply of cheap oil; OPEC did. We didn't pass a bunch of regulations that made us uncompetitive with foreign carmakers for a while; the U.S. Congress did.

Just as educators are not responsible for the breakdown of the family or other social trends that make their jobs so difficult, we weren't responsible for those major causes of *our* failure. Did that matter? Not a bit. When I hear some educators say that they aren't responsible for the quality of the students they get or the social problems that undermine what goes on in their classrooms, I not only sympathize, I agree 100 percent. Then I ask, "So what?"

Twenty years ago, critics pointed out that auto companies in Japan and Europe were doing a better job of making cars than we were. And they were right. Those critics cut us no slack because the problems we faced weren't our fault, and neither did our customers.

Critics say much the same about American schools today, and they are right. I know educators get tired of hearing that. (We in the car business sure did!) Teachers get tired of hearing that they aren't as good at their jobs as their counterparts in Japan and Germany. The comparisons aren't always fair; they're not "apples to apples." But remember, fairness is irrelevant! The end products speak for themselves—end of discussion! Cars coming out of foreign factories were better than ours, and students coming out of foreign schools are better than students coming out of American schools.

If you were Chrysler 20 years ago, you had yet another problem: You weren't even as good as your *local* competition! Chrysler was the equivalent of a public school. The other guys were the better-off private academies—the Country Days and the Our Lady of Smartnesses. These competitors had fewer problems and more advantages, to be sure. But do you think the customers cared? Not a whit! Fairness never entered into it. In fact, I'd go so far as to say you could not find a more extreme example of unfair competition. Chrysler was the basket case of the whole auto industry—so much so that, yes, we twice very nearly died.

To survive, we had to completely rethink the processes we used to develop, manufacture, and market our products. Not only did we reorganize our talent into cross-functional teams, but we empowered our people and took a lot of bureaucracy out of the system (because, ironically, often the best way to put discipline *in* is to take structure *out*).

Totaling up Turnaround #1 and Turnaround #2, Chrysler eliminated tens of thousands of jobs vis-à-vis its head count back in the

1970s, for the simple reason that you cannot survive in a competitive world with people you don't need. Our productivity shot up. We paid off our debts and became the most profitable company in our industry. We produced what just about anybody who knows our business will tell you is the best product lineup of any auto company in the world. And ultimately, the value of the self-transformation we had wrought was confirmed by our ability to add thousands of jobs (more than 20,000, to be exact) as our company grew stronger and prospered.

You could easily make a case that unfair competition almost killed Chrysler two times—once in the late '70s to early '80s and once in the late '80s to early '90s. But you'd be wrong. Unfair competition *saved* Chrysler. It's what forced the company—initially against its will—to face realities and make certain changes that we'd never have done voluntarily. The prospect of failure is a great motivator. It can be a wonderful teacher. In fact, shielding a student from failure is, in short, a form of child abuse as cruel as denying him encouragement!

At Chrysler (and everywhere else I've worked), we didn't undergo fundamental change *by our own choice*. It was *forced* on us. The wisest of people or institutions seldom can deduce, on their own, that change is needed. And if they do, they never muster the courage needed to act on that need—not without barbarians at the gate!

It took the threat of *Sputnik* to put Americans on the moon. Federal Express made the U.S. Post Office self-sustaining. Toyota and Honda made Chrysler a success. Why should the effect of competition on education be any different?

Competition won't kill public schools, but in many cases it will force them to act differently—to adopt different priorities, to make needed changes, to eradicate waste, to reallocate resources to where they will do more good, and to become more customer-focused.

Past theories of education responsible for having produced children who cannot add or spell may have to be modified or abandoned. With any luck, one of the first to go will be the curious notion that nothing so banal as facts could matter. (I call this the *"Switzerland? Hey, Isn't That Somewhere up in Scandinavia?"* school of learning.) It holds, as near as I can tell, that every detail or bit of information Johnny or Suzy might ever need to cite can be summoned up from the nearest computer. Likewise, there's no need to master the details of grammar, syntax, or spelling, since errors will be caught and fixed by spell checks, grammar checks, and other such hygienic programs.

I don't know about you, but I don't see that these programs have made the world a safer place for bad spellers or, in particular, for the homonym-challenged (something spell checking can never correct). Permit me a few examples:

Exhibit A. I have before me a lovely, richly embossed invitation from a leading wine maker to a "seat down" tasting.

Exhibit B. I have a headline from *USA Today* (presumably written by an adult, but with *USA Today* you never know): "*X-Files* lets some light peak through." (Maybe it's the afterglow from *Twin Peaks.*)

Exhibit C. Here's an article in venerable *Time* magazine promising a "sneak peak." (I, for one, can't wait to see that stealthy mountain unmasked!)

Exhibit D. In the car business, you're always getting pinged by somebody for your quality. The "Old Gray Lady" herself, the *New York Times,* did the honors in this one, noting that "Recurring quality problems have left many potential buyers leary of Chrysler products." (I don't know, maybe they were referring to Timothy Leary, the psychedelic drug guru. Or, who knows, maybe they were on drugs at the time themselves!)

Exhibits E, F, G, and so on. Here's a newspaper editorial inveighing against "pierced navals." (Who'd have thought that perforated sailors were that much of a problem?) Here's a journalist congratulating Chrysler for having introduced the Durango with such "promotional flare" (yes, we include one in every trunk). And finally, the writer of a letter—a very senior executive himself—asks if America's "effluent society" will ever fully appreciate the bargain price of the Chrysler Concorde. (Geez, I sure hope not!)

Another educational theory of questionable utility holds that any insistence on correct (or at least consistent) spelling and usage represents a nefarious attempt by America's ruling class to throttle little children's creative expression. Not only should creative spelling be tolerated (so goes this theory), it should be defended.

Believers in this approach might be interested to learn they once had a powerful ally in plutocrat George Hearst—miner, multimillionaire, and father of newspaper magnate William Randolph Hearst. Self-made and self-taught, having had hardly any formal education, Hearst, after he became rich, hoped to run for governor of California. Knowing critics might question his intellectual ability, he offered this by way of self-defense: "My opponents say that I haven't the book learning that they possess. They say I can't spell. They say I spell *bird* b-u-r-d. Well, if b-u-r-d doesn't spell *bird*, what in hell *does* it spell?"

Math instruction has fared no better, wading into waters distinctly murky. Why have as your goal anything so crabbed, unimaginative, and anal as getting the right answer? Why not instead use the setting of the problem as a tool for teaching students the social and ecological realities of life? For a lampoon of this approach, consider the following humorous (but not unrealistic) illustration:

Evolution of a Student Homework Assignment*

1960   A logger sells a truckload of lumber for $100.00. His cost of production is four-fifths of this price. What is his profit?

1970   A logger sells a truckload of lumber for $100.00. His cost of production is four-fifths of this price, or $80.00. What is his profit?

1970 (new math)   A logger exchanges a set *L* of lumber for a set *M* of money. The cardinality of set *M* is $100.00, and each element is worth $1.00. Make 100 dots representing the elements of the set *M*. The set *C* of the costs of production contains 20 fewer points than set *M*. Represent the set *C* as a subset of *M*, and answer the following question: What is the cardinality of the set *P* of points?

1980   A logger sells a truckload of wood for $100.00. His cost of production is $80.00, and his profit is $20.00. Your assignment: Underline the number 20.

1990 (outcome-based education)   By cutting down beautiful
   forest trees, a logger makes $20.00. What do you think of
   this way of making a living? (Topic for class participation:
   How did the forest birds and squirrels feel?)

* *Source: Echoes* (winter 1994), Rose-Hulman Institute of Technology, Terre
Haute, Indiana.

Competition, I submit, will help refocus education on the basics
that students need in order to lead self-supporting and fulfilled lives: an
ability to count, read and write, think critically; the social skills to work
cooperatively in teams; and the intellectual self-confidence to break
ranks with the team when they deduce it's headed the wrong way!

We shouldn't ask the schools to solve society's problems or all the
individual problems that youngsters bring with them. It's tragic when
a kid can't learn or won't behave because of something in his family
or his own personality, but that's not the fault of the schools, and he
shouldn't be allowed to stay in school just because he has nowhere
else to go. I myself, as you'll recall, was once bounced out on my ear
unceremoniously (*after* being held back a total of three years). I didn't
get a high school diploma until I was 22. It took a stern father and the
U.S. Marine Corps to infuse me with the discipline I needed to live a
useful life. No school could do it. It's not a school's job.

One of the worst ideas I've ever heard is that schools should be an
alternative to the street. If you belong in school, you belong in
school. If you belong in the street, you belong in the street. The real
tragedy is when the kid who belongs in the street is in school and
vice versa.

"SERVICE PROVIDERS" WHO DON'T

I wonder why the public, so demanding when it comes to the quality
of cars, TV sets, and cameras, is so relaxed when it comes to situations
where the product is a service.

Remember 20 years ago when we heard ad nauseam that the United States and the rest of the West was finished as a site for manufacturing, that all of that gritty stuff would be handled by Mexico or Taiwan? Our new role was to be the leader in services—transportation, hospitality, banking, and what have you. Yet here we are at the tail end of the century, and what's happened? Manufacturing is stronger than ever, while the service businesses are either facing a rocky road, exploiting their customers, or both. What gives?

Manufacturing was confronted by the "C" word! It was change or die for much of Western industry as it got pummeled by agile and quality-focused Asian competitors. Even executives at German luxury-car manufacturers such as Porsche, BMW, and Mercedes-Benz, who used to say to me so condescendingly when I was at Ford, "This Japanese competition must be really tough on you poor Americans," eventually felt the heat. After 10 years of being shaken, rattled, and rolled by Lexus, Infiniti, and Acura, all carmakers had to change their tune radically.

This hasn't happened in the service industries. Many of the key ones, such as the airlines, are in a situation analagous to Detroit's before the advent of the Japanese. There's a "Big Three" (or Four, or Six, depending how far you want to go back). They *think* they're in a bloody, competitive battle, but they're only fighting with their traditional domestic competitors, who all play by the same rules. They ain't seen nothing yet!

How would it be if Singapore Airlines or Swissair were to operate on domestic U.S. routes? With friendly, informed, and helpful ground staff, immaculate aircraft, smartly dressed and highly professional cabin attendants, outstanding meals in both coach and first class, and invariable precision in both departure and arrival, they'd make mincemeat out of most of our domestic providers.

How long would the American passenger continue to suffer the indignities of surly check-in staff throwing the luggage on the conveyor; disheveled-looking pilots suffering from "Dunlop's Disease" (that's when your stomach "done lop" over your belt), chip-on-their-shoulder flight attendants with steely gazes dispensing only peanuts and pretzels; and flights canceled at the last minute due to "operational reasons" (i.e., the plane wasn't full enough to make the flight profitable)? But for now, domestic carriers continue to enjoy a quasi monopoly. And the attitude displayed by most airline personnel continues to be, "We employees were having a perfectly good day until you darned passengers showed up!" An appropriate slogan for several of them: "*We're* not happy till *you're* not happy!"

Lest anyone think that I get mad only at surly and inadequate American service providers, let me reassure the reader that I am an equal-opportunity complainer when it comes to nationalities.

A trivial but repetitive annoyance, for instance, is the abysmal quality of dry martinis in places outside the United States, particularly in Europe. The dry martini is a uniquely American cocktail, and its translation into other cultures, especially in expensive and traditional establishments not daily frequented by Americans, is complicated by three factors.

First, "Martini" is the name of a popular Italian vermouth, so the first (and not illogical) assumption is that you're asking for the "dry" (i.e., unsweetened) version of that. Second, Martini, Cinzano and Noilly-Prat send an entirely different, colorless, and much less aromatic version of their product to the United States, so if a European bartender goes heavy on the vermouth, it renders the martini pungently undrinkable. Third, the greater the tradition for culinary excellence of the European restaurant, the less they are usually willing to listen to the customer (me!) explain what I want. In this case, "The customer isn't right," not because (as in Law 1) the provider has a more enlightened idea, but because listening and learning and adapting means the restaurant has to face the fact that they aren't perfect.

I've tried using a cross-sectional diagram of a typical booze glass, showing ice cubes, olives on spear, $\frac{1}{10}$ maximum dry vermouth, and $\frac{9}{10}$ gin. This leads to such comments as, "Our bartender is highly experienced and doesn't need your picture" (followed by delivery of a glass of dry vermouth with a lonely ice cube swimming in it). I've had some of the strangest quasi martinis and some of the biggest arguments in my home country of Switzerland. In one case, at a quaint, expensive restaurant in eastern Switzerland, the manager proudly brought me a fluted glass containing what appeared to be pink champagne without bubbles. I said I had asked for a dry martini. She said, "That is one.

Our bartender is very proud of them." "So why is it pink?" I said. "Because of the angostura bitters, of course!"

Me: But dry martinis don't have angostura bitters.

She: Yes, they do, sir. Our bartender has won international prizes. That's the way they're made. It's an old English tradition.

Me: Could I have one without the bitters, and with more ice?

She: Not if you ask for a dry martini, and you'll have to pay for this one.

Me: Look, madam, I came here to enjoy myself. Could I please just have the drink I asked for?

She: You already have it. And if you're going to be difficult, I'm afraid I'll have to ask you to dine elsewhere.

Did I leave? No, it would have complicated my evening too much. Did I ever go back, and did I fail to tell the story to at least a hundred friends and potential customers over the years? No!

Bad restaurants are another blight on our collective quality of life. By *bad* I most certainly don't mean *inexpensive,* for the expectation level of the customer is very directly linked to the price paid: There's such a thing as a delightful experience in an old diner or in a cement-block building next to a rural gas station bearing the word EATS. If the service is friendly, the food hot and, despite its simplicity, *good,* then the customer's expectations are met or exceeded: He's happy. At the other end of the spectrum, one finds the pretentious upscale place with a fancy name, valet parking, pseudochateau decor, a mistake-riddled French menu the size of a cafeteria tray, and a pimply-faced waitstaff in ill-fitting tuxedos behaving as if you, the customer, should be glad you were even allowed in the door. The $11 soup and $17 *salade à la manière du chef* are lousy. Expectations *not* met!

At such places, I often see patrons grumbling. Yet when the manager (slightly older tuxedo-clad person) comes around and asks, "So, how was everything?" they only mumble, "Great, thanks, ver-r-ry good." Why did they accept so bad a product? Why didn't they complain?

Another story: There's a luxurious restaurant and hotel on a lake near Zurich, Switzerland. After the first three hopelessly flawed "dry martinis on the rocks," I whipped out my pen and drew the usual cross-sectional diagram on a cocktail napkin. At that, the urbane-looking restaurant manager who had failed to listen to the first three attempts, completely lost his cool, told me I could keep my insulting sketch, and if I didn't clean up my attitude immediately, I could leave their establishment.

Interestingly, when you take these complaints to a "higher level," i.e., the general manager or owner, the reaction (at least before the 1995 recession hit Switzerland) was "Yes, we're sorry about that, etc., but our establishment is so sought-after, and qualified personnel so hard to get, that, well, we'd rather lose a guest or two than a head-waiter." And this is where it ties in to the U.S. airlines again: too many customers, too sought-after a product, too little real competition.

Now I know some readers will say, "Your 'bad service' stories re-mind me of a trip to *car dealerships,* Chrysler's included." Well, yes, we know that when Chrysler's products suddenly turned red hot, as when the Dodge dealers got the all-new 1994 Ram pickup, some dealers who had spent decades scouring, pleading, and begging for customers were so overwhelmed by the sudden onslaught of drooling customers that, well, they "couldn't handle the psychological transition." After all the scorn, pity, and derisive remarks, they were now in the driver's seat, and by George, they were going to make these *customers* grovel and beg! And while it was a tiny minority of our dealers who behaved this way, it was enough to further reinforce the public's already poor image of car dealers in general.

Car dealers, however, are far from unique in this regard. In fact, the vast majority of automobile dealers today, including Chrysler's, are more reputable and service-oriented than a lot of other businesses out there that aren't saddled with the same kind of negative reputa-tion—even though maybe they should be.

By the same token, though, no business or other organization is going to improve if left totally to its own devices.

It just seems that some businesses and individuals, after years of successfully dealing with adversity, really botch it up when hard-earned prosperity finally arrives!

Sheeplike, we all assumed that complaining about the "service" provided by the U.S. Internal Revenue Service would only bring down on us the wrath of the IRS's famously underqualified personnel. But look what happened: Enough brave souls *did* complain that the problems are finally being addressed! If no patrons protest the bad food at the *Auberge du Reepoff,* it's never going to get better. Nor will the airline fix a broken seat-back or put the missing hinge pin on the tray table if you don't tell them about it.

Every time I check out of a hotel, some assistant manager says, "I trust your stay with us was satisfactory, Mr. Lutz," and I usually hand him or her a list: Phone in the sitting room doesn't work, TV remote has a low battery, lightbulb in the shaving mirror is burned out, and one of the sinks won't drain properly. If the person reacts with ill-concealed irritation or disinterest, you know the place will go downhill—don't bother booking there unless you have to. But if the establishment is genuinely grateful for the information and thanks you for taking the time and effort, you know it is on the path of continuous improvement.

Service industries are an important part of any nation's economic competitiveness. They're also a major factor in our quality of life, which, after all, is the fruit of our competitive striving. If we want services to get better, though, we're all going to have to be a little less tolerant, a little more courageous, a bit more insistent on accountability—in short, more anal!

A Little Fear, in Reality, Ain't All That Bad

NOW, I KNOW WHAT YOU'RE THINKING: HE'S FINALLY GONE TOTALLY around the bend—sort of like the Gordon Gecko character in the film *Wall Street* with his "Greed is good" speech. Well, before I'm accused of that, let me say emphatically that I think fear caused by a manager's capricious, personal whims or self-serving delusions of grandeur has no place at all in today's business world (or for that matter anywhere else!).

I do believe, however, that there's a useful place in all our lives for *legitimate* fear—the fear, for example, of letting down one's team, of bringing embarassment on oneself or one's family, and the very rational fear of what the competition will do to you if you let your guard down even for a minute. *That* kind of fear should never, ever be ignored or sublimated, because if it is, you can bet that an even bigger fear will soon arise to take its place: fear of survival!

Fear keeps an organization awake, on its toes, a little nervous—all of which protects it from falling prey to FDH (the dreaded fat-dumb-and-happy syndrome). I once heard Larry Bossidy, CEO of AlliedSignal, say something that hits this nail exactly on its head: "Tension and conflict," he said, "are necessary ingredients of a healthy company." Not only necessary, but inescapable. It's neither practical nor desirable for a leader to try to purge worry from an organization. Rather, he or she should learn to worry selectively, distinguishing mere bugaboos from serious threats.

FIVE BUSINESS FEARS WORTH HAVING . . .

What follows is my own, highly selective list of things worth worrying about. Worry about these during the workday, and you'll have reason to sleep better at night.

1. Forgetting Who the Boss Is

Authors, consultants, facilitators, and licensed management gurus have been spreading much treacly stuff about "stakeholders" in recent years, all of it informed by the view of shareholders as a sort of greedy lot who don't do any work but get all the profits.

How can you motivate your customers, your workforce, your suppliers, your employees, and your community (goes the stakeholder argument) if all you talk about is *owners* and their rights? Aren't employees our most precious asset? Aren't we supposed to love our customers, respectfully reward our suppliers, and be good, contributing citizens to the communities our businesses call home? Does it not, then, make sense to postulate a more inclusive model of corporate ownership—one called, say, "Stakeholder Symbiosis"—that treats these interdependent constituencies as *equals?* Rewards, after all, need to be fairly divided. Shareholders should respect the fact that they owe these other constituencies plenty.

This, I submit, is utter nonsense. The shareholder votes with his or her pocketbook, easily selling shares at a moment's notice and thus abandoning the whole symbiotic chain of stakeholders the minute the company's financial performance stumbles. He or she owes nothing to anybody!

Proponents of the stakeholder model can (and do) say, "But you can't think *just* of shareholders! You have to satisfy customers, suppliers, employees, and communities or you won't long be able to generate the returns shareholders demand!" This argument is, of course, true, but it's also simplistic and irrelevant. It doesn't change the fact that there is only *one* entity that put up the money needed to make the corporation possible and only *one* entity that "owns the joint." And that's the shareholder.

Balancing the legitimate needs of other constituencies is the job of a management hired by shareholders. It is management's responsibility to make the customers happy, to make them feel they have received value for their money, to make them come back again and again. It is management's job to ensure that employees are capable, permanently, of doing their jobs with optimum efficiency. That precludes both brutal short-term exploitation of employees (which results only in high and costly turnover) as well as excessive coddling designed to make employees feel like "a happy family" (which, if taken too far, only invites waste, inefficiency, an unjustified feeling of entitlement, and a loss of urgency).

What holds true for employees applies just as well to other constituencies: Suppliers cannot be treated as untrustworthy arm's-length adversaries; but neither can the ideals of partnership, trust, and valued long-term relationships be invoked to excuse anything short of flawless performance. As for communities and good corporate citizenship, I'll quote Jürgen Schrempp, the man who turned Daimler-Benz around (and certainly a man who has great respect for the "social responsibilities" of companies), who has said, "Only a *profitable* company can be of service to the community."

The fate of companies that fail to uphold shareholders as their supreme master can be grim: Subpar earnings reduce the value of the stock, which reduces the market capitalization of the company, which can result in a takeover by a stronger or much more focused company that may well wreak havoc on sheltered, pampered employees (or other protectees). As controversial corporate "emergency-room surgeon" Albert J. ("Chainsaw Al") Dunlap himself notes, "The Al Dunlaps of the world would not be hired if top corporate people did their jobs."

2. Being Too Cautious

You can't be blamed for a mistake you didn't make, right? But if, as a leader, you actually "do things" rather than merely perpetuate the status quo, there is a high probability, bordering on certainty, that you will make mistakes. In sports, this fact is accepted. No basketball coach expects his finest star to stuff them all in. In baseball, players who fail 70 percent of the time go to the Hall of Fame! But in business—especially in big business—apportioning blame has become a daily ritual: Who authorized this? Who signed? Whatever made you think *this* would work?

Scorn and criticism are heaped upon those hapless doers who, by the time they are in their late thirties, have learned the hard way that you don't want to volunteer. Only the thick-skinned few soldier on to discover a far greater truth: It is, in fact, better to have to beg forgiveness than to constantly ask permission!

Fear of failure (or more accurately, fear of the career-killing criticism that so often follows failure) is the main reason we find it so difficult to energize people in large organizations. Not only do we punish employees who take initiative, we tend to reward nondoers who perform their assigned tasks the way the company wants them performed (not necessarily the way they *ought* to be performed).

We reward those who look good, appear active, are politically astute, and who excel at writing apparently thoughtful memos (which, if they were ever subjected to hard examination, could be shown to be merely pandering restatements of what senior management wants to hear). Finally and most especially, we reward those who have studiously avoided ever having committed a mistake.

I knew one such individual at one of my former employers. He had risen to corporate vice president based on a skill set like the one just described. On controversial issues, where senior management was going to have to choose between two dramatic alternatives (A or B), he would, prior to the crucial meeting, prepare *two* sets of position papers, one arguing for A, the other for B. After skillfully probing to find out where his bosses' inclinations lay, he would pick up the "correct" pile and make his distribution, saying something like, "Gentlemen, when we took a look at it, the recommendation really became quite clear. I think you'll concur with our conclusions." Who needs people like this, and why pay them high salaries? (Perhaps there's justice after all, though: This particular individual later went on to failure in important positions at a series of ever smaller companies, where his fear of doing things became impossible to hide and where spineless and pontifical memos, however well written, were not seen as contributing to shareholder value!)

Caution isn't all bad. It's just bad when it's excessive, or when the solution to a problem demands aggressive action (as today, with the pace of change accelerating, it's apt to). In these demanding times, I marvel to see how many CEOs are cautious, carefully spoken, and stoically statesmanlike. Boat rockers? Not they. *How,* I ask myself, *can this be, when such dynamic change is needed?* Or, to put the same rhetorical question more informally: What *is* it with CEOs? How can people so powerful and so successful be so timid, so reticent, so given to "on the one hand . . . but on the other" waffling? For all too many, it isn't just that they have no fire in the belly—their pilot light seems to be off!

The reason, I think, is pretty logical: Corporate boards, especially in public companies, have a duty to protect the shareholder. When it comes time for them to pick the replacement for the retiring CEO (and you can assume the business has been going well or his departure would be something other than a "retirement"), they consider the various candidates, and their conversation goes something like this:

> Board member A says, "What about Johnson! What a dynamo! He's bright, he's fast, and he's turned around every bad division we've ever handed him. He's had some great product ideas, and the people in his business group would die for him!"
>
> At this point, the human resources director and the old CEO assume a troubled expression. "Yes, Johnson gets the job done, no doubt about it, but, well . . . he sometimes makes mistakes, bad ones . . . and he kind of pushes his peers around. He's constantly suggesting how they could improve their operations, and they don't feel it's any of his business. In fact, I'm worried that if we went with Johnson, some of our fine, long-service folks might quit. He's great, but he's, well . . . *disruptive!"*

At this point, the board sagely engages in much head nodding and chin rubbing, which precedes its next question: "Okay, who else do we have?"

The "who else" inevitably turns out to be a reasonably talented, thoughtful, always mature individual who "looks the part," will play well in Washington, will win easy acceptance from "the other guys" (no wonder, he never pushed them!) and who, at this watershed in his career, can look back on a decent-but-unspectacular performance marked by a complete absence of mistakes. In stable times, this steady-as-she-goes candidate may seem the wisest choice: The company's formula is working. The board asks itself, "Why take a chance when we have a commanding position in the market? Why go with Mr. Disruptive when Mr. Status Quo is so much more . . . congenial?" Some version of this interior monologue, I expect, was played out in the boardrooms of Eastman Kodak, IBM, Kmart, and many other of America's great blue-chip institutions. (Chrysler, to its credit, did not fall prey to this same mistake: In Bob Eaton, our board chose a change agent of the highest order!)

Then one day, when the formula suddenly stops working because the world has changed with a vengeance, these nondisruptive, change-averse CEOs appear stunned, incapable of taking effective action. And there you have the intrinsic weakness of the all-too-typical CEO: He's unprepared for change. He's loyal to a fault; he knows everything about his own company but little about others; he believes deeply (but too often uncritically) in what his own company is doing and how it's doing it. How, though, could he be expected to believe otherwise? His predecessor and mentor put the universe in place; now he (the successor) nurtures and maintains it. Did the old boss disapprove of outsourcing? Then you can be sure the successor will as well: "We've always made our own widgets here; that way, we can be sure of quality control. It was the Great Founder's way; it's our way! It's what makes us different!" All well and good. But watch out for the day some new competitor arrives whose CEO had different and better ideas on cost control and quality assurance!

What becomes of those "disruptive" number twos who didn't get the CEO's job? Most find themselves actively recruited by headhunters, who then place them with some company in deep, deep trouble whose board has decided that the risk of hiring an outsider with a reputation for change is a lower risk than the risk of slipping steadily beneath the waves with "Steady Eddie" at the helm.

What's most depressing here is that though more and more boards now seem willing to consider hiring a pro-change outsider, most still don't acquire an appreciation for this style of leadership until the wolf is at the door. How much better if they had questioned their love affair with caution earlier (and perhaps better encouraged some of the more dynamic types in the company's own ranks in the bargain!).

3. Being Slow

The story of competition won't, in the future, be about the strong eating the weak; it will be about the swift eating the slow! And yet much of business continues to act as if there were no urgency (a strange fact given the modern world's emphasis on shortened product cycles and reduced inventory turns, but a true one, nonetheless).

A company's (or even a department's) slowness almost always is proof that it lacks talent at its top: an able leader whose vision of the future impels him to make progress quickly and to urge subordinates ahead in that same direction. A good leader feels impatience. He or she wants to meet objectives quickly, so the organization can move on to its next goal.

Absent such a leader, however, management does nothing more than what its name suggests: it "manages"; it administers and carefully maintains the status quo. It doesn't lead; it doesn't drive change. Progress made by "management" means progress at a glacial pace: No one wants to stick his neck out; no one wants to be tagged for a mistake; no one wants to do anything unfair or unpopular (a situation made worse by the recent vogue of 360-degree performance evaluations); and no one, God forbid, wants to be responsible for making a decision without first getting everybody on board.

Thus is born the plodding and ultimately self-defeating "management by consensus" that is almost always guaranteed to offer up the lowest-common-denominator, most predictable, most tried-and-true products and strategies. Worse, it's the form of management guaranteed to waste the most time and to most delay a program's progress. A consensus-driven leadership, faced with having to make (oh, no!) a decision, invariably sidesteps it by suggesting some such procrastinating alternative as, "Let's study it some more," "Let's run some more focus groups," or "Let s all go away, work on this some more, and then get together again next month sometime."

Don't get me wrong. Good leadership isn't shoot-from-the-hip recklessness. Sometimes it's appropriate to send the team away for another look. But a leader with a proper sense of urgency is more apt to say, "I'm disappointed that we don't have a solid recommendation today. I was hoping we could make this decision and move on. Why don't you take three more days and get back to me by Thursday, at which time *I'll* decide if you guys can't?" This approach, of course, requires courage. And subordinates may grumble that it's arbitrary. Papers and analyses will have to be moved ahead. Comforting nose-counting research will have to be abandoned. Tension results, and the leader perhaps gets a reputation for being too "demanding."

For this very reason, people who subscribe to the ideal of team-work and to the moral equivalency of all viewpoints (logical or not) always find it easier to allow more time to pass. Time heals disagreements; and it also, frankly, makes some problems fade away entirely. But as a rule, management's failure to hew to a tight timetable (which implies a pressure to perform, to make tough decisions, to *act*) will seriously degrade a company's performance. Worse, it will drive away its best employees—the future leaders and change agents.

4. Mistaking the "Nice" for the Essential

Most businesses are pretty simple. They incur cost in the form of capital, materials, and labor in order to provide a product or service that, if of competitive price and quality, will attract customers and thus produce revenue in excess of costs.

It would seem, then, that management would make every effort to be lean, to cut out unnecessary steps, to focus on the core business. But it often isn't so. The bigger a corporation grows, the more apt it is to behave like some federal bureaucracy, peopled by hundreds of staffers who churn out endless streams of memoranda simply to justify their existence. I know of one large corporation that had a department called Outside-Speaker Evaluation. Its job was to perform highly quantified analyses of the performances of invited speakers, as measured by audience applause, number of questions asked, and evaluation sheets filled out by attendees. The speaker later would receive a letter giving him a grade, as well as a lot of statistical data showing how his performance compared to that of other speakers.

Needless to say, this company got itself into near-terminal trouble, and I imagine that in the ensuing fight for life, Outside-Speaker Evaluation was unceremoniously dumped. But how had it arisen in the first place? Who ever thought it provided customer or shareholder value? My guess is that it was probably brought about when some senior corporate executive, having just suffered through an especially appalling speech, turned to an underling and remarked, "We've got to find a way to stop inviting blowhards. They waste our time." And so, starting with the best of intentions, even more time and money were wasted.

The difficulty in separating the nice-to-have-but-nonessential stuff from the genuinely important stuff is that you often find yourself operating in gray areas where proof is lacking. (Opinion, of course, is not.) Does corporate sponsorship of a laudable but elitist cultural event make sense for shareholders, or should we cut the cost? How about sponsorship of a sporting event that has little to do with the product or service we provide?

Chrysler for many years was an active sponsor of big-time horse racing. It was expensive, but "well worth it" (I was told by folks in marketing) in terms of exposure to our target audience. Was it? We cut almost all of it without ill effect. (Not too surprising, when you consider we neither manufactured nor sold horses!)

Automobile racing is an on-again, off-again favorite with car companies worldwide, the age-old Detroit adage being, "Race 'em on Sunday, sell 'em on Monday." That might be true, I suppose, if the Sunday and the Monday cars bore the slightest resemblance to one another. Chrysler's do, to the point that its own adage might be, "We race what we sell." Even so, I've gone from being a huge proponent of racing to being fairly skeptical. But I'm positive that spending tens of millions of dollars (or hundreds of millions, in some cases) to win at sports that have little relevance to the people actually buying your products is a waste of time and money.

Nonessential costs, of course, don't just infest marketing and public relations. They can and do take the form of "quality" customers don't care about: embossed floor mats or painting parts of a car's underside the owner will never have occasion to see unless he's run over. They take the form of needless, redundant, and restrictive financial measurements, of idiotic programs often fomented by an overzealous human resources department (a.k.a. personnel department), of well-intentioned but too-frequent "quality awareness days," of company-produced books, brochures, and videos, not to mention some forms of "employee training."

As a leader, what are you to do? You know this waste is part of the company's system, but how best to attack it? How do you distinguish between what's of real, long-term value and what should simply be axed? Here I have bad news for you: No one has ever figured out a reliable method. It reminds me of the old Madison Avenue maxim, "Half of every advertising dollar is wasted. But nobody can figure out which half."

However, there are a few guideposts a leader can follow: First, remind yourself that the most waste-free companies are generally those in the most trouble and struggling for their survival. When properly led, they dump programs the same way a crippled airplane heaves out cargo to stay aloft. At such moments, management's mind is wonderfully focused on the basics: essential product development, manufacturing, and selling. In these circumstances, it's easy to say no to anything that doesn't immediately reduce cost or enhance revenue. There's no point trying to improve matters in some nebulous "long term" that the company will never live to see unless it survives.

But with prosperity, the soft-side, "long-term-payoff" programs creep back in. Some are legitimate, offer good value, and are clearly needed. For example, after Chrysler had survived its second brush with death, Bob Eaton decided, wisely, that we needed to do some "catch-up" in the area of training—not in "underwater basket-weaving," but in such critical areas as statistical process control (in the engineering and manufacturing areas) and advanced software programs in the sales ordering and vehicle distribution areas. Other programs, however, aren't of real value, but they nonetheless are sold, maintained, and defended by their proponents as if they were. Questioning them results in the leader's being inundated with reams of self-serving justification. You then need to ask yourself, "If this were my very own company, with me personally owning every share of stock, would I be engaging in this activity at this time?" If the answer is no, kill it.

5. Forgetting to Look under the Bed

The threats I've just listed are indeed the big ones—those likeliest to do you in. But it's possible, too, of course, to die slowly from "a million tiny cuts." The following probably should be classed merely as annoyances. They're easily pushed under the bed and ignored. Yet a prudent leader will worry about them *a little,* checking every now and then to make sure they haven't grown into something more substantial.

- *Chasing fads.*   When will the business community's appetite for new management fads—each one engendering its own host of gurus, authors, facilitators, and consultants—ever be satisfied? My prediction is *never.* Every day some new, revolutionary theory of "managing by X" (fill in any term) soars, then peaks, then wanes as if it were a pop song, only to expire and be replaced by an even hotter one. What theory will next top the charts? My own expectation is that management, having tested the limits (and then some) of "empowerment" and "teamwork," will next run way too far to the other side of the boat and begin advocating "management by fear and loathing" (with Hunter S. Thompson as the lead guru!). *When,* I ask, will someone start advocating "management by using your God-given intelligence"?
- *Seeking popularity.*   Management seems to suffer from a collective need to be liked and popular, as opposed to being respected and acknowledged as tough but fair. Sure, being tough but *un*fair is the worst of all possible worlds. On the other hand, woe betides the executive team that pays too much attention to employee attitude surveys saying, "Senior management pushes us too hard" or "Senior management is never satisfied" or "We feel we are not given enough resources to do our job." These gripes (when voiced by a minority of employees) are only normal. If no such complaints arise, it's a sure sign an organization is running with way too much slack. Reducing the pressure to increase performance (or decrease costs) may or may not increase the happiness of your company's "associates." But I guarantee it will reduce the happiness of owners, whose displeasure will quickly be reflected in the stock price.
- *Starting to believe your own clippings.*   It's only natural for a business to want to "look good" in the public's eyes, and, at the same time, it's an almost futile ambition, given the antibusiness and anti-free-market bias of much of the press and the entertainment industry. Still, on those rare occasions when praise does come (say, from business and trade journalists), it often tends to be so flattering and with-

out nuance that the praised company winds up believing it really must be able to work miracles. Resist that belief! You're the same company you were before. Just because some news organization pays you a compliment is no reason to let down your guard or become self-satisfied.

MEANWHILE, OUT IN THE BIG, BAD WORLD . . .

What about threats lurking in the world outside your office? A wise leader will keep a weather eye trained on these as well, especially broad social trends that, unless taken into account, can wreak havoc with your planning. You don't want to awaken one morning to find that your best efforts have been rendered futile, and that (figuratively speaking) you've been cleaning ashtrays on the *Hindenburg.*

Of the many worrisome trends at work in our society, I want to draw your attention to four in particular that concern me, since each, I believe, has broad implications for the future of capitalism itself. The first, which I call "The War against the Car" may seem parochial to my own industry; but I assure you it is not. If the enemies of the automobile gain ground, our collective freedom will be curtailed and the power of government—already excessive, in my opinion—will grow just that much greater.

The second threat is the spread of a "victim mentality" among consumers, manifested most clearly in the public's eagerness to sue businesses for wrongs that plaintiffs themselves have often had a hand in causing. The third is a close relative of the second: the decay of the American character (of which a refusal to take personal responsibility is but one symptom). And fourth, we need to glamorize "making things" (as opposed to merely "making money") once again, starting with glamorizing engineering.

The War against the Car

Was the horse, as a means of individual transportation, under attack in past centuries as the car is now? Were our equine friends vilified for nibbling at shrubbery while parked, pounding moist sod into a brownish morass when running, permitting human access to (and subsequent trampling of) forests and glens? And what of horseback-related injuries when people were kicked or thrown? And what of the menace of horse excrement threatening to swamp our cities?

I've never read examples of the press from those times, but if it was at all similar to today, the horse must have been under heavy attack. (Of course, medieval times were not beset by the advent of safety advocates, "shockumentary" TV, and personal injury lawyers!)

The dislike by certain sectors of our society for the personal automobile has always puzzled me, for rapid, comfortable, individual transportation crisscrossing the surface of nations is something only the automobile makes possible. It not only performs vital transportation functions, but provides excitement, leisure, and a sense of freedom and independence. The automobile feeds both our physical and our emotional needs.

And yet every passing year brings forth some new outcry against cars or the people driving them. Most of these objections, after enjoying a moment of spectacular publicity, wither away. Remember road rage? All right-thinking protectors of the public weal were recently beside themselves with worry over car-induced mayhem. Now, in America, no less an authority than the American Automobile Association (good ol' "Triple-A") questions whether road rage was ever much more than a topic for pundits to bewail on Sunday morning TV shows. Statistically, says AAA, it hardly exists, incidents of it killing only about 50 people a year. That puts it on a par with being hit by lightning or bitten by a poisonous snake.

That didn't stop governments from taking action. In New York State, unmarked vans now patrol the highways searching for outbreaks of it. Drivers thought to be perpetrating it are videotaped. New York and six other states are considering legislation to make it (if it's ever found) a crime.

Why this vilification of the car? It is my personal experience, having lived and worked in various nations, that there tends to be a close correlation between dislike for the automobile and an elitist/collectivist political philosophy. The elitist intellectual left wing has always felt that the world would be a better place if only they and a handful of like-minded cronies were running it. That way, we would have the "fair" and "just" society that we never quite attain but all aspire to. The lesson that a market economy, for all its shortcomings, will come far closer to getting us there than all of the world's failed, discredited, centrally directed economies is forgotten or ignored. This time it'll be different, because *we're* in charge and we know what's good for the people and for society.

One of the keys to changing society toward one that is more "inclusive, fair, just, and environmentally wholesome" (to use language typical of the elitists) is to *get people to stay in one place.*

How can you really punish the wealthy with taxes if the victims of taxation can say, "I've had it!," sell their houses, climb in their cars, and move to a place with lower taxes?

How can you establish unpopular but grandiose inner-city planning schemes when people can simply move to the suburbs if they don't like it? That's the real problem with cars: The mobility provided by them has permitted the free world's pesky citizens to "vote with their feet" (as in *"I'm outta here!"*) and look for (sometimes literally) greener pastures.

I'm not saying that every person who worries about urban congestion or the dangers inherent in personal transportation is a nutty, "over-the-top" left-winger. It's just that in my experience I've never found a right-leaning intellectual who vilified the automobile or worried about people escaping the government's benevolent control.

One anecdote from my days at Ford of Germany really brought this home: It was 1975, Helmut Schmidt of the Social Democratic Party was chancellor and, as is not unusual in such cases, the political spectrum of his cabinet ranged from moderate to pretty far left. A woman of the latter persuasion was, I believe, minister of culture. She approached Ford of Germany and asked if we would be willing to expose our workers to a newly minted operetta (government-funded), which, with song and dance, would uplift workers all over Germany. *Why not?* I thought. And since the ministry of culture was picking up the cost to convert part of one of our plants into a vast theater, it would have been impolite to say no.

As the fateful Friday afternoon approached, we handed leaflets to our workers, advising them of the free musical, and we put ads and coverage into the factory newspaper to make sure word got out. When I went to the makeshift auditorium, I could see the ministry of culture's huge, new, white semitrailer units, emblazoned with the name of the production. This was not a low-budget operation!

The seats in the auditorium were empty to a disconcerting degree, though. There were a half dozen or so senior Ford of Germany executives, as well as the pro-socialist elected union representatives and most of the Ford Cologne Works Council. As CEO of Ford of Germany, I gave a little welcoming speech, followed by one from the minister, followed by the musical, which was a deadly dull affair, heavily political and urging workers to devote their free time to political activism. Afterward, the senior people were invited to a champagne reception in a back room. Here the minister of culture really let me have it.

Why was there no audience? Where were the workers? This was an outrage, an embarrassment, an affront to the government! I tried to calm her down. I explained what all we'd done to ensure an audience, including letting folks off work early. But, seeing as it was Friday afternoon, they had gotten in their cars and driven off, presumably towing their boats to some of the nice lakes in the region. "Can't you control your workforce?" she demanded. We don't try to when they're not at work, I replied. Didn't I understand the sheer materialistic emptiness of rushing off in cars to go to a weekend cabin instead of staying in town and working politically for the betterment of the proletariat's lot? I said this was a choice we left to the individual. At this point, she drew herself up to her full height and, focusing a death-ray stare on me, said, "We observed this program in East Germany and adapted it, and believe me, when the communist CEO said, 'You will remain at work after hours to see a government-produced musical,' they *stayed*!"

My reply was that under Communism they didn't have the cars to drive off in. "Is that the kind of society you want?" I asked her. She then uttered these (to me) totally unforgettable words: "Those of us who are entrusted with the power must do what's right. Many times, people don't realize where their true happiness lies, and it's up to us to *force* them into this happiness if necessary."

And there you have it—the caring, intelligent, elitist person of the left who knows what's best for all of us! Often, the master plan works so much better if we can make that darn automobile go away.

Whether it is the "Our trees are dying" (killer automobiles causing conifers to lose their needles) hysteria of Europe in the early '80s, the current "voodoo science" about the automobile's causing global warming (immobilizing every car and truck on the planet would reduce carbon dioxide output by a whopping 0.4 percent), alleged "killer" sport utility vehicles (again, that nasty customer deciding he or she would rather have a large 4×4 than an environmentally correct microcar), or "demon air bags," the message and its underlying intent is frequently the same: Cars are simply inconvenient to leftists bent on effecting social control. To control, you must first immobilize. Communism failed at it, and so (if lovers of the automobile remain vigilant) will efforts by the environmental extremists to achieve the same goals through a different ideology. Call me paranoid if you wish. But I have a favorite phrase: "Just because you're paranoid doesn't mean they aren't out to get you."

The American Legal System: What? Me Responsible?

In the room where I am writing this, the radio has just broadcast the following bulletin: "The 'Twinkie defense' has been upstaged!"

In case you're not familiar with the phrase, it first came into use some 20 years ago when defense lawyers for Dan White, a San Francisco man accused of murdering San Francisco Mayor George Moscone and Supervisor Harvey Milk, sought to explain (read *excuse*) the crime by claiming it had been brought on by an upsurge in his blood sugar, triggered by his having eaten (among other things) Twinkies.

Now the radio was telling me the Twinkie defense had been topped by the "tick defense." A New York State man, accused of having shot his neighbor to death, is seeking to mitigate his responsibility by claiming (or his lawyers are claiming) that he acted in a Lyme disease–induced rage. *Don't blame me, blame the tick who bit me.*

Where is this trend leading? To a "bad-hair-day defense"?

As recently as 40 years ago—less time than it takes most Yuppies to reach a midlife crisis—the United States had a different attitude toward personal responsibility: If you shot yourself in the foot, your first thought was likely to be "Ouch," not "Those shoe bastards . . . if only they'd put steel plating in my loafers, this never would have happened. I'm going to sue them for every cent they're worth."

Today no child who rides his trike down a flight of stairs and sustains a cut knee can emerge from this traumatic experience without winning at least a million-dollar settlement for mom and dad: Mom suffered "mental anguish" seeing her child go bouncing down the stairs, and dad was denied an anguished mom's "marital consort."

Nothing any longer is an individual's own fault. (Not even, by the way, what one does to relieve oneself. A few years ago, the Illinois Supreme Court reinstated a $1.5 million verdict against the Chicago Transit Authority in a wrongful-death lawsuit brought by the family of a man who, while inebriated, electrocuted himself by urinating on the electrified "third rail" of the Chicago El. Poor guy. Obviously a victim of a "bad bladder day.")

Americans' eager hunt for scapegoats isn't the result of some mysterious change in their genetic programming. In large part, I think, it's a rational response to the advent of a new "industry"—one that both frightens consumers with news of immediate (or pending) harm and, at the same time, reassures them that generous cash rewards await anyone affected. The mainspring driving it is our legal system's contingent-fee system, which offers plaintiffs a convenient sue-now-pay-if-you-win plan: attorneys charge no up-front legal fee, taking instead 30 or 40 percent, say, of any recovery.

This literally operates as an industry, with three distinct phases of product manufacture: First comes target acquisition, in which safety advocates or environmental watchdogs (their motivations dubious) insinuate that some product or service deserves a hard look. In the next phase, awareness-heightening, sensationalist TV shows (such as *20/20, Dateline NBC, Eye on America,* or my own personal nonfavorite from the poor side of TV Town, *Hard Copy*) provide a highly selective "investigation," in the process spreading the insinuations to a mass audience. Finally, trial lawyers, having smelled blood, pounce on the beleaguered product or service, soliciting consumers who've been "wronged" by it. TV producers and tort lawyers actually enjoy a symbiotic relationship, since lawsuits provide grist for TV's news mill, and the news provides grist for lawsuits.

It all amounts to full employment, not just for lawyers, but for "expert witnesses"—usually people fired by their past employer for incompetence, dishonesty, or mental instability—who crop up like kudzu around the country in the wake of trial attorneys, attacking that same employer in exchange for fat fees.

The rest of the world thinks we're crazy! They marvel at the American public's increasing unwillingness to accept personal responsibility for its actions. They chortle over manufacturers' desperate attempts at self-protection: champagne corks that bear a small slip of paper reading, "Danger! Popping cork can cause severe eye injury! When opening, do not point bottle at self or others!"; air conditioners with the warning, "Please do not drop out of window"; or this, from a child's sled: "Warning: This product does not have brakes!" One more? This, from a child's Batman cape: "Warning: This does not enable the user to fly." (The chortling may be short-lived. Trial lawyers, even now, are trying—you guessed it!—to export the American contingent-fee system, promising their legal brethren in other countries vast riches if they can introduce enabling legislation.)

Ridicule, however, we could endure. Far worse is the extra economic cost we're forced to bear. Manufacturers pass on to consumers the bill for increased liability insurance—$100 added to the cost of a $200 football helmet, for example, or $20 to the cost of a $100 stepladder. In Washington, D.C., the sainted Girl Scouts, for heaven's sake, have to sell an extra 87,000 boxes of cookies every year just to pay their $120,000 liability insurance.

In many industries, the rising cost of liability insurance has proved especially onerous. It did, for example, almost totally wipe out the once-flourishing U.S. general aviation industry (which is recovering today due only to special protective legislation). Its role in driving up health care costs has been well publicized: Premiums for malpractice insurance have forced more and more doctors out of private practice, as has the legal need to have witnesses present during even the most routine medical consultations. Add to that the cost of painful, needless, and redundant lab tests in order to avoid any later recriminations in a court of law ("Tell me, doctor, would it not have been reasonable and prudent to have ordered such-and-such a test? And why did you fail to do so?"). But worst of all is the cost of stifled innovation of medical or surgical advances withheld for fear of suits; product improvements withheld because an improvement damns the prior product in the eyes of a trial lawyer: By implication, the old, unimproved product was somehow (pick one) dangerous, harmful, poisonous, or given to cause anything from heart attacks to itching.

Finally on May 20, 1996, the tide seemed to turn in favor of common sense. That was the day the U.S. Supreme Court, for the first time ever, struck down a punitive damage award as excessive.

That case centered on a Birmingham, Alabama, oncologist who in 1990 bought a $41,000 BMW 535i that had been repainted by the manufacturer prior to delivery due to some acid rain damage the car had sustained back in Germany. There was not, at the time of the purchase, any law on the books in Alabama saying that companies such as BMW *had* to disclose this type of relatively modest, in-factory repair, and BMW's own policy was not to tell customers about repairs worth 3 percent or less of a car's retail value. The paint refinishing in this particular case was valued at $601. An Alabama state court jury, however, not only awarded the oncologist $4,000 in compensatory damages (to compensate him for the supposed decrease in the car's value), it in addition awarded *$4 million* in punitive damages to punish BMW.

This incredible award became, understandably, a cause célèbre in the business community—not just in Alabama but nationwide— neatly underscoring two of our legal system's more amazing (and in my view, destructive) features: the lack of any consistent standard governing damage awards and juries' unbridled power to award damages of *any* dollar amount from zero to infinity.

When the U.S. Supreme Court eventually overturned the BMW decision, there was, for the first time, real hope that common sense might be returning to U.S. courtrooms. In fact, the general counsel of the U.S. Chamber of Commerce, quoted in the *Wall Street Journal,* went so far as to say, "This is the victory business has been waiting for," calling the decision "a nail in the coffin of excessive punitive damages awards."

That nail didn't hold very well!

Just a year later, we at Chrysler had our own cause célèbre: A jury in Charleston, South Carolina, ordered us to pay *$262.5 million* to the parents of a six-year-old boy, Sergio Jimenez, who died when the 1985-model Dodge Caravan he was riding in collided with another vehicle and rolled over, ejecting him. It was the largest product liability judgment ever against an automaker—$12.5 million in compensatory damages and $250 million in punitive damages. And it epitomizes, I think, several of the flaws in the American tort system most dangerous to business.

The death of young Sergio Jimenez was a tragedy—as would be the death of any youngster. This tragedy, however, was turned into a legal farce. The plaintiff's lawyers, who stand to reap nearly $100 million for themselves from the case, managed to persuade the jury that Sergio had been ejected through the van's liftgate, which, they maintained, had been thrown open as a result of a design flaw in its latching mechanism. Chrysler, they contended, had knowingly and wantonly ignored this flaw.

Was this what truly happened? As for how Sergio had been ejected, eyewitnesses gave conflicting accounts: Some said he had gone out the liftgate; others said he had been ejected through a smashed side window. Strong scientific evidence supported the latter possibility. And no matter how he may have left the vehicle, government-compiled statistics on fatal vehicle ejections showed Chrysler minivans to be safer than cars in this regard and twice as safe as other minivans.

The plaintiff's lawyers made much of the fact that Chrysler had modified the design of its latching mechanism in 1988 by adding a flanged head to the tailgate striker. This, they felt, was the ultimate "smoking gun"—irrefutable proof that our minivans had contained a design flaw.

We had indeed modified the liftgate. But so what? We make changes in the design of our vehicles constantly. Chrysler added air bags to all our cars in the mid-'80s; does that mean that its cars built before were *defective*? Of course not.

Far more interesting to me than any of the facts introduced in the case were the ones *not* introduced (or dismissed as unimportant): First, Sergio's mother, by running a red light, had precipitated the fatal accident. She was thus suing for "grief and suffering" she herself had helped cause. Second, Sergio's father had at one point filed a wrongful death suit against her for the loss of their son's life. And third, Sergio had not been wearing his seatbelt. Had he been wearing it, there's every reason to believe he'd be alive today.

Chrysler has appealed the court's decision. Meanwhile, what can we—or any potential defendant—do to rein in the excesses of the U.S. legal system? Make no mistake: Contingent-fee lawsuits and sky's-the-limit punitive damage awards are cancers eating at society, dangers to commerce, killers of intelligent risk taking and innovation, and disincentives to improvement. You, as an American—whether publisher, doctor, dentist, or manufacturer—owe it to yourself and to your country to go on record in favor of meaningful reform. Support politicians who favor setting reasonable limits on the size of punitive damage awards, capping rewards for noneconomic losses (e.g., "loss of consortium"), reducing the percentage of awards that contingent-fee lawyers can collect, and forcing losing parties to pay litigation costs.

Even if won, however, such remedies would address only the legal aspect of a problem that in actuality goes far beyond the courtroom. Is it not, at base, a problem rooted somewhere in our national character?

Author Charles Sykes, in his 1992 book, *A Nation of Victims: The Decay of the American Character,* postulates that our "everybody-is-a-victim" mentality stems in part from Americans' unwillingness to acknowledge the limitations and disappointments inherent in the human condition—our tendency to see "the immemorial questions of human life as *problems* that required *solutions.*" As a result, he suggests, modern Americans have enshrined "the infinite expectation for psychological gratification, self-actualization, self-realization, and happiness not as a goal to be won but as an entitlement."

I think Sykes may be on to something. And I think his insight is being played out not just in our court system (where, more and more, personal responsibility is seen as a quaint relic of the past) but in our culture at large—including in our schools and in our families.

Me! Me! Me!

No matter where I look, I see ever more Americans uttering what has become practically a new national cry: "Me! Me! Me!" Have we ever before, as a people, been so self-absorbed and inward-looking? So divided into interest groups and exclusionary ethnic enclaves? So unapologetically selfish?

I don't think so. When I was growing up, leaders and teachers inculcated in young people what were known as the martial virtues:

love of country, self-sacrifice, courage, dignity, honor, self-discipline. These virtues were upheld not just in the military but in civilian life. The cry of the land wasn't so much "Me!" as "Us!"

Long before many of the consequences of "me-ism" had become as familiar as they are today (rampant drug use, fatherless families, worsening racial tensions, and the gutless nihilism of a TV show like *Beavis and Butt-head*), I personally witnessed (from a ringside seat) the beginning of our slide into this abyss.

It was the early 1960s, and Berkeley was playing host to the famous Free Speech Movement. The sons and the daughters of a generation that had fought to rid the world of *real* oppression (in the form of Hitler, Tojo, and Mussolini) were crusading against what they, with their limited worldview, regarded as oppression. Everyone, it seemed, was marching for free speech, free love, free housing, free health care, free everything! And, of course, it wasn't long before the entire country caught Berkeley's fever, and what had been, until then, a counterculture eventually became America's *dominant* culture.

Ol' R.A. Lutz—ever the disruptive, even then—stood out in this sea of permissiveness like a pork chop on a kosher menu. I was older than most undergraduates, sported a crew cut and well-shined shoes, and carried myself with military bearing. Since I often wrote letters to the school newspaper, *The Daily Californian,* I sort of became the resident "right-wing" speaker at debates and discussions. The free-speech types didn't want to appear exclusionary, so they put this obviously wacko, lunatic fringe conservative (me) on their panels, just to even things out. The funny thing was, I was very much a *moderate!* I only looked conservative compared to those whom I debated.

What began at Berkeley in the '60s as a well-intentioned, if misguided, social experiment has, in my opinion, proved itself all but bankrupt by the 1990s. In our naive attempt to create a society that is totally free, we have ignored aspects of the national character that ultimately make freedom possible, including self-discipline and the capacity to sacrifice (if only temporarily) one's own selfish interests for the good of a greater community, whether city, state, or nation.

Luckily, there is a stronghold where many of these necessary attributes are still alive and well: the U.S. military—and my own favorite branch of it in particular, the U.S. Marine Corps.

The chairman of one of Chrysler's largest advertising agencies, Leo Kelmenson of Bozell Worldwide in New York, is a fellow former Marine. And not too long ago, he brought to my attention an article from the *Wall Street Journal* that I think sums up this country's present situation (vis-à-vis its military) quite well. The article was entitled, "Separation Anxiety: 'New' Marines Illustrate Growing Gap Between Military and Society."

The piece pointed out that the Marine Corps, like the rest of the military, hit what probably was its all-time low point in the 1970s, following the Vietnam War. As the article put it, "Riven by military defeat, racial tension, drug abuse and widespread insubordination, the Marines came close to being a broken family."

But a truly remarkable thing happened: Unlike American society at large, the Marines (and the rest of the military) rebounded. While civilian society slipped further and further into the muck of laziness and selfishness, the men and women of the military found the courage to confront their problems, both personal and institutional (including race and drug problems) in remarkably effective ways. The Corps did it, not by pandering to the baser instincts of humankind (such as greed and self-interest), but by appealing to what poets call our "better angels"—things like pride and patriotism, plus a good healthy dose of what (for lack of a better term) we might call "family values."

As a result, the Marines are now what conservative columnist George Will calls "hard people in a soft age." He further calls them "today's counterculture," which, frankly, can be either a good thing or a bad.

It's a bad thing if society at large doesn't come to its senses soon and begin to emulate the military by restoring discipline and personal responsibility to everyday life. If that doesn't happen, then I'm afraid that the military will remain a counterculture and that, as a result, it will find itself more and more at odds with the society it's supposed to be protecting. Not good!

On the other hand, though, I'm an optimist. I believe in the power of good ideas overcoming bad. Just look at what we went through at Chrysler: You might say we got into trouble the second time because we'd strayed too far from our basic values: We'd diversified into financial services and corporate jet manufacture. We'd lost our discipline for cost control. And, worst of all, we'd sort of put our product development on autopilot, which resulted, as you know, in a string of bland, look-alike cars and trucks.

But Chrysler, like the Marines, rebounded. And like them, we did it by appealing to our own better angels—which in our case meant teamwork and employee empowerment, tempered (in true Marine style) by a strong dose of good, hard, clear-eyed discipline.

In our new, teamwork-oriented culture, our teams were given almost total autonomy in determining the "how" of a project. And, believe me, they appreciated the freedom they get from that substantial grant of power. They also recognized, however, that it's up to them to exercise the self-discipline necessary to get the job done, and that it's still top management's prerogative to set the "what" of a project (team goals and objectives). All of which means that at Chrylser teamwork and empowerment aren't in any danger of degenerating into anarchy!

Chrysler now has what many people consider to be the fastest-moving, most efficient, and most successful product development organization in the auto industry. And one big reason for all that, I'm convinced, is that as a company Chrysler has strived to achieve the same unique mixture of personal empowerment and group discipline so well exemplified by the U.S. Marine Corps.

I'd be delighted to see the Marines' "counterculture" become, as it once was, the *dominant* culture in society at large. One way to do that is for companies to do what we did and deliberately emulate the Marine model. Another way, of course, is for us to encourage our young people to relearn self-discipline. That needn't mean, in every case, that a young man or woman should take the step of enlisting in the Marines (or some other branch of the service). But it's not a bad idea!

One of my daughters served in the Corps, to her considerable benefit. A former Marine captain (like me!), she's now an executive with Korn/Ferry International in Geneva. My stepson Elliott is benefiting, too. After borrowing perhaps the wrong leaf from the Lutz book (the one covering my misspent teenage years), Elliott found himself living up to something less than his full potential. My sympathy for his predicament was, as you can imagine, strong, since I had had my own problems at his age. Elliott's mother and I decided to enroll him in the Marine Military Academy in Harlingen, Texas.

What the Marine Corps did for me, the Marine Military Academy has done for Elliott: His grades became good. He was on the drill team. And, for perhaps the first time in his life, he discovered the true joys of self-confidence and self-respect—enough so that, on graduation from MMA, he was qualified to enter Michigan's very fine Hillsdale College.

If we could just give *all* of America—especially America's youth—a taste of that same pride, discipline, and self-respect, then this country, in my opinion, would be a better place.

Am I suggesting we revive the draft?

I've always believed that America started coming unglued morally and attitudinally with the demise of the draft, which had served as a powerful instrument for social integration.

The military threw together rich and poor, smart and dumb, black and white, and made them think as a team. I was, and still am, amazed at what the Marine Corps did for me and 80 other raw recruits at boot camp on Parris Island. Race discrimination? Not tolerated! Your buddy—whatever his background or ethnicity—was a Marine, period! Color was irrelevant: Anybody able to make it through on the basis of ability, courage, intelligence, and integrity earned—and got—respect. Living in close proximity with people of all kinds built a cohesive bond between us.

This same benefit accrues to other countries that have a draft. Switzerland, though smaller geographically than New York State, has two religious factions (Catholics and Calvinist-Protestants), a German-speaking northeast, a French-speaking southwest, and a third region that speaks Italian. As if that weren't diversity enough, there's the ancient Romansh culture of the mountains, which bears no resemblance to the other three. Yet these culturally and linguistically disparate groups mesh easily, making Switzerland one of the most effective democracies in the world. A major reason, I suspect, is the fact that Switzerland never has abandoned universal military conscription (i.e., the draft).

The requirement of the Swiss constitution that all males from ages 20 to 45 must serve a minimum of 330 days in the armed forces (over a period of at least 22 years) helps unite Swiss of all languages, regions, and socioeconomic backgrounds. Friendships formed in the military link citizens together in a delicate, elastic web, putting unifying pressure on a social system that otherwise might be as tattered as our own.

U.S. youth today need something they're not getting from our schools—something Theodore Roosevelt put his finger on when he warned, "To educate a man in mind and not in morals is to educate a menace to society." Another leader whom I much admire, General C.E. Wilhelm, made much the same point recently when he addressed the Marine Military Academy. With the General's permission, I'll relate a little of what he said. He began by quoting Herbert Spencer:

> Education has for its object the formation of character. To curb restive propensities, to awaken dormant sentiments, to strengthen the perceptions and cultivate the tastes, to encourage this feeling and repress that, so as finally to develop the child into a man of well-proportioned and harmonious nature—this is alike the aim of parent and teacher.

If only that were true of our schools today! General Wilhelm went on to tell his young audience,

> There are those who will tell you that your own personal feelings and self-gratification are the goal of your existence. The old "if it feels good, do it" theory of life. This self-centered me-ism is destructive to any society, even one as free as ours. The fact is that it takes standards, self-sacrifice and a firm foundation in the concept of right and wrong to build and maintain a civilization. Make no mistake: That is what we are doing here today, maintaining a civilization.

Amen! He noted that civilizations, badly tended, die and that history is replete with examples.

I don't want America added to that list!

But who is going to ensure that the necessary values and discipline are instilled in our young? Schools aren't doing it. Neither are many of today's busy parents. Wouldn't it make sense for this nation's self-indulgent, unfocused, and often "valueless" young people to spend, say, six months in the service of the nation that has provided the freedoms they take for granted? Wouldn't many, if not most of them, benefit from a regimen that teaches them the virtues of teamwork, discipline, and honor? And after acquiring these virtues, would they not make better citizens, leaders, and employees?

I think they would. If restoring the draft would help restore the American character, I say let's do it!

Too Few Engineers, Too Many MBAs

We need more nerds! And we need to stop thinking of our nerds *as* nerds. We need to think of them instead as an endangered population—like gazelles, maybe.

Granted, engineering isn't as sexy a vocation as being a poet or an actor. Young girls may never quiver at the prospect of a moonlit walk with an engineer quite the same way they would with Leonardo DiCaprio. But the U.S. balance of payments is not riding on Leo. It is riding on the ability of our economy to manufacture things—a process to which engineers (need I say it?) are essential.

In Japan, engineers are revered almost as if they were gods. And pretty much the same holds true in Europe. I well recall from my own upbringing in Switzerland that mere businesspeople were thought to be much lower in the social order than engineers. Engineers were and are exalted personages in Europe.

Yet turn on U.S. television, and you see not just engineers but anybody competent in math or the hard sciences depicted as a doofus, right on down to his or her stereotypical pocket protector. Engineers, to quote Rodney Dangerfield, "don't get no respect"—even to the point that *engineers* love to tell jokes about engineers.

Chrysler's own François Castaing, when he was vice president of engineering, liked to regale audiences with a story about an aristocrat, a doctor, and an engineer who, in revolutionary France, were being taken to the guillotine. Now, the French (at least in François' story) have a rule that during executions any malfunction of the guillotine shall be viewed as proof of divine intervention, and the intended victim shall be set free. The aristocrat—first to confront his doom—is led to the machine, and his head placed on the block. The executioner pulls the chain. But the guillotine malfunctions: Its blade hangs up, and the aristocrat is set free. Ditto with the doctor: The guillotine jams, and the doctor lives to overbill his patients another day. Now comes the engineer. He takes his last fond look around, glances up at the glistening blade, and says, "Hey, fellas—I think I see what's wrong!"

All jokes aside, I think the popular image of the engineer needs to be rehabilitated. That's a tough proposition, however, since the root cause of engineering's poor image goes deep into our culture: We have glorified consumption to the point where, in the popular mind, we have very nearly *denigrated* production (a.k.a., "making things"). Where this mind-set came from is hard to say. Part of it, I suppose, comes from the consumer movement. And part of it may derive from the antipathy for big business that began in the '60s.

For the longest time, the United States didn't much need to concern itself with production. After World War II, the nation enjoyed a virtual monopoly on world industrial power. The United States was, in a sense, the captain of the team, not because it played a better game, but because it owned the ball! By the 1980s that power was beginning to wane badly, yet America kept itself going forward through the expedient of massive budget and trade deficits. It was almost as if (as one writer put it) the country were the cartoon character Wile E. Coyote in the old *Roadrunner* series, running straight off the side of the cliff but somehow managing to stay suspended in midair for just a moment! Well, "suspended animation" stopped working in the '90s, as we discovered at Chrysler and as thousands of other U.S. businesses discovered at the same time. That all of us collectively were able to claw our way back by sweat and brainpower is a testament to the resources still latent in the American character.

Today the threat America (and much of the rest of the Western world) faces is different. We're almost *too* well-off! And we, in our complacency, seem to assume that our productive edge will just somehow maintain itself. Our young—most especially the best and brightest—turn up their noses at stodgy old engineering or manufacturing and scamper off to business school, having heard the siren's call of Wall Street and careers in "sexy" fields like finance. It's a "brain drain" that takes talent from our most productive industries. To compensate, the United States has had to borrow engineering brainpower from abroad, as evidenced by the increased numbers of Asians in U.S. engineering offices.

I'm not a member of that club that views MBAs as largely unproductive. I'm *president* of that club! And I can report we have some very distinguished members, including Steve Jobs, who, toward the end of his first hitch at Apple Computer, lamented that Apple had hired perhaps one too many "professional managers." Sure, said Jobs, the MBAs knew how to manage, but they couldn't *do* anything. Highly productive filmmaker George Lucas apparently subscribes to the same view. Reminiscing in 1994 about his early years in the movie business, he told the *International Herald Tribune:*

> When I began, you'd go to a studio and there'd be three or four people and they'd say, "Okay, do the movie," or "Don't do the movie." But once Wall Street took over, their way of operating was to create a huge middle-management structure. These are people more interested in stock options than in making good movies, people *pretending* that they were experts in making movies—and they weren't. They fostered the idea that "the talent" doesn't know anything, that the talent are idiots or idiots savants. I mean, it's crazy.

At Chrysler, we tried to wean ourselves a bit from the MBA habit. It used to be the case, for example, that a Chrysler engineer, in order to get ahead, would have to get his very own almighty MBA. We changed that. We began to encourage our engineers to get additional *technical* training—either an M.S., a Ph.D., or even a second B.S. in a branch of engineering different from their first bachelor's. We figured the United States had enough MBAs already.

Actually, there's nothing wrong with an MBA or, for that matter, a law degree. And I must admit that I myself have an MBA (though I sort of regard it the same way sailors do their tattoos—I got it before I knew any better!). If the United States is going to maintain the marvelous competitive position we've won in the world, however, we're going to have to keep ourselves focused on production and encourage more of our young to opt for careers that make production possible. The MBA degree will cover itself in glory the day its letters stand for "*M*ust *B*uild things *A*gain."

More of our universities need to offer programs in manufacturing and industrial management. We need to put engineers on a pedestal. And our young people need to be taught that there's something noble about engaging in value-creating activity. Twenty or thirty years from now, when their grandchildren ask them, "What did *you* do in the great economic war?" they shouldn't have to answer, "I was a *bond trader.*"

CHAPTER 13

Leadership Is All About Common Sense, Which, Unfortunately, Is Not All That *Common*

IF BY NOW YOU'VE GOTTEN THE IDEA THAT I VIEW LIFE AS A BATTLE—OR AT least as a heated conversation—you're right. In previous chapters, I've laid out a few of what strike me as the more significant struggles being waged right now, not just in the workplace, but in our courts, classrooms, and public institutions. In each, who will prevail? Ten years from now, will the tort system be more equitable or less so? Will children's spelling be better or worse? Will we, as a society, have rediscovered self-discipline or declined further into laziness? Not being a crystal ball gazer, I'll pass up this chance to forecast the future. But I'll confidently predict one thing: In each skirmish, the side with the better leadership will win.

Leadership has been a hot topic lately, and several different models of it have been propounded, each claiming to have captured the essence of this art. I've encountered most of them, I think. And if there's one thing that separates the good models from the bad, it's that the good ones never drift too far from common sense or get too fancy. One of the very best, in fact, comes from a big, yellow book

161

with an unpretentious title, *Managing for Dummies,* which draws a useful distinction between leaders and managers.

"Managers," it says, "push their employees to achieve the goals of the organization. Leaders, on the other hand, "challenge their employees" to achieve them "by creating a compelling vision of the future and then unlocking their employees' potential." Under a section called "What Leaders Do," the book says leaders "inspire action," "communicate," and "support and facilitate." Not a bad description!

Yet how difficult it is to master principles that sound so easy. Sometimes the best way for aspiring leaders to learn their craft is to put aside their books and study how an actual leader gets results in the real world. Fifty years ago, the world gave us an outstanding example of just how much strong leadership can accomplish, even against daunting odds. The story, as told by *Aviation History* magazine, illustrates several of the points I'm going to be making, so I'll relate it in detail.

THE BERLIN AIRLIFT

It was June 25, 1948. On that date, the Cold War can fairly be said to have begun. The former Soviet Union advised the Allied Commanders of West Berlin (surrounded by Soviet-controlled East Germany) that their city's vital road links to West Germany would be "closed for repairs." The shutdown was designed to force the United States, France, and Britain out of the divided city, thus flouting the terms of the treaty ending World War II. The Soviets seemingly held all the cards and could sit back and wait for the Western enclave, deprived of supplies, to collapse.

Yet the commander of U.S. troops in West Germany, General Lucius D. Clay, refused to give in. So effective and so inspiring was the way he and his officers mounted their resistance that Berlin's fight for life serves as one of the best examples of what strong leadership can accomplish.

Clay first contacted General Curtis E. LeMay, commander of the U.S. Air Force in Europe. He asked him if the Air Force could airlift supplies into Berlin. LeMay declared flatly, "Sir, the Air Force can deliver anything." But could it? The 2 million inhabitants of West Berlin consumed, every day, some 13,000 tons of food and coal. It was estimated they could get by on a ration of 2,000 tons of food and 1,439 tons of coal daily.

No one, including the U.S. Air Force, had ever moved so much tonnage so quickly.

LeMay began by using the aircraft that he had at hand—twin-engined C-47s (the military version of the Douglas DC-3). With one plane landing in Berlin every eight minutes carrying 2½ tons, an average 1,000 tons a day were delivered during the first 10 days—far short of the 3,439-ton minimum. The Soviets, watching, ridiculed the American effort as futile.

By mid-July, however, deliveries had been raised to 1,500 tons per day. By August, LeMay was able to bring larger C-54s into service, and daily tonnage climbed to nearly 4,000. The pressure on crews and aircraft was tremendous: eight hours of flight time followed by eight hours of ground duty, with mechanics working nearly around the clock. In September, the full capacity of Berlin's airfields was reached; but the city lacked bulldozers large enough to build more runways. To tackle that problem and others spawned by the unprecedented size of the airlift, LeMay called in Maj. Gen. William H. Tunner, who, during World War II, had organized the airlifting of supplies over the Himalayas from India to China.

Tunner was a remarkably resourceful leader, as he quickly demonstrated by his solution to the bulldozer problem: At his order, big bulldozers were cut into smaller, air-transportable sections, then rewelded on the ground in West Berlin. He insisted all pilots, whether flying in good weather or bad, fly only by their instruments, thus ensuring that every plane would stay exactly in position from takeoff to touchdown and boosting the system's overall efficiency.

Yet as tonnage rose, the morale of badly overworked troops began to wane. To bolster it, Tunner introduced a host of measures, including mobile snack bars staffed by beautiful Berlin girls and a special newspaper—the *Berlin Airlift Times*—which celebrated feats accomplished and records broken. By using the *Times* to excite a friendly rivalry between crews, Tunner gave the Berlin Airlift the trappings of a competitive sport. To say he made the Airlift fun is not to patronize his leadership. Quite the opposite! By keeping his troops' spirits high and their competitive instinct aroused, he pushed their results ever higher.

In March of 1949, a record 234,476 tons were lifted into Berlin, more than 7,000 tons a day—twice the survival level. It was many times more than anyone had thought possible. But Tunner, in the spirit of true leadership, felt his men needed a new challenge to shake off any tendency toward complacency. He set an arbitrary, "impossible" goal of 10,000 tons in one day. His challenge, publicized in the *Times* by the slogan "Tonnage for Tunner," caught his troops' imagination. They strove to find new ways to make the impossible possible, recognizing that working harder would not, by itself, be solution enough. Smarter ways to work were tried: Loads were prepositioned for faster movement.

On Easter Sunday, April 16, 1949, the impossible was accomplished, and 12,940 tons were delivered to Berlin! Shortly thereafter, on May 12, the Soviets—recognizing that it was now their own blockade that was futile—restored access to Berlin.

What hallmarks of strong leadership were illuminated by this impressive victory? From the outset, the protagonists decided to fight aggressively rather than to accept the status quo or rationalize away their possible defeat (e.g., "West Berlin really isn't of huge strategic importance. Why risk a lot of American lives so soon after the end of World War II to save a town the average American doesn't care that much about?"). Generals Clay and LeMay took full responsibility for their assignments and began executing them with imagination and discipline. Most especially, the victory celebrates the demanding (but never overbearing or inhumane) leadership style of "Tonnage for Tunner" Tunner, who not only challenged his men to meet ever higher goals but made the meeting of those goals a sport. Strong leaders, through their bearing and their communication skills, make the surmounting of difficulties seem attractive—even fun. (While inculcating that attitude helps boost productivity, it's doubly useful in a crisis situation, where it reduces stress and tension.)

The single greatest attribute of Tunner's leadership style, in my opinion, was its insistence on constant change. When he saw that the maximum benefits of following visual-flight rules had been reached (and that Berlin still was getting only its minimum ration), he chucked those rules and ordered his aircrews to switch to instrument flight, which permitted higher efficiency and higher tonnage. Seeing the need for new airfields, he ordered the weld-cutting, airlifting, and reassembly of bulldozers. And he experimented constantly with innovations (such as the *Airlift Times*) designed to improve motivation and instill teamwork. By cajoling his men to meet an "impossible" goal (10,000 tons a day), by posting "scores," and by celebrating exceptional achievements, he fostered a "Super Bowl" mentality that made attainment of the goal possible. That the goal was exceeded by more than 20 percent shows just how much can be achieved by average men and women, overworked though they may be, if they believe in their mission and receive strong leadership.

WHY DO WE NEED LEADERSHIP ANYWAY?

We used to study management—how to analyze complex situations, how to establish budgets, how to do accounting, how to market. We taught the individual skills, similar to teaching the members of a basketball team how to shoot and dribble or teaching military recruits how to march and how to handle firearms. But just as dribbling and shooting alone do not make a great basketball team and close-order drill and marksmanship do not make an effective fighting force, so it is that an aggregation of great business skills does not, of itself, make for an outstanding company. A group of disparate musicians, no matter how skilled, needs a conductor to become an orchestra. A basketball team, to become a contender, needs a strong coach. The military unit needs its designated leader to transform a group of militarily trained people into a fearsome group of dedicated warriors.

This is why managing, supervising, or overseeing just aren't enough. Sure, finances and budgets need to be managed, but people must be *led*. Product development, marketing, sales, manufacturing, even the finance function—all require strong, visionary leadership in order to effect continuous improvement and meet ever greater competitive challenges. The reasons these entities require leadership is that they tend to be large, diverse in skill and education, multifaceted, sometimes geographically dispersed, and, most challenging of all, saddled with several seemingly conflicting objectives (such as "improving quality while reducing cost," "delighting the customer while maximizing shareholder return," "creating great new products while minimizing new investment"). Without a leader who can make order out of seeming chaos, who feels accountable, and who selects and defends the right priority ranking among a list of must-haves and nice-to-haves, the organization will simply cease to move forward. Instead, it will churn helplessly in place, trapped in an endless re-do loop beginning with "proposal/rejection" and progressing to "modified proposal, failed consensus," "new proposal, counterproposal," and finally arriving at, "what we really need here is more research and more study time before we can achieve the kind of closure that will allow all our constituencies to buy in." (My God, how I hate these waffle words!)

An organization that lacks strong leadership is like a lake: It may be deep and large and contain much potential energy, but as long as the ground beneath it remains flat, its energy will remain just that—*potential*. Now comes a strong, "disruptive" leader who tilts the landscape. Suddenly the same water becomes a river, able to turn turbines and produce power!

Mechanical analogies abound. Take the enormously complex systems that comprise today's military fighting aircraft: a high-thrust, computer-controlled engine, fly-by-wire flight controls with no mechanical linkages; a sleek, beautifully designed and executed airframe; an incredible array of passive radar-warning and infrared sensors, decoy systems, target-acquisition radar, autopilot, offensive weapons, and on and on. These aircraft can be managed, in that it is possible, by installing radio controls, to fly them, without a pilot, from the ground. It's easy, and, for target drones, it's done all the time.

But this superb accumulation, representing the pinnacle of human technology, is essentially a useless $30 million lump of aluminum, steel, and plastic hurtling through the sky unless it is in the hands of a trained and motivated human pilot who directs it, maintains situational awareness, senses emerging patterns, engages the enemy under his terms if possible, selects the appropriate weapons, and closes for the kill—thus accomplishing the mission. The individual elements of this organization we call the *airplane* all do their jobs and make their contribution. Wings lift, radar observes, rudders and elevators steer, computers inform, engines thrust. The leader sits in the cockpit. The pilot can't get it done without a superb aircraft. And the superb aircraft can't get it done without the creative, adaptable, goal-oriented intelligence of the pilot.

General George Patton (a strong leader if there ever was one) understood this point perfectly. He wrote:

> Success in war lurks invisible in that vitalizing spark, intangible, yet as evident as lightning—the warrior's soul. . . . It is the cold glitter of the attacker's eyes, not the point of the questing bayonet, that breaks the line. It is the fierce determination of the driver to close with the enemy, not the mechanical perfection of the tank, that conquers the trench. It is the cataclysmic ecstasy of conflict in the flier, not the perfection of the machine gun, which drops the enemy in flames. Yet volumes are devoted to arms; only pages to inspiration.

Why, in aerial combat, do a small minority of pilots typically bag a majority of kills? The aircraft are the same, but each pilot flies his own plane more aggressively or less so. Only 20 percent of pilots, let's say the most inspired, are "leading" their weapons systems. The other 80 percent make do with a weaker style. No guts, no glory!

ARE STRONG LEADERS BORN OR TRAINED?

Both, of course—just as would be true if we were discussing musicians, writers, athletes, or artists. Some people may find they have the requisites for leadership as an innate—maybe even genetic—gift: that curious blend of courage, insight, communication skills, and willingness to accept personal risk. Yet there is no question in my mind that almost anyone of normal intelligence—those born with or without these attributes—can be *trained* to be a far more effective leader than he or she could ever have been naturally. Training makes the bad less awful, the good better, the better best.

To return to a topic raised earlier in this book, lately—I'm happy to say—I've noticed that the U.S. Marine Corps has been cited increasingly in books, newspapers, and magazines as being one of the best, most effective machines ever devised for the production of leaders. One reason: They recognize that training improves leadership at every level of an organization, that a private in the Corps (or an hourly worker in a corporation) is every bit as susceptible to being a better leader as the most medal-bedecked general (or CEO). However good a leader may be, he or she always can be better.

In the Marine Corps, training never really stops. Men and women who graduate from officer training discover they have only begun a process that will last for as long as they stay with the Corps. Ever higher levels of instruction lead eventually to the War College, school for future generals. Is it any wonder, given this mix of natural aptitude and ceaseless training, that the Marine Corps is now regarded by many as one of the best schools for leadership in the United States, if not the world? Nor should it be surprising that men and women trained in the Corps (and other branches of the military) have gone on to excel as business leaders. Distinguished Marine alumni in business that I have personally known include Don Petersen and Phil Benton of Ford, not only Leo Kelmenson but also Mike Vogel at Bozell, Hugh McColl of NationsBank, and George Black of Ingersoll-Rand; and I'm sure that Chrysler's Tom Stallkamp credits his own military service (with the U.S. Coast Guard) as instrumental to the success he's had in his career.

I sometimes have been tempted to give corporate human resources people the following hypothetical challenge: I could put 20 senior Marine Corps officers, disguised as civilians, in a room with 20 vice presidents of Fortune 500 companies, and HR's task would be to interview these 40 people on non-job-specific subjects (e.g., no esoteric finance or military tactics questions) dealing only with self-expression, imagination, ethics, fairness, motivation, how to get the best performance out of an organization, how to mete out criticism, how to reward and punish, how to measure, how to train, and so on. The purpose, at the end, would be to rank these people by HR's perception of their ability to lead a corporation to new prosperity. My own bet is that almost all of the top 20 would be Marines! They might not have the industry-specific knowledge or the experience of the civilian VPs, but their sheer ability to lead would put them on a higher plane.

Why am I postulating this outcome? Senior Fortune 500 types are almost all well-educated, dedicated professionals and specialists. They were selected from the universities based on their grade-point averages, reports from their professors, and their proficiency in their functional specialties. Employers seldom even ask about leadership ability or skills! Give us your finance whizzes (say employers), your bright marketing minds, your computer-literate engineers, your huddled time-and-motion experts yearning to breathe free; but don't let's waste time searching for something so nebulous (and potentially disruptive) as a strong leader.

Happily, all this is changing. Maybe not fast enough, but we, in industry, are on our way to relearning many of the oldest truths that have served elite military organizations around the world through the millennia.

CHARACTERISTICS OF GREAT LEADERS

Defining great leadership is as hard as trying to define charm, charisma, or beauty, and yet you know it when you see it. Probably the best way to get at its heart is to describe what leaders actually do, the traits they share, and the principles they follow.

Flexibility

We've all read a lot of books and articles about the advantages of one style of leadership versus another, as in, say, the benefits of a participative (or collective or coaching or collegial) style of leadership versus a more authoritarian style. I've given a lot of speeches (and now I've written a book) on the demise of the authoritarian style at Chrysler and the very real blessings that flow from a more sharing, team-focused approach. That approach not only reduces fear, but taps the creative power of many brains (as opposed to just the consummate cranium of the big leader).

A lot of the discussion about leadership style sounds to me like carpenters arguing about whether saws are better than hammers, or artists arguing about whether red is better than blue. All styles are *potentially* useful. Since no two situations are ever alike, the leader must use whatever style is appropriate for each. If things are in a real mess, as in an emergency clinic where patients are suffering life-threatening injuries, the need for immediate action is so acute that the senior doctor must make all the key decisions quickly: Who gets treatment first? Second? The leader must make fast life-or-death deci-

GUTS

sions on his own, relying on team members to feed him necessary information.

A military platoon that is suddenly ambushed by a numerically superior enemy must respond unhesitatingly to the authoritarian commands of its lieutenant. Once the worst of the crisis is over and the men are temporarily safe from death, the lieutenant who's a good leader takes time to discuss the next moves with his experienced platoon sergeant and perhaps even other noncommissioned officers. Having the luxury of time is what now permits him to use a more participatory style of management.

The rule, of course, for leaders to follow is that participation in the leadership process should be inversely proportional to the severity and immediacy of the crisis. That's just another way of saying that leadership is always a skillful blend of top-down direction and participative empowerment. The trick that effective leaders master is knowing how much of each is needed given the circumstances or the task to be achieved.

While a good leader can and does command a spectrum of styles, he or she should *never* succumb to consensus-driven management. That, to me, is a place leaders don't want to go! Continuously diluting and modifying a proposal until it wins everybody's endorsement wastes huge amounts of valuable time. On top of that, the consensus-driven version is apt to be so homogenized, pasteurized, diluted, and blended that its merit is lost. Everybody, perhaps, experiences the warm feeling known as "closure" and believes we've made progress. But we haven't! The most insidious thing about consensus leadership is that it stifles initiative and creativity; it risks destroying the good solution in favor of the one nobody hated enough to kill.

Sometimes, consensus has its place: for example, in boards of directors, where a show of unity and solidarity with the elected officers can be of great legal and psychological importance (though I do admire board members who occasionally buck unanimity and either abstain or perhaps vote against a proposal they can't, for legitimate reasons, support). And of course, consensus is a requirement in a negotiating process with someone outside your organization. There, consensus is a sine qua non: no agreement, no deal. But that's got nothing at all to do with internal leadership.

170

An overly solicitous, democracy-driven, consensus leadership style will also demotivate and effectively neutralize the more junior leaders in the group. They see no possibility and no point in acting as leaders in an environment where even the disinterested, the uninformed, the indolent, and the lovers of the status quo have as much influence over the outcome as those who want to move ahead.

Communication

Communication is the conduit through which the leader passes on a vision or a big idea to others so that they comprehend it the same way he or she does. Sometimes, leaders are great orators. But the elegance or cleverness of their delivery is less important than that they open themselves up. The most effective communicators are those who offer audiences a glimpse of their soul and who engage in honest give-and-take. In this way, the next level of management becomes energized, since they feel they've given the leader their own input and are now sure they know where the leader stands. How maddening are bosses who play their cards close to the vest, won't communicate honestly, won't give their true reactions, and respond to every input with varying degrees of acquiescence. Nobody ever knows where they or their projects stand. It's like hitting tennis balls into a backboard made of cotton candy. The balls disappear in a sugary puff, never to come out again!

Even worse, though, is the leader who responds with scorn and derision, or even anger, to subordinates' input. After a few exposures to the great leader's devastating negativism, there won't be much more forthcoming in terms of new ideas.

And then we have the worst of all: dishonest communication, in which the leader, in careful one-on-one conversation, embraces several opposing viewpoints, with each subordinate believing that he and only he has the boss's full support. These underlings then attack each other with a vengeance, sure that "the force is with them," while the leader sits back, watching the carnage with interest to see which of his pit bulls is the last one standing. *Divide et impera* (divide and rule) is the operative phrase here, and it's legitimate when dealing with your enemies. But only the most insecure of leaders would put direct subordinates in that category!

Oratory can be one of a leader's most powerful tools, enabling him to cast a kind of spell over those he needs to follow him. It's also a skill that can be learned. You may think me a little eccentric, but I personally enjoy watching the technique of revival-style preachers like Jimmy Swaggart. I study such preachers' gestures, their range of tone, the pacing they use to keep an audience on the edge of their seats—everything from staccato bursts of invective to soothing and mellifluous discourses. (Not, by the way, that I'm the world's greatest public speaker—but at least, unlike many of the preachers, I've stayed out of jail!)

The aspiring leader should remember, though, that many a great orator is *only* that. Such people may have communication skills, may be able to energize a crowd, get it fired up, sell ideas, and foment positive or negative revolution. But if the gift of gab is their only skill, they'll never make the grade. Glibness on the podium is less important than the other attributes of leadership we'll consider here, including integrity and openness.

A leader's writing (like his verbal communication) must above all else be clear, so that people of all levels of intelligence and sophistication can immediately get the message. To use jargon is sometimes to invite misunderstanding and confusion. Yet see how many executives love buzzwords and windy phrases!

I got so exasperated with needlessly complex phrases when I was executive vice president of truck operations at Ford (the job I had just before coming to Chrysler) that I circulated the following guide for inventing more of them. In a memo that accompanied it, I warned our division (tongue in cheek) that we risked being thought of as out of date unless we started using new terminology. Not only had such familiar words as *agreement, objective,* and *participants* been replaced by *buy-in, desired outcome,* and *stakeholders,* I noted, but some new words were already in their second and third generations. For example, *participative management* had already been displaced, first by *facilitative management* and then by *transformational management.*

Thanks to the following handy-dandy Lutz Language Guide, everyone now could sound au courant. By simply combining (from left to right) any word in column 1 with words from columns 2 and 3, they could dispense with such dull, outmoded phrases as *initial agreement,* and serve up *preliminary cross-functional buy-in* in its place!

Lutz Language Guide (or the "1-2-3 list")

Enhanced	Conceptual	Vision
Interactive	Cross-organizational	Technique
Iterative	Postadversarial	Substructure
Facilitative	Synergistic	System
Supportive	Transitional	Process
Shared	Transformational	Buy-in
Team-oriented	Reciprocal	Contract
Preliminary	Cross-functional	Outcome
Cooperative	Interdisciplinary	Consensus
Underlying	Participative	Communication

I also—just for the heck of it—added a quick-use glossary for my Truck Ops brethren:

Instant "New for Old" Guide

Some selected "1-2-3" combinations and their old-fashioned counterparts:

State-of-the-Art-Speak	*Outmoded Term*
Team-oriented interdisciplinary buy-in	Everybody is interested
Cooperative participative consensus	Agreement at working level
Shared cross-functional contract	Agreement at higher level
Interactive synergistic substructure	Committee, group
Enhanced synergistic substructure	Bigger committee, group
Facilitative transformational process	Good change
Enhanced transformational process	Better change

Shared transformational process	Agreed change
Iterative transformational process	Repeated change
Shared conceptual vision	Agreed plan
Enhanced conceptual vision	Your superior's plan
Underlying conceptual vision	The real plan
Shared cross-functional outcome	Objective, goal
Enhanced cross-functional outcome	Next year's objective, goal
Team-oriented postadversarial substructure	Employee involvement group
Preliminary conceptual communication	Draft
Enhanced conceptual communication	Draft after staff review
Interactive cross-organizational communication	Sending memos back and forth

Not only do great leaders tend to be jargon-free, they practice a deceptively simple form of communication that, on its surface, may seem to be a waste of time: storytelling (or anecdote telling).

In the Bible, it was the parables. In the Marine Corps, knowledge about the values of the Corps is passed down via so-called sea stories—illustrations that, while basically true, have become better polished or funnier with each retelling, making them useful devices for driving home a point. What these leaders are doing with this type of storytelling is essentially to say, "Look, I don't expect you to believe me on principle. But it dawned on me that I had once faced an analogous situation in my own career, and here's how it went . . ." The leader is thus transmitting knowledge and understanding by way of a personal case study. The subordinates now share the leader's past and understand his or her thinking, reactions, and logic path. While the time-consuming aspect of leadership-by-storytelling can be overdone (as when an absentminded elder statesman retells the same war stories!), it is an outstanding technique by which a coach can pass on his or her vision, knowledge, and motivation to subordinates.

One I frequently tell (maybe too often!) is designed to illustrate the folly of "talking to yourself" in advertising or PR (that is, of bragging about internal achievements that are of no earthly interest to the buyer). The event was Fiat's introduction in the United Kingdom of the new Ritmo (Strada in the United States) in the late '70s. Immensely proud of their new automated body shop in Italy's most modern facility, the Fiat U.K. folks decided on a launch theme of "New Fiat Ritmo: Hand-built by robots." Great line, cute ads, poor results. Why? Customers don't care whether people, machines, or a blend of both made the car! They just want to know how it looks, what it does, how much it costs, and how good the quality is. (Imagine a famous restaurant advertising "All meals are cooked in our new Ajax Z-4000 ovens!")

In short, *how* a leader communicates with subordinates is less important than that he connect emotionally with them, transferring his will into their minds, hearts, and souls.

I always liked to begin every meeting with jokes or venting about politics or retelling something funny I heard or a bit of industry gossip—anything but the subject at hand. If one of the participants was host on a dealer incentive cruise (a nice perk!), I'd ask how it was. ("How much did you have to suffer for that great tan?") If some of them were at a superbike race-training session, I'd get them to talk about that. The tougher and potentially more divisive the subject of the meeting, the more time and energy I'd devote to the warm-up. I used to hate myself for doing this, believing I was simply procrastinating because I didn't want to tackle the tough stuff. While that may have been my original reason, I came to realize the usefulness of limbering up the channels of communication. The feeling of good humor and comradeship produced by those few minutes of irreverent banter can help resolve some really contentious issues, with far less chance of aggressiveness or defensiveness getting in the way.

Ability to Deal with the Press

Many leaders shun reporters automatically, having been burned once too often perhaps by stories they considered inaccurate or sensationalized. They're not wrong to be a little wary. Even the press itself, I notice, occasionally acknowledges its list toward shocking news, whether or not it is backed up by facts. I recently enjoyed a cartoon making this same point in the *Cincinnati Enquirer* by cartoonist Jim Borgman.

Funny? Sure. But not if you happen to be in the sock business, metaphorically speaking. Chrysler went through times when no matter what we did, we just couldn't seem to get good press. Every decision we made—in the opinion of business reporters and Wall Street analysts—was wrong. It got so unremitting that, for comic relief, I concocted the following explanation showing how the pundits' interpretation of various news events affected Chrysler stock. (It must have hit a nerve, by the way, because the *Wall Street Journal* ran it in its entirety!)

Chrysler Stock Performance—Understanding Same

Event	*Interpretation*	*Effect on Stock*
Chrysler raises dividend.	Market seeks value, not yield. Bad use of cash flow.	Down
Chrysler holds dividend.	Yield is unacceptable.	Down
Chrysler spends more on product.	Management is irresponsible, departing from prudent financial strategy.	Down
Chrysler spends less on product.	Management is irresponsible, too short-term oriented.	Down
Chrysler accelerates pension funding.	Imprudent allocation of cash that might be needed elsewhere.	Down
Chrysler does not accelerate pension funding.	Management still does not grasp true magnitude of this serious debtlike liability.	Down

So, you see, I've been there myself! Nonetheless, I also have learned that a personable executive who knows his business and is respectful of the First Amendment–protected job the press has to do can make a huge difference in the way a story gets played. By "respectful," I mean such things as listening carefully to questions, eschewing condescension, avoiding jargon, and speaking, when appropriate, not only truthfully but with extra candor.

You can usually tell the motivation behind a story by listening carefully to how questions are asked. "Are you confident that the company can maintain its dominance in minivans despite all the new competition?" sounds a lot different from "As your minivan business suffers under the competitive onslaught, how can the company possibly offset the profit reduction?" Most negative questions give the interviewee a chance to educate the journalist in a way that genuinely provides new information or depth of insight. If I hear a question that sounds like a statement (and a *wrong* statement), I invite the journalist to examine the question's underlying assumption. I treat him or her as a fellow professional just doing his or her job—someone with whom I can intelligently discuss the issue. The interviewer will not be indifferent to this, especially if he or she senses you are speaking with sincerity and candor—especially *candor,* as I've discovered from being in the company of world leaders.

Prime Minister Margaret Thatcher, during the period when I was chairman of Ford of Europe in the early '80s, enjoyed having senior businesspeople come by Number 10 Downing Street for one-on-one conversations. If the meeting was in the afternoon, she would inevitably offer a glass of scotch, and there was no reticence on her part to having a large one herself. She was incisive, direct, and able to put the visitor at ease instantly. She was a good listener and had a very quick wit. She greatly enjoyed being told the truth, and she was able to create an environment in which it became easy to be open. That's because I and her other listeners always felt that she herself was open. She would give us her honest reactions, sometimes of necessity separating her personal views from those dictated by official policy, so that we, as her visitors, never got the sense that she was giving guarded or perfunctory responses. Not only did her manner put me at my ease, I'm sure that she herself, because of the uninhibited talk, learned a great deal she might otherwise have missed (because, of course, *we* opened up as well, following her lead).

With reporters, you can increase your credibility enormously by not wasting time defending the indefensible. Saying "Yes, that model isn't selling too well because we didn't get the details quite right; but we're addressing that now with some changes," works a lot better than insisting everything is perfect and the only reason competitors are outselling you is that they're giving the store away. Acknowledging such points will only strengthen your credibility when, later, you may need to set the reporter straight on some matter of greater consequence.

Journalists, being people, like leaders who have the human touch, show a sense of humor, don't take themselves too seriously, and—above all else—come across as "real." How they must hate the pompous, self-congratulatory, stuffy big shots they so often have to interview, especially when all they get from them are tired, oft-repeated tidbits of the company line doled out in a condescending way. If your joie de vivre manifests itself by your having an office filled (as mine is) with photos, posters, car models, toy airplanes, and other expressions of your personality (in my case, that meant a hulking life-size plastic reproduction of a Lamborghini V-12 engine!), do not attempt to make it intimidatingly stark or orderly for an interview. Why? Leaving it in its natural state, I think, constitutes a form of candor; and I can't help but notice, when I visit TV stations and pressrooms, that creative clutter seems to be the decor journalists themselves prefer!

Finally, though, if you ever do find yourself on the receiving end of a true media hatchet job, *take 'em on!* When a story appears with which you take righteous exception, don't hesitate to dispute its content or conclusions publicly. Your own PR people may caution you against this; and sometimes you may be better off heeding their advice. But in many cases, you really should fight back; you owe it to your company. When the TV show *Dateline NBC,* for example, accused GM of manufacturing explosion-prone fuel tanks, GM not only rebutted the accusation but proved that *Dateline* had caused fuel tanks to explode by artificial means for purposes of the TV show! GM won considerable public sympathy, and I'll bet viewers never again accepted a *Dateline NBC* story with quite the same credulity.

Courage and Tenacity

I didn't know it at the time, but one day in 1966 I exercised a key trait of strong leadership. I was visited in my small office at GM's German subsidiary where I then worked, Adam Opel, by a GM executive vice president from Detroit who was on a supervisory visit. I was awestruck, flattered. He proceeded to explain that I was doing an outstanding job, that I had had a major impact on the company's European operations despite my lowly status, and that my tenacity and unwillingness to accept harmful compromise had resulted in some really progressive and profitable new products.

He went on to tell me that my talent was well recognized by higher-ups, that I was on a fast track, and that a future job in the top management group of the company was "mine to lose." So? "We want you now to stop exposing yourself to so much internal risk. Every time you win one, you alienate some of the old-timers. You're always right, but someday you'll be wrong, and they'll get you. We don't want that to happen. So, please, you don't have to prove anything anymore. You're designated. Just play along with the system, pull in your oars, and let yourself drift downstream." It was sincerely meant, friendly advice from a gentleman who really wanted to help my career at the company. But I couldn't stay there—not after that! How do you tell a kid who is on a crusade to make dull old Opels into respected predators on the speed-is-social-status autobahns that he's done enough, has demonstrated enough, and should now slip quietly into the risk-averse mode? You can't, and, after a few more years of being told as well that riding a motorcycle and racing cars on weekends did not fit the pattern of well-regarded executive behavior at GM and receiving instruction on "executive hair" (as opposed to my USMC flattop), I was willingly recruited away by BMW.

Strong leaders win respect by sticking to their guns. Subordinates hate phonies. And the worst phonies in the leadership profession are the ones who look great, sound great, and talk tough in the locker room, only to fold up (or worse, radically change positions) the minute the big boss appears to be on a different wicket.

I remember meetings early in my GM career where several layers of bosses (I was senior analyst and thus, despite the "senior," lowest on the totem pole) would agree emphatically on a position I had written. "This time, we're really armed with convincing arguments. . . . Let's go see big boss X." Big boss X would arrive in his conference room 10 minutes late, would ask what the meeting was all about, would delicately be introduced to the subject, and would then grunt, "It's a dumb idea, I don't want to do it." At this point, you can play spot-the-leader.

In my case, it certainly wasn't the second most senior guy present, because he was saying he didn't like it either, he just wanted to run it by the others. And all the others, nodding furiously, were throwing stern "how-could-you-be-so-stupid?" glances in my direction.

On several such occasions, I would say, "Excuse me, sir, but we knew that 'no' was your original position, and still we felt there were some salient facts you weren't aware of. Because we think that, when we lay out all the facts, you may not want to reject it." Expressions of awestruck horror combined with morbid curiosity would cross the faces of the assembled apparatchiks. How could this incredibly unimportant person speak across five levels of hierarchy and *directly challenge* the big boss? Easily, if you're tenacious, reasonably polite, have a ferocious belief that you are right, are proposing the right thing for the company, and believe that your arguments will convince a reasonable person.

More than once in this type of scenario, the big boss would grumpily read the memo and finally utter, "Well, I guess that puts a different light on it. Is this what all of you think?" Again, an enthusiastic chorus of "absolutely," accompanied by much nodding.

All leaders display courage. It can be mental or emotional courage (the courage to risk a superior's wrath), or it can be physical. In business, it usually takes the form of a man or woman being willing to challenge the all-too-seductive groupthink, to take intelligent risk, to accept responsibility—in short, to do the exact opposite of those craven executives who immediately embrace whichever "solution of the moment" seems to be winning! Note that *courage* is not to be confused with *recklessness* or with unwise acceptance of excessive risk. Leaders who are reckless are like overaggressive drivers who pass slower traffic on blind curves: They may make headway, but not if there's a semi coming the other way! Good leaders don't recklessly endanger their troops in the military, and they don't recklessly endanger the jobs of their employees or the assets of their shareholders in the corporate world. On the other hand, they don't just sit on their assets, either.

Humility and the Common Touch

Strong leaders, cognizant of their own ability and worth, have no need to play the aloof big shot to confirm their status. They know they give nothing away by being "just one of the folks" in informal situations, sharing jokes and anecdotes with people many organizational levels below themselves. I'm suspicious of leaders whose only friends seem to be well-known celebrities (at whatever level of life); it sounds as if they're members of a support group for the insecure.

The leader ought to view himself as *different* from the troops—but not *better*. They have their skills; he has his. Though he needs their support to get anything done, the reverse is less true: A symphony orchestra probably can muddle through at least one evening's repertoire minus its conductor.

In the military, the leader's job is not only to command. He must also serve as his troops' coach, teacher, mentor; he must do everything in his power to ensure they are kept as safe as possible, commensurate with the mission that must be accomplished. That is why the Marine Corps (and the military in general) upholds the tradition that, when in the field, no officer may stand in the food line until all his troops have been fed. It's a gesture of respect, of "downward" loyalty, of humility, of caring, of a leader's feeling of deep responsibility for those he leads. How different from the corporate world, where too often an imperial, "don't-touch-me-I'm-a-star" type of leader, through his or her every gesture—through every erg of body language, in fact—conveys the message, "I make a lot more money than you do, and, by God, I deserve it because I am incredibly intelligent." These guys can't wait to get to a washbasin after shaking hands with hourly workers. Do the workers pick up on their disdain? Of course they do. No style of leadership is more powerfully antagonistic or demotivating.

What about the perquisites of office—reserved parking spaces, corporate jets, executive dining rooms, and the like? Should a leader, in order to win greater respect from subordinates, turn his back on such trappings? Not necessarily. Subordinates don't want their leaders to be *exactly* like themselves, nor do they begrudge them rewards won for leading them to victory. And though it's probably politically incorrect of me to say so, privileges still exert a powerful, positive motivating force, especially on junior members of a team. When I was an aspiring leader, I *wanted* a reserved parking space (and worked hard to merit one). As for the corporate dining room, I say hooray!—

at least for Chrysler's, which allows executives to accomplish far more work during mealtime than they ever could amidst the bustle and distraction of a commercial restaurant or typical corporate cafeteria. Perks that help a leader to be more efficient and more productive are hardly perks.

It helps to remember that subordinates see a leader very differently from the way he (or she) is apt to see himself. They see only the imposing outer shell, the great figure, the title, the rank. They can't see the self-doubt, the nagging insecurities that leaders, being human, drag around. It's up to the leader to take the initiative to put subordinates at their ease. He or she may have to make a conscious effort to show some vulnerability, to open up. A little self-deprecating humor can often do the trick.

Something I always liked to do in large meetings was to address comments or questions to the most junior people at the table. This accomplished two things at once: It demonstrated that I didn't consider myself too important or exalted to talk to the younger folks (who probably had done most of the actual work), and it gave them a very real feeling of being noticed and appreciated. When in the plants, walking the floor, I've always been astonished at how much great communication can be established by asking some tough-looking, tattooed worker if he really owns a Harley or just the tattoo. It was the same with cigar smokers, who loved to share opinions and stories on their smokes. Observing and reacting to such personal messages (frequently on T-shirts!) gives the leader a huge opportunity to break down the perceived gulf in rank or social station. (Sometimes, you even get a chance at education: I observed one obviously bright, energetic young worker whose baseball cap carried the words, "You obviously have mistaken me for someone who gives a shit." I gently took him aside and said that I couldn't believe his cap reflected his attitude. He assured me it didn't. I suggested it might create a bad impression. He agreed, thanked me, folded the cap and tucked it in his waistband.)

Integrity

"Fish begin to stink at the head," say the Greeks, meaning corruption in an organization usually starts at the top; and it's true. Leaders must set the tone—morally, ethically, in dress, in every other way. They personally must uphold and manifest the same standards they expect their subordinates to embrace. Earlier I quoted General Patton, so it seems only fair now to quote his adversary Erwin Rommel, who grasped the importance of this point:

> Be an example to your men, both in your duty and in private life. Never spare yourself, and let the troops see that you do not, in your endurance of fatigue and privation. Always be tactful and well mannered and teach your subordinates to be the same. Avoid excessive sharpness or harshness of the voice, which usually indicates the man who has shortcomings of his own to hide.

To be accepted as a natural leader whom people *want* to follow, you must impress subordinates as being not just as good as they are, but better! Followers want to be led by someone they can look up to. By "better," I mean superior in those qualities that entitle a man or woman to lead: intelligence, resolve, tenacity, loyalty to subordinates, and, above all, honesty and integrity.

How can subordinates look up to a person who cuts corners, who preaches purity yet is on the take (e.g., that little antelope-hunting safari to Africa) from suppliers, who preaches truth yet willingly lies, who preaches frugality yet lavishes excess upon him- or herself? The simple answer is: They can't! They may obey orders, they may show up for meetings, but their obedience is uninspired and perfunctory, given grudgingly only because their superior holds a higher position in the organizational chart.

Does it really matter that the leader have impeccable integrity? You bet it does! Again, the reason is that people want to follow a superior who genuinely is *superior*. You wouldn't want a stock broker who'd committed a felony to be running your portfolio, no matter how good his or her stock picks. You wouldn't want a teacher for your children whose performance as a professional might be impeccable, but who, in private life, has been convicted of statutory rape. So it's completely natural that we should lose trust in leaders who show a willingness to lie and cheat (even about so-called small things and "everybody-else-is-doing-it" things) but who claim that these deficiencies do not affect their job performance.

Though we seem to have become numb to the apparent transgressions of our highest elected officials, I can tell you that the corporate world is not so tolerant of behavior so unbecoming a leader. If, for instance, any Fortune 500 CEO stood accused of half as much general impropriety (with a similar nonexplanation) as President Clinton, he'd be out of office in a second.

Perhaps for that reason, I have never found lack of integrity to be a problem in the executive suites of the American companies I have worked for. Whether at GM, Ford, or Chrysler, I always found senior management who took a strong, personal interest in ensuring that corporate integrity was absolute. They accepted no favors from suppliers, and they insisted on the utmost honesty in reporting data (on finances, safety, emissions, or what have you) to the U.S. government and Wall Street. I know that many of the country's lawyers and investigative journalists would have you think otherwise, but it's simply not true.

Overseas, though, it's sometimes a different story. When I was executive vice president for sales and marketing at BMW in the early '70s I encountered several situations for which my previous experience had not prepared me.

I discovered that our advertising agency, for example, was engaging in fictitious billing—funneling billed-for (but unspent) money to accomplices inside BMW marketing. I fired them all—both the agency and the whole marketing department.

Another instance concerned a "creative" manager of a BMW-owned dealership and his wife. The manager had his wife (posing as a customer) offer to buy a well-worn VW Beetle convertible that had come to the dealership on trade. Her offer, thousands of marks below the car's real value, amazed the salesman, who called the manager for approval. "Sell the nice lady the car, you idiot," said the manager-husband. "It's been around long enough!" Some time later, the wife brought the car back and complained about the paint, the top, the interior, and the tires being worn. She wanted the car refurbished at the dealership's expense. Again, outraged refusal by the sales staff countermanded by approval by the boss-husband, who proclaimed that BMW's high standards of customer satisfaction demanded nothing less. A few weeks later, the wife in customer's clothing stopped by again, this time to sell the car back for a price three times higher than what she had originally paid. The dealership's hired hands, in shock, told her she was nuts: Who had paid, after all, to restore the car? But the managing director again said, "Pay the lady the price! That cream puff of a convertible will be a valuable advertisement for how well we recondition used cars!"

How were these crooks found out? The manager's abysmal lack of personal morality finally bit him, but in an indirect way: As deceptive in his personal life as he was professionally, he had been carrying on a longtime affair with his secretary. When he ended this relationship in a particularly unfeeling and one-sided manner, the scorned woman told me all his misdeeds so that Hell's full fury could be visited on him. The manager admitted to his dealings, but shrugged, "So what? Every transaction was one I was legally empowered to make." The fact that he had enriched himself at the company's expense did not seem to trouble him. Nor would he accept an "unfair" dismissal: Just look at his great results; how could I possibly fire him? Easily!

My next moral adventure came in the form of a bribe, the terms of which were almost comic in their shamelessness: A soon-to-be-former BMW distributor offered me a trip aboard his yacht with a countess and her beautiful teenage daughter, plus $10 million deposited to a Swiss bank account. I politely declined, making sure we never did business with him again. This, plus a few more firings, eventually spread the word that BMW was serious about integrity. The place got cleaned up, and I have every reason to believe that BMW today is as ethical an operation as anyone could want. I tell these old anecdotes not to single out BMW, but to illustrate by general example how important integrity is, how easily it can be lost, and how unmanageable an organization becomes without it.

When a leader encounters immoral dealing, he or she must root it out immediately. And don't be quiet about it! The rank and file pay close attention to who gets punished and who gets rewarded, seeking in these actions clues to their leader's personal beliefs.

Fairness

Leaders can't afford to play favorites, even though (being human) they have their own personal likes and dislikes. Every subordinate must believe he or she is being evaluated purely on merit. We hear a lot about diversity these days, and certainly a workplace that is totally devoid of discrimination and that offers true equal opportunity to all is not only desirable, it's smart business. At the same time, however, I think what is even more important is diversity of *ideas—good* ideas. What does it profit an organization, after all, to achieve a cosmetically diverse workforce made up of people who all think alike? A leader who promotes racial and sexual equal opportunity will have struck an important blow for a more just society; but a leader who promotes *intellectual* equal opportunity will have conferred upon his or her company an incalculable competitive advantage. Original thinkers— "disruptive" people unafraid to challenge conventional wisdom—are a powerful asset.

It's not unfair for a leader to criticize those parts of an organization that he or she views as not adding value, so long as this criticism is kept institutional, not personal. The people in a department, after all, may not be there of their own free choice. Furthermore, they may understand the department's problem only too well but be constrained by their lack of seniority, say, from doing much about it. I well remember the evident frustration of young staffers when Chrysler was conducting a debriefing for me and other top managers of the drive characteristics of our 1995-model Chrysler Cirrus and Dodge Stratus midsized sedans. After project leaders had extolled the sporty ride of the test cars, I weighed in, strongly disagreeing. As I explained what I found deficient about the cars' ride, I could see the heads of young back-benchers nodding in silent agreement. By their body language they were telling me what they dared not say out loud to their immediate bosses—or, perhaps, what they *had* said but that had gone unheeded.

In meetings, when talk turns to the shortcomings of "those guys in sales" or "those guys in manufacturing" (or whatever department is not being represented), it's tempting to join in. A strong leader, however, will try to resist, knowing that such finger-pointing is at best a divisive pastime. My own favorite whipping boy has always been "product planning," the breed of folks who, in my opinion, had more to do with almost wrecking the U.S. auto industry than the financial "bean counters" ever did (and I say all this even though I myself began my career in the auto industry as a forward-model product planner for GM!).

The typical planning group staff numbers several hundred people, all of them churning out ideas or potential ideas for new products. Once they've done that, they come up with investment estimates on the cost of making the product, piece-cost estimates, and volume estimates. They do this more or less on their own, without much interaction with the rest of a car company's management. And when they're done, they put a gun to the head of management and say, "The new product X plan will cost you $2.7 billion, will involve three assembly plants, is going to sell 400,000 units a year, and you'll be happy with it because it will make you a lot of money. Now . . . if you don't like the plan, if you think $2.7 billion is too much, we can give you the $1.5 billion version, but you're not going to like it." Senior management never has any input other than saying yes or no at the end.

In my experience, the function usually produced huge, expensive vehicle programs that never quite recovered their investments. Over my years at Chrysler, I never passed up an opportunity to voice my low opinion of this practice.

Then one day I was advised that the product planners, many of them excellent young people, were concerned about my "dislike for them." I decided to go into the lion's den, and invited all of Chrysler's product planners to a meeting in which I addressed them without notes.

I apologized for making them feel I disliked them personally, which of course had not been my intent, and I went on to explain my institutional concern with their department: that it was using an entirely too simplistic approach to planning what was basically a psychology-driven product. I enumerated what I saw as their department's most erroneous projections and most spectacular failures, and I made suggestions for reform. I'm not sure I healed every wound, but I did let them know what had been behind my criticism, why I felt the way I did, and what they could do to change my opinion. Having faced them openly and in person, I think, made them feel they now were being treated fairly.

What's the lesson here? That being fair and evenhanded does not mean that the leader can or should treat all activities, groups, and staffs equally to avoid the perception of favoritism. Some activities *should* be de-emphasized. Some people *do* deserve more of a merit increase than others. Some perceived unfairness is the price of change, and to try to avoid any ill feeling or sense of persecution on anyone's part simply invites stasis. But the good leader knows the difference between arbitrary, judgmental unfairness and that which has to be imposed on the organization in the interest of attaining its goals.

My favorite example of "fairness" *mis*applied comes during budget-cutting time: "Let's just give everyone the same 10 percent cut right across the board, so it will be perceived as being fair." Right? Wrong. How can this be fair when you know that some of your direct reports have padded their numbers by 10 or 15 percent in anticipation of a future cut (or, worse yet, just mindlessly grown willy-nilly in size over the years), while others have given you a true, rock-bottom figure (and/or have managed the way they were supposed to all along)? Or when you know that, in tough times, departments such as marketing and public relations may need *more,* not less, money?

Here's a simple test to help you determine if an action or decision you want to make is fair: Could you explain your rationale for it to the very people who stand to be most hurt? Could you get them to agree, however grudgingly, that if placed in your position, they might make the same decision? Then it's fair.

Optimism and Esprit de Corps

When the going gets tough and the situation appears hopeless, that's when inspirational leadership is the most needed and the most effective. A classic example? General Douglas MacArthur saying, "I shall return," when it seemed unlikely he ever could. When subordinates see bravery and defiance of the odds by their leader, they acquire new inspiration. The hope of winning begins to replace the crushing, paralyzing fear of defeat. Lee Iacocca was the archetypal emotional leader during Chrysler's bout with near bankruptcy in the late '70s and early '80s, always optimistic, always proclaiming future prosperity, even when it appeared totally unrealistic. When the *Wall Street Journal* told Chrysler to die with dignity, Iacocca's response was, "*Screw* the *Wall Street Journal!*" It was infectious. It made people believe.

Naturally, when your world is crashing down around you—when your boss is dissatisfied or the board starts asking pointed questions—

being truly upbeat can become tough. That's when *acting* kicks in— the good, old Hollywood kind. The leader can't show him- or herself to be despondent in front of his or her subordinates. Concerned and angry? Sure. Indignant that "they" are trying to do us in? Absolutely! But defeatist? Never. (Remember, defeatism is contagious, too.) I've found humor to be an extremely effective weapon against defeatism. Why so? Perhaps because subordinates assume anybody able to make jokes can't be too badly scared.

There's another reason the apprentice leader should remain optimistic: What feels like a disastrous setback very often isn't! What you consider to be *bad* luck may, in fact, turn out to be the best thing that ever happened to you. To paraphrase Lutz's Law of Life (from the Prologue of this book): What you think you *want* in life and what you really *need* are often indeed two different things.

I learned the truth of this early on—30 years before I had to face those flashing camera strobes with Bob Eaton in 1992. I was visiting London with one of my professors from U.C. Berkeley in 1962. I was helping him do some research into the mathematical modeling of business decisions, and we were going to have lunch with a senior official of the British Iron and Coal Board, which had been very successful at developing quantitative formulas for raw materials futures purchasing.

We met at the Reform Club, one of the venerable London gentlemen's clubs, steeped in cigar smoke and tradition. At lunch, I ordered calves' sweetbreads, usually served in portions the size of a hockey puck, breaded, sautéed, and served in drawn butter. (I still ate meat back in those days.) What arrived and was served with a flourish was an enormous, gray, lobed monstrosity that resembled, for all the world, an elephant brain. It hung over the edge of the plate and had an overpowering smell of "organ." Our English host leaned over appreciatively, gazed at the thing, and said "My word, that *does look good!*" I bravely ate about half, held up my end of the discussion and, on the way home, decided not to accompany my professor to the museum but to "go lie down for a while." I was *not* feeling good.

Barely in the room, I was sicker than ever before in my life. Between frequent trips to the bathroom, I flicked on the tube and got the news: Khrushchev was mad as hell, Cuban missiles were pointed at the

United States, and our president, John F. Kennedy, was shown live, laying down his ultimatum for the removal of the missiles "or else."

Between bouts of severe nausea and diarrhea, lying in bed in a completely dehydrated and exhausted state, I contemplated the end of the world as we then knew it. And here was the hard part! For the past seven years, I had been trained—physically and mentally—to be a conventional *or* nuclear weapons attack pilot. My fevered brain was conjuring up images of all my buddies being called to active duty, their Douglas A4 Skyhawks catapulting skyward, straining under a load of ordnance, going to what probably would be certain death for many of them in the early days of the long-dreaded World War III. How I wished I weren't dying in a London hotel room (for I was certain I was expiring from food poisoning). How I longed to die *usefully,* in an airplane, in the service of my country, so my parents could be proud, as opposed to finding my smelly remains on a London hotel room mattress!

I recovered. No Marine pilots died that day. And what I thought was a missed opportunity or being in the wrong place when the action was somewhere else turned out to be a nonevent. So relax! What seems like it may be the end of the world (literally or figuratively) probably isn't.

Command Presence and Bearing

This attribute is a touchy one to write about, since anyone advocating it runs the risk of being called "appearance-ist." Yet that's the furthest thing from what the U.S. Marine Corps, for example, intends when it insists leaders have "command presence."

Leaders who have this attribute come in both genders, all sizes, all colors, all ages, with and without hair. They range from handsome to ugly. What distinguishes them from their undistinguished brothers and sisters is a certain bearing, a body language, that is neither cocky nor aggressive, but quietly self-confident: a facial expression, say, that is neither puppy-dog friendly ("I want you to love me") nor overtly challenging. A gaze that is steady and focused, respectful but unflinching. And a posture that doesn't slouch apologetically, or shuffle around, or involve hand-wringing or palm-wiping on one's trousers. (And, of course, whether we're talking uniforms or business attire, neatness counts.)

Such externals tend merely to reflect the inner prerequisites of command presence: the self-confidence that comes from training, experience, or background; the inner harmony that comes from being at peace with oneself; and the calm that comes from having no lies to cover up, no secret agenda to hide.

A person who possesses these traits (and they are not innate) tends to attract favorable attention in any gathering. If, when he or she begins to speak, the content of the thoughts matches the impression created visually, then respect and confidence are born. Interestingly (but perhaps not surprisingly), blustery, self-serving arrogance in those first few minutes of verbal intercourse can quickly destroy the initial impression created by the favorable bearing: The individual now is seen as a vain peacock or a strident bantam rooster, depending on size. But an initial touch of humility or self-deprecating humor from a person of seeming power is highly effective in cementing the first impact of command presence. Thinks the subordinate, "This person must be supremely confident—otherwise how could he poke fun at himself and his mistakes?"

I've known a lot of "positional" leaders (i.e., the titular leaders of organizations who have done an adequate job of *managing* without command presence), but I've never met a true leader who didn't have it.

If I've made the art of leadership sound too buttoned-up and left-brained in this chapter, I apologize, because that isn't my intent. It's perfectly okay for leaders to be a bit off the wall at times. It lends color, displays passion, and perhaps, when "off the wall" is off the *wrong* wall, it shows the human frailty that, provided it doesn't interfere with the mission, can draw the subordinates closer to the leader. I'm sure it didn't hurt our standing as leaders of Chrysler that Bob Eaton and I eagerly donned racing suits and competed with celebrities and other executives in Chrysler's annual Neon Challenge Cup race. Or that all our officers regularly fought ferociously for the last ⅒ of a second in lap times at the end of our regular "ride and drive" (vehicle evaluation) sessions. It's a lot better than to be remembered by the organization as the man who stole hundreds of the little hotel room-service jam pots because he was too cheap to buy jam, as was the case with a leader in one of my previous companies.

And of one other thing I'm sure: Given the intensifying level of competition in all fields, the daunting and seemingly intractable problems facing industrialized societies around the world, the growing complexity of interactions between the media, government, the public, and industry, we, in the future, are not going to squeak by on better management or more administration. We're going to need that exceptionally *uncommon* mix of attributes that is strong leadership!

CHAPTER 14

SOME SQUEAKY WHEELS DON'T GET THE GREASE, OR PROS AND CONS OF BEING A CHANGE AGENT

WE HAVE A CHILDISH FASCINATION WITH CHANGE TODAY. WE SEEM TO THINK we discovered it, Heraclitus notwithstanding. More than 2,500 years ago, he wrote that nothing is constant except change and that you can't step in the same river twice. Why do people get all excited about change? Change happens. Deal with it!

I live about 600 miles from the nearest saltwater, and yet my land used to be at the bottom of an ocean. Later on, it was under a glacier. So why should I be amazed when I pick up the paper and read that some guy who calls himself a scientist has come to the startling conclusion (probably after years of exhaustive research) that Earth's climate is changing?

We have a minor environmental crisis in Michigan caused by mute swans, immigrants from Europe earlier this century. There are about 2,600 of them in the state. They mate for life, live up to 30 years, leave enormous feces wherever they roam, and aren't really mute. They hiss and grunt when they get mad, sometimes attack swimmers, and are particularly nasty to black terns. Three wildlife biologists were quoted in the *Detroit News*. One said, "The mute swan doesn't belong in Michigan at all." Another said, "They are dominating this ecosystem." And a third said, "Terminate them with extreme prejudice."

What ever happened to evolution? If the mute swan is the strongest, isn't he supposed to run the pond? Corporations have come to approach change with a raging prepubescent innocence. First they bring in the latest thinker, author, lecturer, or change maven who has discovered that, sure enough, there's change happening out there. He or she speaks to management and warns of the impending crisis. Committees are formed. Retreats are held. Brows furrow with the weighty realization that change is bearing down on the company like the Mongol hordes. It will be here any day, and we have to get ready! What to do? Hire consultants, that's what! *Change agents,* that's what we need!

In the old days, change agents were called "leaders." The first responsibility of leaders is to manage change. That's what they do every day, all day. Thus it has always been. There is nothing new about it.

One of the most disturbing features of our current preoccupation with this pedestrian phenomenon called change is the presumption that all change is good and therefore must be accepted. Look at the language that the human resources people put on appraisal forms today. They ask, "Does the employee *embrace* change?" I conjure the image of a fast-tracker desperately looking in every nook and cranny of the company for some undiscovered and unembraced dollop of change that he can put his arms around and squeeze. You have to be a change-hugger or you are going nowhere.

That's silly, of course. Change has no inherent normative value at all. Some change is good. Some is bad. People ought to be evaluated based on whether they can tell the difference, not on whether they obediently and mindlessly embrace unexamined change. High marks should be given to those who resist change that is bad as well as to those who champion change that is good.

I've already said what I think of many changes taking place today, from outcome-based education to casual dress in the office. Most of the changes I saw taking place at Berkeley in the early '60s were dumb, and so were the people embracing them. Civilization didn't get this far by *embracing* every screwball idea that came along; it got this far by accepting certain changes that were inevitable and certain others that were demonstrably beneficial, and by opposing, sometimes violently, changes that would have imperiled the species. So a good leader has to be a change *killer* as well as a change agent, but it's the latter role that I'll focus on in this chapter. And I'll start with the disagreeable cusses who usually are best at effecting *positive* and *needed* change.

· · ·

Every fighting force has an elite cadre specially suited by training, temperament, or both to tackle tough assignments. The Navy has its SEALs, the Army its Green Berets, the Marines their Force Recon. Among leaders, too, there exists an extra-hardy (and perhaps foolhardy!) minority. These are men and women who attempt to move an organization in the direction they know it needs to go, but in which it may not want to go. Such people, by definition disruptive, are indeed known in today's business jargon as "change agents."

No one, to my knowledge, has ever written a job description for this type of leader, but any draft would have to specify that the change agent needs to be a man or woman of unusual courage and conviction: Even when their own team members question their judgment, they have to have the fortitude to persevere, with or without agreement of the team members. Leaders must adhere single-mindedly to their vision of where the organization needs to go.

Sometimes the course a change agent sets will take the company down the same road a competitor has followed—as when benchmarking (for example) has shown that the competitor is using a superior system. At these times, the leader can expect to hear a litany of reasons why doing business that way is untenable: "They have lower labor costs than we do." "Their cost of capital is lower." "The government is helping them." "Our old boss would never have approved!" To such cries he or she must turn a deaf ear. When change is the imperative, the change agent must forge ahead, neutralizing opposition.

The question is, how?

The change agent's job is twofold: First, he must overcome his organization's disinclination to change—the natural inertia that impedes any institution. Second, he must be ready to exercise two completely different sets of leadership skills, depending on where an organization needs to go: Is it an overly left-brained institution suffering the ills of bureaucracy and stasis? Then the manner in which the change agent puts forward his program will be quite different from the one he would use to move a disorganized operation toward greater discipline and accountability.

What else should this job description include? Most definitely a note of caution: Being a change agent can be a marvelously rewarding and gratifying experience, especially when your vision finally is vindicated and your company has been set on a new, more successful course. But just as in chemistry, where a catalyst can itself be consumed by the reaction it causes, the human change agent can find himself diminished by the process. Battles leave lingering resentments. No matter how impressive the changes wrought, you may not find your next promotion to be exactly "greased." (In fact, sometimes you may even *get* greased!) If that happens, you will have suffered the all-too-frequent fate of the disruptive person. For this kind of leader, that's sometimes the cost of doing business.

THE ORGANIZATION, DESPITE YOUR MOST CONVINCING ARGUMENTS, SIMPLY DOES NOT WANT TO CHANGE

Driving an organization toward beneficial change requires enormous energy, conviction, persuasiveness, and, ultimately, stubbornness.

There are many reasons that people in an organization resist positive change. Let's start with the one easy to empathize with: Some well-meaning individuals will be sincerely convinced that a monumental mistake is in danger of being made, that the letter of the company's core values is being violated (even though the spirit isn't), that traditions are being broken, and that disaster awaits unless management desists. This well-intentioned (as opposed to malevolent, which I'll deal with in a moment) opposition will manifest itself in notes, questions at staff meetings, and (especially in cultures steeped in fear) anonymous epistles to senior management or even board members from "concerned employees." How to deal with such resistance? Here, leaders diverge.

Some prove so uncritically self-confident and unshakable in their beliefs that they plow ahead regardless. Such an approach, though it gets the job done, may prove dangerous in the long term: The doubters, every now and then, might just be right!

Other leaders waffle. These are people who may be great in the locker room (great at making their case to small groups of acolytes or to the board), but when beset by the cries, moans, and sometimes surprisingly persuasive counterarguments of the affected masses, these leaders quickly lose faith in their own judgment and side with the majority. These leaders have so little self-confidence and conviction (or so little willingness to accept the unpopularity that goes with getting the job done) that they will have little lasting influence on an organization. Subordinates will inevitably smell a weakling; and the next change initiative, when it comes along, will be met by even stiffer resistance.

The well-intentioned often fight change because they think the organization is successful as it is. Why experiment? Why venture into the unknown? This attitude was much in evidence at Chrysler in the late '80s when, as part of our adoption of platform teams, we first instituted our horizontal approach to engineering. Drawing small groups from different specialties to engineer a whole vehicle was deeply threatening to partisans of the traditional system, even though we were all living under a wasteful, error-prone, five-year process. And frankly, the flood of anonymous letters from these partisans to Lee Iacocca was impressive, both in quality and quantity. It would have been easy for management to have flinched. Instead, we persevered, relying on countless, no-holds-barred "town hall" meetings to allay workers' fears, to explain why change was necessary, and to impress upon workers and managers alike that we were adopting one of the hallmarks of what was then Japanese superiority. (Lee himself, by the way, conducted a countless number of these town hall meetings, enduring his fair share of the grief along with the rest of us.) The forces of conservatism, however, remained strong. These sincere traditionalists were joined (as so often happens in large organizations) by opponents whose motives were far from pure—insecure, bad managers who worried that their status was in jeopardy. And it was! Their power and influence, tied to the old fiefdoms, stood to be reduced the moment personnel from these groups were split up and reassigned to platform teams. But the soon-to-be toothless still had power, and some of them waged war (both covert and overt) against our new direction.

What to do? We had already eliminated giving in as an option, because, well, our gut told us we were right. (Well . . . we were almost sure we were right! We knew all-out, team-based product development worked for the Japanese, but of course there was still the question of whether it would work in Chrysler's culture.) Sure, we could have deferred it for further study (a popular escape route for timid leaders who cannot bring themselves to make any faction unhappy). But what would that have accomplished? We knew we would only rehash everything again, assign more people to reassess the pros and cons, and, in the end, only further delay the action we knew was necessary.

In such circumstances, the correct thing for a change agent to do is calmly press ahead, continuing to explain the why of change but, at the same time, forcefully implementing action. It's explaining and selling at the same time. Plus, it's remarkable how quickly resistance crumbles once the first tangible successes of the new approach become evident. As step follows step, subordinates, despite their initial misgivings, come to see that they are indeed being led to a better place!

Do not be at any pains, however, to make the pace of change too comfortable. In today's highly competitive global environment, "gradualism" can spell death if a slow-moving company comes up against a faster, more agile, more aggressive competitor. For this reason, change agents, early on, must develop an attractive and compelling vision with which to spur their troops. It must then be sold aggressively. (How much time you will have for salesmanship, of course, will depend on the urgency of your situation.) If time permits, listen to the naysayers: There may be value to their arguments. If you tailor your program to take note of these misgivings, it will succeed all the quicker and more smoothly. Next comes action! No giving in for the sake of popularity or tranquillity. No "let's study it again, and we'll decide in a couple of months." That's a sure way to create waste and lose respect. In extreme cases, when the opposition is powerful, permanent, and crippling, key figures in the old system will have to be removed.

MANAGEMENT DOES NOT FEEL COMFORTABLE RELINQUISHING ENOUGH CONTROL TO ALLOW FOR GREATER CREATIVITY AND EMPOWERMENT

In any organization that has been dominated by an overbearing senior management, the move to greater empowerment will be a difficult one. The reasons can be both logical and emotional—"logical" in businesses where even the smallest error may be prohibitively costly or where past abuse of freedom has lent legitimacy to the imposition of inflexible rules. People still tell the story of the large computer manufacturer that, during an especially "empowered" phase of its political evolution, launched a major new system, only to discover to its dismay that the computer was a failure, incapable of reaching any of its market targets. The logical knee-jerk reaction was for senior management to declare, "Let's make sure that never happens again," institute many new rules and procedures, and stifle creativity. It was years before this company introduced anything new again! (To harken back, for a moment, to Lutz's parable of the kid in the pool, this redoubling of rules is tantamount to the kids' parents redoubling Johnny's straps and belts in a doomed effort to assist his swimming prowess.)

In the 1960s and 1970s, a profusion of new safety regulations for military pilots owed its origin to just this sort of logic. For the moment, a higher premium was put on accident avoidance than on combat readiness. New Catch-22-like edicts (e.g., "No pilot shall fly night formation unless he has done so within the past 60 days") were issued, leading wags among the younger pilots to recast them with their own brand of humor ("You may not do so unless you have already done so").

Then, too, there is an overpowering human tendency to regulate any activity the free and desirable exercise of which occasionally causes waste, mistakes, or (in the case of such a high-risk activity as military flying) death. The left brain, to its credit, wants to eliminate risk wherever possible.

The Soviet armed services in general attempted to do that, strictly limiting the freedom of junior commanders, destroying independent thought or initiative, and forcing everyone (except the enemy, of course) to adhere to a rigid script. Leadership was highly centralized, in contrast to the U.S. habit of empowering (through training) even the most junior noncommissioned officers to lead their units autonomously should senior officers be incapacitated. Soviet fighter pilots were given an especially short leash. They routinely flew with flight recorders, not so that the recorders could be used later for accident investigation, but so senior officers could monitor how closely pilots adhered to official procedure. Big brother was always there in the cockpit, actively monitoring any and all changes of altitude, speed, and course. To say the least, this discouraged the kind of envelope-stretching practice sessions that made America's Top Gun pilots so superior in combat.

Probably the best example of this overcontrol was the downing of Korean Air Lines Flight 007 in 1983 by a Soviet pilot and his superiors on the ground who apparently didn't have the flexibility to deviate from their standing orders, which, of course, were to shoot down intruders. Ironically, this tragedy may have speeded the end of the Cold War because it told us that the Soviets' highly regimented command-and-control system didn't work very well, and even more serious, it told the Soviets that the West knew it didn't work!

These examples of overcontrol, however distasteful they may be to a right-brained person, at least spring from the noble desire to prevent misfortunes and accidents. One can argue (as a good right-brainer certainly would) that the price paid for greater stability was prohibitive, but one must admit that imposing extra control seemed logical to those who insisted on it.

Control freaks, on the other hand, deserve no such sympathetic consideration. A worship of control for its own sake, in fact, denotes a company badly out of balance.

Though different today, the Ford Motor Company I worked for in the '70s and early '80s was control-obsessed and inhospitable to those unwilling or unable to master not just the minutiae of their own jobs (a reasonable expectation) but the minutiae of fields far from their own areas of responsibility. Creativity? A knack for grasping the big picture?

These attributes mattered less to an executive's advancement than his or her capacity for memorizing facts by rote. Executives about to make a presentation to senior management studied fact sheets and formulaic "Q&A" responses for days before the big event. In fact, one "useful" thing staffs did for bosses was to generate huge lists of potential questions (and answers) that could be memorized. But memorization alone was not sufficient; major presentations called for preparation of immense black binders involving up to 100 or more tabs, each tab providing schedules or supplemental data.

When a victim thus equipped was set before them, Ford's senior reviewers delighted in playing a high-stakes game of "20 Questions," trying to see how many levels of trivia the poor presenter could offer up, how quickly he could access the right tab out of the massive book: "Yes, I believe I have that for you, gentlemen, if you'll . . . be so kind as to . . . bear with me for a moment . . . yes . . . right here at . . . [suddenly a note of triumph!] Appendix C, Schedule 2, page 5.7(a), paragraph iii!"

The most skilled players of this game were widely praised for knowing their operations and being on top of the details. But when I looked at the real-life performance of their operations in terms of creativity, daring, intelligent risk taking, and courage (not to mention results), some of these heroes were sorely lacking. A system that encourages people to describe a wooded plot as "exactly four thousand three hundred and eighty-seven trees" (with backup schedules on each tree's size, health, age, type, and location) rather than as "an 18-acre forest" is creating serious waste. The waste goes far beyond the time taken to memorize data that was generated needlessly. The real, monumental waste occurs when good employees—treated for years as if they had no brain, no creativity, no judgment, and no honesty— either leave or, worse, stay and degenerate into what management has groomed them to become: dispassionate drones.

Changing an environment of excessive control (i.e., trying to move an extreme left-brained organization more in the direction of left-right balance) is not an easy task, even if you are leading it or are a member of the leadership team. Fear of the unknown, fear of loss of control (with all the horrors that term implies), will make change extremely hard.

Since such a shift usually cannot be ordered, the would-be change agent indeed has to sell his or her vision of a more enlightened, empowered, and hence more efficient organization. Sometimes, though, your listeners won't listen. When that happens, a frustrated agent should consider using some or all of the following techniques:

1. Solicited comment.   When overly left-brained organizations get into trouble (and they almost always do, sooner or later), they undergo a period of self-examination during which they ask, "What's wrong with us?" Comment may be solicited from persons below top-management level. Take this as your chance to tell it like it is, orally or in writing. In particular, a brilliant piece of writing, at the propitious moment, can have tremendous influence. The most dramatic case I know of happened in the Marine Corps in the 1950s, when an encroachment on officers' authority by innumerable bureaucratic checks resulted in badly bruised officer morale. The "special trust and confidence" with which Marine officers are invested by their commander in chief was dying a death of a thousand cuts, each seemingly harmless and trivial, administered by enlisted clerks only doing their job. Eventually, a Marine colonel named R.D. Heinl Jr. had had enough. He wrote an article titled (appropriately enough), "Special Trust and Confidence" for the *Marine Corps Gazette*. Its publication triggered a wholesale reappraisal of the system, eventually leading to its reform.

2. Unsolicited comment.   Such comments, being uninvited, may fall on less-than-fertile ground, especially if the organization does not yet understand it has a problem. And they expose the critic to a degree of risk. But take courage! Remember, if you are frustrated by the overly analytical nature of your organization, you probably are not alone. You may, in fact, discover you have sympathetic friends in high places. (Just don't be a jerk about it!)

3. Benchmarking.   This exercise was instrumental to Chrysler's second turnaround, as you know from having read the first part of this book. We fully appreciated that we had to change—that our long-established ways were proving insufficient. Yet we were not sure which model we should use to replace them. Nor did we see a way, politically, to wean our old guard from its familiar habits: How were junior people to tell senior management its methods and philosophy were headed for the scrap heap? Benchmarking helped us out of this quandary. By benchmarking the highly successful Honda Motor Company, we could show objectively that Honda's methods (or some of them at least) were superior to our own. No junior managers were shot, since, ostensibly at least, they weren't directly criticizing Chrysler—they were just reporting how Honda went about making cars. It's not too much to say that the Honda study was our single greatest instigator of change.

4. Consultants. We all know the cynic's definition of a consultant: someone who travels 1,000 miles and charges $5,000 a day to tell the boss what you already know. In fact, I've always been more than a bit wary of consultants myself—to the point that I felt like hanging a medal on the chest of a friend of mine who's on the board of directors of a large corporation (not Chrysler) when he told me his response to the CEO's announcement that he'd hired an outside consulting firm to write that company's strategic business plan: "Look," he told the CEO, "This board is certainly willing to pay for a business plan. Now, we can either pay *you* to do the strategic thinking for this company, or we can pay the *consultant*—but we're only going to pay *once!*"

Nonetheless, consultants (or at least *good* ones), just by virtue of being outsiders, can often get your colleagues' attention in a way that you, being familiar and in-house, cannot. If you're a change agent, you can use them to get a message across. At least you can *sometimes!* I tried this strategy at Ford in the early '80s with mixed results. Dismayed at Ford's slowness and lack of teamwork in product development, I invited Kelly Johnson to address us. Johnson, legendary head of Lockheed's "Skunk Works," had produced America's first jet fighter, sketch to flight, in just 100 days, partly by cutting his engineering group from 8,000 to 800. I felt his message might help shake things up. For an hour, he held forth on teamwork, elimination of waste, fast prototyping, and all the other virtues that today's product development experts hold dear. Yet the speech got hardly a rise out of Ford's executives, one of whom asked aloud, "Whose idea was it to invite this guy, anyway? None of what he talked about was related to our business." Ah, well. Maybe someone in that room was influenced, because Ford, ultimately, *did* change!

5. *The working example.* Sometimes, change can be effected through a nonthreatening example or a working experiment. Rather than attempt to convince the "control holders" to lighten up on the whole place at once (which might be an unacceptable risk), effort may be better expended in obtaining permission to try a small model where normally applicable procedures (if they are not useful) can be ignored, where teamwork and trust can flourish, and where behavior can be guided by a desired common objective rather than by malevolent supervision. "If it works," you tell the bosses, "we may learn something. If it doesn't, we won't have put the company at risk."

After our Honda study, when Chrysler knew it was broken but didn't yet know how to fix itself, a working example helped show us the way. The story of the Viper (our 10-cylinder, 400-plus-horsepower supercar) you've read about already in Chapter 3, so you appreciate that as radical as this car may have been in its appearance, the process by which it was designed and built made it a still more remarkable departure from our corporate norm. Rather than entrust Viper to Chrysler's traditional chimney system of production, we selected a small team of about 80 volunteers, gave them floor space and some goals, and told them they could do anything to bring this car to market fast, provided it wasn't illegal, immoral, or in clear violation of policy.

The experiment, as you know, ultimately proved to be a huge success: This fabulous retro car, the fastest and most expensive vehicle ever mass-produced in the United States, was brought to market in three years on a modest budget of $80 million. The program wasn't perfect (and neither were the first Vipers), but the champions of change (in this case, the use of platform teams) had been vindicated beyond dispute.

MANAGEMENT DOES NOT FEEL COMFORTABLE IMPOSING ENOUGH CONTROL TO ENSURE ORDER AND CONSISTENCY

It happens infrequently, but it happens: Too much creativity, too much freedom, too much empowerment, and before management can reassert control, a company spirals into financial or administrative chaos. How did it happen? The causes can be many. It might merely be a case of bad leadership—of a boss distracted from his duties either by personal problems or by his having fallen in love with his ancillary duties (hobnobbing with politicians, serving on commissions, etc.), or maybe both. Absent clear, strong leadership, a "cat's away mice will play" atmosphere can easily prevail.

This drift in otherwise successful and intellectually balanced companies is easily corrected: The boss either comes to his senses or his bosses appoint his replacement. Interestingly enough, such breakdowns most often occur not in empowered organizations, but in companies that still depend on a high degree of top-down leadership. More rare (and more challenging) are runaway companies whose cultures revere creativity and support empowerment. Such companies tend to belong to industries that demand unceasing innovation and rapid new-product (or new-service) cycles, and garner huge rewards for being first. Examples include advertising agencies, movie studios, and biotech and computer companies.

Advertising agencies present an especially interesting case, since a single firm, in the course of its life, may swing cyclically from right-brain to left and back again to right. Almost by definition, an advertising agency provides its client with advertising designed to portray the client's product or service in a novel or provocative way. Agencies that do the best job are those that nurture a strong right-brained culture and obey all seven of Lutz's Laws. They understand that "the customer isn't always right," because their creatives know that the kind of advertising asked for by a client's ad manager (often a left-brained middle manager, recycled out of sales) isn't usually the advertising best calculated to move the product.

Likewise, they know that "teamwork isn't always good," because they know that advertising generated by committee, with all its edges sanded smooth, seldom has power or energy. And they know that "disruptive people are an asset," because they've got legions of them in-house. Many of them look and act eccentric, are often critical of their own agency and sometimes even clients, but prove their commercial worth every time they hatch a breakthrough campaign.

Such agencies grow and prosper, acquiring new and more important clients; they expand internationally, often acquiring smaller agencies along the way. Finance and internal controls become important, and a full-time treasury function becomes essential to the management of cash flow and the maintenance of an increasingly complex balance sheet. Previously informal mechanisms for hiring, firing, and employee appraisal give way to a personnel and organization department, while the ubiquitous legal department grows apace. Senior management increasingly adopts the demeanor and outlook of its largest corporate clients. In fact, senior agency and senior client managers become interchangeable. Thus does the successful agency awake one day to find it has become all the things it vowed it never would: bureaucratic, ponderous, risk-averse.

Now the backlash sets in. Young creative people, fed up with the glacial pace of developing new campaigns, repelled by the slavish demurral to client demands ("listening to the customer"), and out of sympathy with the agency s preoccupation with the bottom line ("the purpose of business isn't to make money"), decide to leave, feeling themselves unappreciated and viewed as disruptive.

They strike out on their own, form a new agency, and swear they will do nothing but great advertising using off-the-wall, risky ideas; they will reject clients who won't allow them that creative freedom, and they will never again cynically produce less-than-great advertising just because their number one client, Megacorp, isn't quite comfortable with their best stuff. Also, while they take their oath of excellence, they decide to eschew all trappings of their corporate past: those pesky staff people, all those "Dr. No" lawyers, the nit-picking controllers, and the non-value-added personnel and organization types.

So begins the life of a new agency, conceived as a right-brained refutation of everything its old, left-brained progenitor stood for. It soon grows to be the hot new shop in town, attracting a bevy of fast-growing, risk-embracing clients (including maybe even a big fish or two, tired of bland creatives from competing Megagency) who, thanks to the new ads, achieve spectacular improvements in sales. The hot new agency grows by leaps and bounds, takes on new clients, hires people and . . . in many cases, heads for near collapse. Some just go off the end of the chaos scale entirely, losing all logistic, financial, or personnel control. The sad part is that, at some point, even the close relationship with the client suffers, as meetings are botched, new people are poorly trained, and follow-up falls through the cracks. Financial problems follow, and now this entity (here an advertising agency, but just as easily a small biotech start-up, a software boutique, or almost any kind of company) is in deep trouble.

How to get it back on course? If the free spirits don't recognize they need help, it's probably too late. Chances are, though, that they know they've got a problem. Their banker or their most important client may have told them to shape up. Or perhaps they've found themselves reabsorbed, amoeba-like, by the lumbering and stodgy company against which they originally rebelled. (It's not uncommon, for example, for Silicon Valley companies to acquire small start-ups created by their former disruptive employees who, after having developed a better widget on their own and having sold their company to their former employer, then settle back into their old cubicles.)

However it may come to pass that the too-right-brained company gets a wake-up call, the problem of saving it from its own yeastiness and restoring order takes special finesse. The fact is, managing creative people really is, as the saying goes, like "herding cats."

Deft leadership again supplies the key. But here the leader should be a person who feels comfortable in both the left-brained and right-brained world—what I would term a "levelheaded hybrid." He or she must play the role of a wolf in sheep's clothing, imposing control and restoring order, but doing it in a manner specially tailored to the needs of right-brained people. The reason is simple: If an overly logical, overly authoritarian, top-down leader is imposed, he or she will either be unsuccessful (rejected) or entirely *too* successful (everybody is whipped into line, costs are down, control is perfect, the disruptives are fired, but the "creative company" is a goner—operation a success, but the patient died!). The muscular approach of an Al Dunlap—sawing off limbs willy-nilly in an overgrown bureaucracy—may be inappropriate when what's called for is more akin to trimming back a right-brained organization's delicate but unruly blooms. Good leadership, after all, is about nothing if not *balance*. Some patients indeed require amputation. But others may only need a transfusion.

Here the ideal leadership style is friendly, but deadly serious; light in style, but earnest in substance; understanding and accommodating when it comes to symbolic trivia (free gourmet coffee, for example, if employees really do appreciate it and drink it), but tenacious and implacable in controlling basics (meeting client deadlines, making budget).

The right-brained company's ills cannot be cured by a "do it my way because I said so" leader, because creative people naturally resist a too-authoritarian approach. While leaders of every stripe need to be excellent communicators, no situation requires greater sureness or subtlety of tone than the one in which a change agent must try to save a chaos-bent mob of right-brainers from themselves.

To state what might seem obvious, right-brainers need to be addressed in a right-brained way. "Look, guys, we're in serious trouble here, and we're going to have to cut some of this cost, and you're going to have to help me do it. If I try to do it alone, I might get in the way of the very thing that makes this company so outstanding at what it does, and I don't think any of us wants to take that risk. We don't want to destroy morale, either, because that's part of where creativity comes from. So what do we do? I'm open to suggestions. But remember my bottom line: I'm here to get the place turned around, so 'let's do nothing' is not an option."

That, as a going-in position, will work far better than a memo reading as follows:

To: All Senior Associates
From: New Leader
Subject: Cost Control

Inasmuch as I have been given the responsibility to return this company to profitability under a very difficult set of circumstances, I am requesting the following take immediate effect:

1. All senior associates will meet with me individually to rejustify all projects currently in progress.

2. All work on any project not reviewed and reapproved by me is herewith suspended.

3. All company travel, except in the most unusual circumstances (my approval), is curtailed.

4. All amenities (coffee, doughnuts) at corporate meetings are to be eliminated, effective immediately.

5. No new customers are to be solicited pending a full review of our processes.

I contrast these two extremes because they seek to solve the same problem in two different ways. Neither one is necessarily right or wrong. Circumstances determine which will get you the results you want. Who are the employees you're dealing with? A group of controllers or accountants, in a dire situation, might react better (in fact, with relief) to the blunt memo (as, frankly, did most Chrysler people to my infamous "Waste Is . . ." memo during our dark days of 1988, the poison-pen letters I got notwithstanding). A group of overwrought right-brained creatives, on the other hand, will almost certainly respond much better to the first approach.

Having made initial contact and gained a degree of trust, the leader can't back off. One appeal won't do it. He's got to be persistent without being abusive, pushing for change and for more order unrelentingly. (And maybe later he'll need to add a harder edge to his insistence.)

What all this means is that change agents must be supremely good at sizing up a situation, sensing quickly which style of leadership will be most effective.

A senior trainer I know who works for an international consulting company has the twofold task of teaching Japanese-style lean production methods (requiring great order and discipline) to Americans, while, on other occasions, teaching Japanese executives how to be more creative. (The Japanese, he says, admire Westerners' ability to act on hunches and think out of the box, as opposed to always following a strict, conformist, step-by-step approach.)

"I'll tell you," he says, "It's a hell of a lot easier teaching order and discipline to a creative person than it is the other way around."

That's his experience, of course. But my own has been that neither challenge is exactly what I'd call a picnic! True, it's probably easier to teach a right-brained creative person to achieve orderliness. But on a broader, organizational level, it's a lesson fraught with peril: If circumstance demands that the leader achieve results quickly, the organization (through rough handling) may suffer serious damage when its talent bolts and finds employment elsewhere. Creativity is a precious and delicate creature, easily bruised, even by someone acting with the best of intentions.

Remember, I never said achieving right-brain/left-brain balance was easy! It's hard knowing when to support and facilitate, when to inspire action, when to seek creative looseness, and when to tighten up on discipline. In the real world, I've found, leaders must be able to do both at once. They must possess not just an understanding of, but a real sympathy for, the workings of the right brain and the left in order to get them into harness and working side by side. Perhaps it goes without saying that leaders who accomplish this are people who have done the same job in the privacy of their own craniums. They're "schizophrenic" (in the good sense!). They've personally mastered the skill they're demanding of their organizations: thinking "right" and "left" at once!

F. Scott Fitzgerald once wrote: "The test of a first-rate intelligence is the ability to hold two opposed ideas in the mind at the same time, and still retain the ability to function." He might just as well have been speaking of organizations, far too few of which ever learn the trick. Those that do, however, earn rich rewards. The Marines did. Today they're taking the lower third of the Beavis and Butt-head generation and turning them into high achievers and good citizens. And we did at Chrysler—as Chrysler's employees and shareholders can attest. Holding "two opposed ideas" in the mind at the same time is, I believe, the yin and yang of leadership, the result of hard work, hard thinking, and, yes, *guts*.

DaimlerChrysler: The Beginning of a New World Order for Business?

THE MAY 7, 1998, ANNOUNCEMENT THAT CHRYSLER AND DAIMLER-BENZ intended to merge generated, to say the least, an avalanche of interest throughout both the business world and the world at large. And for good reason: It was to be, after all, the largest industrial merger in history, initially valued by the two companies at some $92 billion. Jürgen Schrempp, the chairman of Daimler-Benz, called the creation of DaimlerChrysler a "marriage made in heaven," and I, for one, think that he's most likely right (and not, by the way, just because I happened to have a hand in picking the final name for the new company—a moniker far classier, I submit, than either "Daimsler" or "Chrysbenz"!).

For starters, this "Jeep meets Mercedes" union is, truly, a merger of equals. Unlike so many deals of this sort where one strong and one weak company (or, sometimes, *two* weak companies!) link up, this is a coming together of two very strong companies that could have easily survived quite well separately, but that chose to follow the principle underpinning all good marriages: that the whole really *can* be greater than the sum of the parts. And the fact that the new company will be run by a management board consisting of eight Chrysler executives and eight Daimler-Benz automotive executives and that there will be dual headquarters in Stuttgart and in Auburn Hills, Michigan, further underscores that this is indeed a "different" type of merger.

But what has really captured the interest of headline writers and onlookers around the globe, in addition to the size of the merger, is the fact that it's the first alliance anywhere near this scope to be transnational (i.e., to involve companies from two different countries, on two different continents). The pundits have talked about how this portends everything from "the first global car colossus" to "the first sign that globalism is reshaping Europe" to the beginning of "a new type of capitalism" to, in the words of a *Wall Street Journal* headline, a "New World Order" for global business.

Most commentators on the merger have been upbeat—some downright euphoric. In fact, I take it as a bellwether that the leadership of both the United Auto Workers union and the Canadian Auto Workers union reacted positively to the initial news of the merger. That, I think, says a lot right there about the new company's growth potential!

At the same time, however, there have been some discordant voices—actually, expressions of uneasiness—having to do with this issue of the breaking down of national borders. Most people, it seems, long ago accepted the idea of globalization in all sorts of industries, but not everyone is yet comfortable with what author and think-tank guru Daniel Yergin calls the condition of "globality"—a world economy in which "traditional and familiar boundaries are being surmounted or made irrelevant."

Those who like to look at life through the rear-view mirror can be heard saying things like, "What about national sovereignty?" and "What about social justice?" (referring, I assume, to the old canard that "bigness equals monopoly"—even though, in the case of Daimler-Chrysler, the company will *still* not be as large, in terms of vehicles sold, as General Motors, Ford, Toyota, or Volkswagen!). What they're really concerned about, of course, is what they see as the rise of the dreaded (to them) "corporate state"—entities that care more about meeting the needs of the real people who make up markets than about the anachronistic pipe dreams of economic nationalists such as themselves.

But, what's so bad about that? What's so bad about bringing the world closer together through commerce? Following the old maxim that "people who trade with one another are a lot less likely to go to war with one another," isn't that, in fact, a step in the right direction toward world peace, among other things?

The business world, I submit, is far ahead of some sectors of the political world in recognizing the many benefits to mankind of "globality." In fact, allow me to make a prediction: Within five to ten years, cross-border alliances such as the one between Chrysler and Daimler-Benz will seem passé. And they'll seem that way because *consumers* will embrace them for all the benefits they deliver. In the brave new world of the twenty-first century, the kingdoms of yesteryear will be replaced by a new king: the customer!

That's not to say, however, that this particular deal doesn't carry with it both tremendous challenges (for the parties involved) and tremendous potential ramifications (for competitors and others). Herewith, in no particular order, is Lutz's List of same.

CHALLENGES FOR MEMBERS OF THE DAIMLERCHRYSLER FAMILY

For the Combined Management

Of the differences in style between Chrysler and Daimler-Benz, oft-quoted auto analyst Maryann Keller has said, "I can't imagine two more different cultures." I don't think Maryann is totally accurate on this one, in that beneath Chrysler's "freewheeling" corporate culture lies a strong foundation of business pragmatism (as I hope I've shown in this book), and behind Daimler-Benz's Teutonic image there resides a company that is every bit as dynamic as, say, Jack Welch's General Electric. Nonetheless, I do think that managing the cultural issues will indeed be the toughest part of making this marriage work. And the challenge, as always, will be getting the cultures to really meld *below* the level of seniormost management.

In September of 1997—a full decade after Chrysler merged with American Motors and several years after our (in part) AMC-inspired platform teams proved to be a smashing success—*Automotive News* ran a story entitled "Chrysler Die-Hards Still Won't Accept AMC

Alumni," which anonymously quoted, among a few others, one Chrysler middle manager who referred to certain AMC-ers as "carpet-baggers." That kind of sentiment (though certainly isolated) not only bothers me, it baffles me: Hey, guys, the "them" you're shooting at is "us"—and, meanwhile, there are plenty of *real* enemies out there!

I hope that the former Chrysler and the former Daimler-Benz are able to overcome these kinds of all-too-frequent human tendencies. I know that one of the major reasons Jürgen Schrempp wanted to merge with Chrysler was to *get at* Chrysler's creativity (i.e., to have some of it rub off on his own people), just as one of Bob Eaton's major reasons was to access Daimler's legendary technical prowess and attention to detail. What a shame it would be if either group were to squander the very thing they did the deal to get!

I don't think that's going to happen, though. In fact, a few years down the road, I don't think you'll be able to tell if DaimlerChrysler is an American company or a German one. Instead, I think it'll be sort of a "Mid-Atlanticer," just like yours truly!

For the Unions

From my years spent in the European auto industry, I happen to know a fair amount about Europe's "co-determination" system of labor-management relations. Some parts of the system I think make sense, and some parts, quite frankly, I think are pretty antiquated. It's highly instructive, for instance, that a big reason Daimler-Benz was able to pull off its own stunning turnaround in the mid-'90s was its unions' willingness to forsake tradition and to show flexibility in the area of pay and work rules—and, as a result, Daimler's workers have certainly shared in the company's ultimate success. Likewise, I think that Chrysler's major unions, the UAW and the CAW, have been on the right track in recent years in supporting what we came to call "modern operating agreements" and joint quality initiatives in Chrysler factories—again, a win-win situation for *all* parties involved. If, as some pundits are predicting, the creation of DaimlerChrysler also leads to some kind of federation between the labor groups on both sides of the Atlantic, I would hope that everyone involved keeps in mind that the customer (whether American, European, or from Timbuktu) cares about only one thing: a great product at the right price.

For Suppliers

The creation of DaimlerChrysler should be a bonanza for the world's auto suppliers—for the *good* ones, that is. It's a company that intends to grow, and with growth should come increased opportunity for those suppliers that can meet the company's exacting demands for quality, technology, delivery, and price. But those demands are certain to get even tougher in the future—if for no other reason than increasing competition among automakers themselves. (Don't think for a second that Toyota, Ford, and BMW are going to roll over and play dead just because Chrysler and Daimler-Benz are getting together!) The critical issue on this front will be a cultural one as well. Chrysler has proven in recent years that browbeating suppliers doesn't necessarily lead to higher performance (in fact, often just the opposite). On the other hand, suppliers have to go through a cultural change themselves if they're to be deemed worthy of greater trust— for the flip side of greater trust has to be *greater accountability* if the system is to work.

For Dealers

Bad news for Chrysler dealers: If you were thinking of getting your hands on a Mercedes SLK convertible as your "pool" car, you're still going to have to *buy* one! That's because both Bob Eaton and Jürgen Schrempp have—wisely—stated that they have no intention whatsoever of blending the brands of the new company. Both understand that a company's brand names are among its biggest assets, and DaimlerChrysler's portfolio of automotive brands—Mercedes-Benz, Jeep, Chrysler, Dodge, Plymouth, and Smart Cars (the new Daimler-created microcar franchise in Europe)—is certainly among the strongest in the world. Plus, and perhaps best of all, there is very little overlap among the brands. So, don't look for any needless overlap to be created (e.g., don't look for a Dodge Ram pickup to be standing next to a Mercedes in the showroom anytime soon). But, who knows, maybe somewhere down the road you *might* see a Mercedes V-8 under the hood of a Chrysler luxury car . . . or maybe Mercedes-badged (but Chrysler-built) light trucks on sale in markets outside Europe and North America. The possibilities in that regard are, as they say, endless!

RAMIFICATIONS FOR EVERYBODY ELSE

For Competitors

The most important message for competitors in the marriage of Chrysler and Daimler-Benz is, I think, a simple one—and it has nothing to do with press reports about "global car giants" or "regional players shoved to the shoulder of the road" or predictions that today's 40 automobile companies will be combined into just 20 in the next century ("the twenty-first century 20," as it's been called). The simple, important message is this: Free-market capitalism works! This is a message, I believe, that ought to have particular resonance these days in Asia, where an economic model approaching "crony capitalism" has proved itself bankrupt.

It's worth noting, I think, that the seminal event that led to this "merger of equals" between Chrysler and Daimler-Benz—other than Chrysler's getting its act together in the 1990s—was Daimler's getting *its* act together by adopting, in the mid-'90s, American accounting rules. This begat a new era of openness and accountability in Daimler's financial reports, which in turn begat a willingness of investors around the world (including America) to invest without fear in Daimler stock, which in turn begat a twenty-something price-earnings ratio for the stock, which in turn begat a $92 billion merger that was done *entirely* with stock. That, to reprise a couple of terms that I used earlier in this book, is the house that corporate *perestroika* and corporate *glasnost* built! And, oh yes, it was all aided by a monetary union in Europe that reflects this same kind of modernity. Which brings me to . . .

For Governments

The message for governments around the world is: It's time to get with the program! The times they are a-changin', and governments—despite recent positive steps such as the creation of the euro—really are trailing behind business in recognizing this. The most egregious examples are the administrations around the world that literally define terms like "crony capitalism" (including those in places like Malaysia and Indonesia with their heavily subsidized "national car programs")—plus, of course, those "managed economies" (including

Japan and South Korea) that Chrysler railed against in the '80s. But even Western governments have a long way to go. One of the big reasons DaimlerChrysler will be incorporated in Germany rather than in the United States or elsewhere is that German law forbids German companies from "sharing their sovereignty" with companies from a foreign country. The bottom line is, such vestiges of economic nationalism do nothing to aid modern global commerce—and, therefore, do nothing to aid government's constituents (who are also, of course, consumers).

For Wall Street and Other Financial Types

Simple message here as well: Auto stocks (at least in the United States) are valued too low. It just doesn't make sense that—to cite just one of many possible comparisons—Chrysler earned $2.8 billion ($4.15 per share) in 1997 on revenues of $61 billion while Daimler-Benz earned $1.8 billion ($3.42 per share) on revenues of $69 billion, and yet Chrysler's price-to-earnings ratio just before the merger was announced was less than a *third* that of Daimler's. A lot of the economic nationalists have made much of the fact that DaimlerChrysler will be 57 percent owned by former Daimler-Benz shareholders and 43 percent owned by former Chrysler shareholders. There's the reason right there: Their stock was worth more—which, in a stock-swap deal, makes all the difference in the world. (Even though, I should point out, the actual American ownership of stock in the new company will be roughly *equal* to that of the European ownership, since a lot of Americans owned Daimler stock to begin with—yet another example of "it's a small world after all!")

Some commentators have suggested that the DaimlerChrysler deal may wake up Wall Street—and investors—to a proposition that I've long believed: that cyclicality ain't what it used to be in the auto business, and that auto stocks are, in fact, a screaming bargain!

For the Media

Ah, my friends in the media! You may have the best time of all in the years ahead. And that, simply, is because you're surely going to have a *lot* to write about! This really may be the beginning of a New World

Order—both for business and for humankind. I, for one, certainly hope so. And I also think we all have a lot more reason for hope than for fear. All I ask as you cover it is, *please* try to get it right!

. . .

The fact is, the announcement of the DaimlerChrysler marriage has already made history—and I'm certain it's going to make a whole lot more. And, having helped the "bride" (or is Chrysler the "groom"?) make it to the altar "all dressed up," I just wish I were 10 years younger so I could be there to watch that history unfold first-hand!

INDEX

Advertising, fad avoidance in, 82
Advertising agencies, right- and left-
    brained management of, 207–209
American Motors Corporation,
    Chrysler acquisition of, 16–17, 31
Anecdote telling, as communication
    technique, 174–175
Asian partners, small-vehicle
    production of, 16
Assembly plants, Japanese in United
    States, 15
Auto industry:
    cyclical nature of, 14
    failure of, 120–121
Automobile racing, relevancy to auto
    industry, 139
Automobiles:
    convenience of, 143
    vilification of, 142–146
Automotive rebates, 17
Auto stocks, valuation of, 219

Balance, right- and left-brain, 212. *See
    also* Left-brained thinking; Right-
    brained thinking
Benchmarking, 34, 204–205
Benton, Phil, 168
Berlin Airlift, 162–165
Bidwell, Ben, 24
Black, George, 168
BMW, 22–23
    integrity issues at, 185–186
    punitive damages suit, 149

Bossidy, Larry, 131–132
Brand management, 27
Broeding, Laurie, 112
Business:
    and enthusiasm, 73–74, 77
    fundamental problems with,
        113–114
    for serving needs of people, 5
    teamwork-based, 26–27
Business plans, and vision, 76
Buying decisions, right-brained, 68

Cab-forward design, 24–25
Caldwell, Phil, 11
Canadian Auto Workers union, and
    DaimlerChrysler merger, 214, 216
Car dealers, service orientation of, 129
Castaing, François, 32–34, 50, 157
Caution, and business productivity,
    135–137
Change, 11, 195–196
    constant, 164–165
    forced, 122
    pace of, 200–201
    for resistant organizations, 198–201
Change agents, 97–100
    as an asset, 187
    and business success, 135–137
    leadership styles of, choosing, 211
    responsibilities of, 196–198
Chaos, 111–112
    avoiding, 206–212
Chimney system, 27–29